The Sidekick Comes of Age

Children and Youth in Popular Culture

Series Editor: Debbie Olson, Missouri Valley College

Children and Youth in Popular Culture features works that interrogate the various representations of children and youth in popular culture, as well as the reception of these representations. The series is international in scope, recognizing the transnational discourses about children and youth that have helped shape modern and postmodern childhoods and adolescence. The scope of the series ranges from such subjects as gender, race, class, and economic conditions and their global intersections with issues relevant to children and youth and their representation in global popular culture: children and youth at play, geographies and spaces (including World Wide Web), material cultures, adultification, sexuality, children of/in war, religion, children of diaspora, youth and the law, and more.

Advisory Board

LuElla D'Amico, Whitworth University; Markus P. J. Bohlmann, Seneca College; Vibiana Bowman Cvetkovic, Rutgers University; Adrian Schober, Australian Catholic University, Melbourne

Titles in the Series

The Sidekick Comes of Age: How Young Adult Literature is Shifting the Sidekick Paradigm, by Stephen M. Zimmerly
Female Adolescent Sexuality in the United States, 1850–1965, by Ann Kordas
Tweencom Girls: Gender and Adolescence in Disney and Nickelodeon Sitcoms, by Patrice A. Oppliger
Representing Agency in Popular Culture: Children and Youth on Page, Screen, and In Between, Edited by Ingrid E. Castro and Jessica Clark
The Feeling Child: Affect and Politics in Latin American Literature and Film, Edited by Philippa Page, Inela Selimović, and Camilla Sutherland
The Rhetorical Power of Children's Literature, Edited by John H. Saunders
Children in the Films of Steven Spielberg, Edited by Debbie Olson and Adrian Schober
The Child in World Cinema, Edited by Debbie Olson
Girls' Series Fiction and American Popular Culture, Edited by Luella D'Amico
Indians in Victorian Children's Narratives: Animalizing the Native, 1830–1930, by Shilpa Bhat Daithota
The Rhetorical Power of Children's Literature, Edited by John Saunders
Misfit Children: An Inquiry into Childhood Belongings, Edited by Markus P. J. Bohlmann
The Américas Award: Honoring Latino/a Children's and Young Adult Literature of the Americas, Edited by Laretta Henderson
Critical Childhood Studies and the Practice of Interdisciplinarity: Disciplining the Child, Edited by Magdalena Zolkos and Joanna Faulkner

The Sidekick Comes of Age

How Young Adult Literature is Shifting the Sidekick Paradigm

Stephen M. Zimmerly

LEXINGTON BOOKS
Lanham • Boulder • New York • London

Published by Lexington Books
An imprint of The Rowman & Littlefield Publishing Group, Inc.
4501 Forbes Boulevard, Suite 200, Lanham, Maryland 20706
www.rowman.com

6 Tinworth Street, London SE11 5AL

Copyright © 2019 by The Rowman & Littlefield Publishing Group, Inc.

Permission to reprint parts of *Finding Balance Through Friendship: Reading A WIZARD OF EARTHSEA* by Stephen M. Zimmerly (2018), published by Taylor & Francis Group (https://www.tandfonline.com).

All rights reserved. No part of this book may be reproduced in any form or by any electronic or mechanical means, including information storage and retrieval systems, without written permission from the publisher, except by a reviewer who may quote passages in a review.

British Library Cataloguing in Publication Information Available

Library of Congress Cataloging-in-Publication Data

Names: Zimmerly, Stephen M., author.
Title: The sidekick comes of age : how young adult literature is shifting the sidekick paradigm / Stephen M. Zimmerly.
Description: Lanham : Lexington Books, 2019. | Series: Children and youth in popular culture | Includes bibliographical references and index.
Identifiers: LCCN 2019006802 (print) | LCCN 2019009861 (ebook) | ISBN 9781498586801 (Electronic) | ISBN 9781498586795 (cloth) | ISBN 9781498586818 (pbk)
Subjects: LCSH: Young adult fiction--History and criticism. | Sidekicks in literature. | Heroes in literature. | Friendship in literature.
Classification: LCC PN3443 (ebook) | LCC PN3443 .Z56 2019 (print) | DDC 809.3/927--dc23
LC record available at https://lccn.loc.gov/2019006802

Table of Contents

Acknowledgments	ix
Introduction: Using Young Adult Literature to Study Sidekicks	1
1 Four Classic Sidekick Roles: Exploring Sidekicks as Narrative Gateways, Devil's Advocates, Comic Relief, and Foils	15
2 Family Ties: An Investigation into the Potential Familial Relationships between Heroes and Sidekicks	41
3 The Secondary Hero: Neville Longbottom and Tenar as Sidekicks-Turned-Heroes	69
4 The Sidekick Sequel: Reinventing Sidekicks through Parallel Novels	91
5 The Self-Aware Sidekick: Studying Sidekicks in First-Person Sidekick Superhero Stories	117
Conclusion	139
Bibliography	143
Index	149
About the Author	155

Acknowledgments

Christopher Kuipers, for his support and feedback over the years.

Lindsey Falk, Judith Lakamper, and Lexington Books, for the opportunity to publish this book.

Rachel, Nolan, Ephraim, August, and our new baby girl, for being the best sidekicks a guy could ask for.

Introduction

Using Young Adult Literature to Study Sidekicks

The importance of the "character" in literary criticism and theory has been regularly assumed since the creation of distinct characters. This importance in literature itself is obvious: where would stories be without the characters that occupy them? However, the meta-attention paid by literary criticism and theory to the nature of character in literature has often been minimal. For instance, Alex Woloch writes about several influential theorists on the paucity of literary studies devoted to character. He cites Jonathan Culler: "Character is the major aspect of the novel to which structuralism has paid least attention and has been least successful in treating."[1] Another is Seymour Chatman: "It is remarkable how little has been said about the theory of character in literary history and criticism."[2] Woloch leverages these statements to set up his own argument—that there is a relative "distribution of attention" on major over minor characters within any story's narrative.[3] His approach is to study the "character-system" and "character-space" as it occurs within the novel—a goal that sounds close to structuralism in nature.

While minor characters have failed to receive attention at different times in literary history, there have been times when character studies were given some due consideration, such as during the vogue of archetypal studies about fifty years ago: elements of a heroic archetype can be found in wide-ranging cultures, literatures, mythologies, and societies. Anthropologists, mythologists, literary critics, and psychologists alike found a character that sounded and seemed like a universal concept. Another archetypal character that occurs almost as universally as the hero is the sidekick: a close companion or friend, usually understood to be in a subordinate or deferential position to another. The sidekick is already present in the first recorded work of world literature, the Babylonian epic *Gilgamesh* (twenty-fifth cent. BC): he is Enkidu, the tamed wild man who accompanies Gilgamesh on his adventures until tragically killed (in good sidekick fashion). The advent of the secondary character in ancient drama was also very early—as Aristotle writes, "the number of actors was first increased to two by Aeschylus, who curtailed the business of the Chorus, and made the dialogue, or spoken portion, take the leading part in the play."[4]

Plato's crafting of dialogues like the *Phaedrus* around the dialogue of Socrates and the titular, but very secondary Phaedrus shows yet another early literary dimension of the sidekick, here in philosophical discourse.[5] Many other ancient examples of "right-hand men," if you will, include Moses's Aaron in the Bible and Achilles's Patroclus in *The Iliad*. Despite their evident usefulness, importance, and proliferation, it seems as though the study of sidekicks has generally, in one form or another, fallen victim of its namesake—being kicked to the side—until the late twentieth and early twenty-first centuries. Now, thanks to the influence (and legitimization) of things like comic books and popular films, the study of sidekicks has begun a resurgence and might finally get the attention it deserves. Fresh in the public zeitgeist are richly developed sidekicks like Bucky Barnes (*Captain America: The Winter Soldier* [2014]/*Avengers: Infinity War* [2018]), Mr. Spock (*Star Trek Beyond* [2016]), Chewbacca (*Star Wars Episode VII: The Force Awakens* [2015]/*Solo: A Star Wars Story* [2018]), Dr. Joan Watson (CBS's *Elementary* [2012–]), and countless others. The influx of interesting and multidimensional sidekicks like these has allowed cultural and literary history to make a shift in focus, to promote the sidekick in new and interesting ways—a shift which I will explore.

I begin this exploration by arguing that there are four classic sidekick roles: "narrative gateway" through which the reader can better understand an enigmatic protagonist; as a "devil's advocate" to provide conflicting views; as "comic relief" to an otherwise serious hero; or as a "foil" to contrast with the protagonist. At the same time, however, I also recognize the difficulty of pigeon-holing sidekicks into only four definitional roles, especially considering the changing nature of literary works (which, it must be noted, resonates with the very core of this project). Authors continue to look for ways to stretch their media and find new ways to tell stories. It is also a difficult task to choose only one of the four roles for many sidekicks, since the roles do not only overlap and combine, but they can shift, especially for sidekicks who appear in extended storylines. For example, a character like Samwise Gamgee from *The Lord of the Rings* delves (at appropriate times) into the roles of comic relief and devil's advocate: some comedy comes early on in the trilogy, and then the devil's advocate palpably arrives as the Ring takes hold of Frodo and the two hobbits find themselves at odds. The advantage in using "only" four roles, then, is to establish a definable starting-place for future conversations to build upon. A deeper structuralist study could be (and perhaps should be) performed to more completely define the different kinds of sidekick roles, which in turn would undoubtedly lead to a post-structuralist challenge to those roles, and so on.

For the most part, I use Young Adult Literature (YA) to illustrate and study how these roles are changing, as I believe this is where the truly cutting edge of sidekick development may be found. YA has embraced the sidekick, recognizing the particular power the secondary character can have for adolescent readers in experiencing growth and finding one's place in the world. Consequently, I would argue YA has been, and will continue to be, at the forefront of sidekick character studies.

Regardless of this recent flowering, the literary sidekick has yet to have a significant critical study. Literary sidekicks are typically only recognized when their characterization offers support for a researcher's major focus—gender studies, multicultural studies, or any other approach that questions power-placement in relationships. More often than not, these scholars include the sidekick in the form of footnotes, endnotes, or incidental recognitions—an act that leaves this vein largely unresearched. In light of this practice, a plethora of opportunities exist regarding the sidekick. For example, as sidekicks inherently occupy a "one-down" position, any and all conversations regarding power, oppression, marginalization, and "Othering" come into play. This position also can include discussions of race, identity, gender, and intersubjectivity when understanding how sidekicks have often been used to attract a minority audience, be it racial, cultural, or sexual. Although these opportunities exist, I intentionally choose not to pursue them at this time in an effort to first establish a study of sidekicks' narrative position and characterization. The result is a foundation that will better enable specialized research opportunities throughout various academic disciplines. In fact, part of the natural reaction to this study is to encourage (and in some cases challenge) scholars to take a more focused look at sidekicks through a unique literary lens. As it is nearly impossible, as well as irresponsible, to entirely ignore issues of power or gender, there are moments in this study where these conversations are begun, touched upon, briefly explained, or alluded to. In the interest of maintaining usable parameters in a study that might otherwise become unwieldy, however, I leave deepening these ideas for future consideration and attempt to bring the conversation back to the original focus.

Another choice that keeps the focus of this study narrow is to view the sidekick as he or she appears in YA. Because of how YA has embraced the sidekick, placing it on the cutting edge of literary history, partnering the two not only makes sense but also reveals a rich literary synergy. Firstly, YA readers typically struggling to find their position in the world relate more easily to a secondary hero of a traditional text than the primary hero. Secondly, so many sidekicks recognizable in the popular, public consciousness are male; female heroes tend to be in short supply as well. The opposite is the case in YA, as it has consistently and deeply connected with audiences through female heroes and female sidekicks. Thirdly, a rising trend in YA novels is to make the sidekick the protagonist by telling the story from the sidekick's perspective (which is, of course, a long-standing tradition in other genres, notably detective fiction). This paradoxically allows a sidekick to host the readers' experiences of finding a place in the world while still alongside a stereotypically more capable individual like the hero. (Although not studied in-depth here, another rising trend is the influence fans and fandom have had on focusing on secondary characters.)

It is my assertion that the story of growth included in most YA texts, in direct correlation to its core readership, allows the sidekick as a literary entity to "grow" beyond its literary-historical origins. This idea, the need for YA readers to continue their maturation and growth alongside their literary counterparts, is supported by considerable YA scholarship: it is clear that as the sidekicks grow, the readers can grow with them. I find and illustrate three different and distinct avenues through which this growth occurs in literary sidekicks, with the intention to help establish sidekick scholarship as a burgeoning field in and of itself, as well as its place within the scope of YA. Additionally, I believe the advanced development of the sidekick in YA demonstrates its creativity and effectiveness in reaching the YA audience.

Because one of my goals is to help establish sidekick scholarship, I freely acknowledge here the dismissal inherent in the term "sidekick." Other monikers used to describe the friendly deuteragonist include "secondary character," "supporting character," or, according to Peter Coogan, "assistant," "partner" (in a platonic sense), or "pal."[6] All these terms, however, imply at least on some level that the sidekick is an afterthought. Even when used as a marketing term—thinking of the vehicle by Suzuki called the Sidekick, the T-Mobile/Samsung cell phone called the Sidekick, or any number of software applications that "help" manage information, actions, or security—there is a connotation of usefulness, but not necessity. The unfairness of such a situation has begun playing itself out in different literary scenarios, to include J. Michael Straczynski's graphic novel *Sidekick,* a story of a superhero sidekick driven insane by his inability to escape the shadow of his once-great, now-thought-deceased hero. Over the subsequent pages and chapters—except when quoting other scholars—I have chosen to eschew the use of "supporting character," "assistant," "partner," and "pal," as I feel all fall short of the importance of the character they describe. I use "sidekick" for most conventional uses, and eventually "secondary hero" as it applies later on. I use "sidekick" with some reservations, however, as the terms still may sound dismissive. It is not my intention to continue relegating sidekicks to a subservient status, but rather to make a connection to the commonly held understanding of the character in the general consciousness.

An examination of the underexplored role of the sidekick begins in the established and much explored role of the hero, surely the most-often studied variety of main character. The hero is, in the traditional sense, the character placed in the forefront of the action—the one who embarks upon a quest, or finds him or herself entrusted with protecting the innocent in the face of evil. The extensive literary theory of the hero is based in archetypal studies: the heroes we have come to know and love (and expect) are based on universal attributes found throughout histories, mythologies, and literatures of many cultures. One entrance into the world of archetypal studies comes through Northrop Frye's *Anatomy of Criticism: Four Essays* (1957). Frye begins the study of archetypes in "a world of myth, an abstract or purely literary world of fictional and thematic design, unaffected by canons of plausible adaptation to familiar experience." In this way, Frye suggests the study of archetypes (as they are inherently outside the realm of achievability) works best when coupled with the study of myth since it too is a sort of unattainable reality. Furthermore, Frye contends myth is "the imitation of actions near or at the conceivable limits of desire." To illustrate actions pushing the boundaries of what we consider "conceivable," Frye offers an image of how "the gods enjoy beautiful women, fight one another with prodigious strength, comfort and assist man, or else watch his miseries from the height of their immortal freedom."[7]

While not exactly the gods of ancient mythology, the superheroes of the twentieth and twenty-first centuries are certainly akin to the gods of old. In fact, Superman fits Frye's image of the divine archetype perfectly. He romances beautiful women (Lois Lane, Lana Lang, Wonder Woman), and the strength he uses to fight unstoppable villains like Apocalypse from *The Death of Superman*[8] increases the longer he stays under Earth's yellow sun, making him "invulnerable," as in Mark Waid and Alex Ross's *Kingdom Come*,[9] among others. Moreover, Superman's goal has always been to assist the people of Earth, and his Fortress of Solitude often lets him internalize "his miseries" as it is a symbol of the height of his "immortal freedom." If superheroes fit so well into the role of mythic god, what role would a sidekick fulfill, or what about sidekicks would we find inconceivable? For at least a partial answer to these questions, I turn to Joseph Campbell.

While his writings on the hero archetype are now somewhat dated, Campbell still offers one of the most accessible definitions of what makes a hero. *The Hero with a Thousand Faces* describes the "monomyth," the nucleus of any number of mythic heroic tales. If Campbell's description is the minimal core of all adventures, only three steps are needed: to venture forth, encounter fabulous forces in battle, and a return with power. Of these three, the venturing out and return seem definitive and certain. Much greater possible variation stems from the "fabulous forces" that the hero encounters while venturing from the known world. One part of the narrative of fabulous forces is "Supernatural Aid," briefly defined as "the unsuspected assistance that comes to one who has undertaken his proper adventure."[10] This aid often comes in the form of a "protective figure," described as a crone or old man.[11] Campbell, as he does with most of his assertions, provides examples of these figures from myths collected from various cultures. In addition to the supernatural protective figure(s), Campbell references those simply called "helpers," of which some "give magical aid."[12] It is interesting to note that the supernatural aid comes from mentoring figures such as aged men or wizards: older, wiser, and in some ways more powerful than the hero. The remaining helper characters, those without empowering abilities, are the sidekicks. Notably absent from the illustrations Campbell provides to visually represent the heroic cycle, these sidekicks exist outside of Campbell's scope. Understandably, Campbell's intention is to present the monomythic role of the *hero*, not of the helper. Regardless, Campbell either does not find it necessary to include any sidekick figures, or simply did not bother to record any in his study of ancient mythologies. Both possibilities tell of the subsidiary consideration of sidekicks in literary history.

A third prominent version of archetypal criticism can be found in the work of Carl Jung and his theory of the collective unconscious. Like Campbell, Jung postulates the basis of all similarities found within cultures, artifacts, and memories. Unlike Campbell, who analyzed the literary similarities between myths, Jung analyzed the psychological (or psychiatric, and arguably spiritual) origins of the human "universal."[13] In short, Jung began by offering the archetype as evidence of a "psychic system of a collective, universal, and impersonal nature which is identical in all individuals."[14] The archetype, in this instance, refers not just to the motifs found in mythological research—for example, Campbell's heroic cycle. Jung takes it one step farther, calling the archetype motif a "pre-existent form . . . recognized and named in other fields of knowledge."[15] Whether or not one subscribes to Jung's postulate of a shared, universal, and subconscious archetype, the evidence supporting the theory marshals convincing psychological evidence that there are recognizable universals found in the classic hero myths.

While Jung and Campbell worked from (or towards) applications of a universal archetype, Claude Levi-Strauss dismissed this idea—at least as a way to understand myth. Specifically, Levi-Strauss objects to any assertion, Jung's or otherwise, that the archetype *itself* contains "a certain meaning."[16] Levi-Strauss makes it clear that in linguistic terms, this is akin to suggesting that sounds have inherent meanings apart from their formation of words.[17] Instead, Levi-Strauss intends to show how archetypes exist as the semantic building blocks from which myths are made: "myth, like the rest of language, is made up of constituent units."[18] This is not surprising, given his assertion that myths function (and exist) as a form of language, or even as language itself. Levi-Strauss strips myths down in the same way he might pare down the phonemes, morphemes, and sememes of a particular language. Continuing in his discussion of these constituent units, Levi-Strauss asserts that myth uses these units to "produce a meaning" by way of bundling and combining them.[19] If we were to use Levi-Strauss's system of mapping "gross constituent units"[20] as a way to trace out the utilization of sidekicks throughout myth and history, it would undoubtedly prove worthwhile. As heroes hold a position as a constituent unit of storytelling, so too can sidekicks, according to the semiotics of Levi-Strauss.

In a similar vein, children's literature scholar Maria Nikolajeva offers an interesting structural reinterpretation of how main characters and secondary characters hold varying positions in their relation to the plot. Nikolajeva builds upon previous work done by W. J. Harvey's *Character and the Novel*, suggesting that the "common and simple division of characters into main and secondary does not seem quite sufficient."[21] Her solution, then, is to further subcategorize secondary characters into "supporting characters," "satellite characters," and "backdrop characters."[22] The supporting characters exist as both plot-central characters (with the protagonists) and plot-peripheral characters (alongside satellite and backdrop characters). Her argument is that "the plot cannot develop" if main or supporting characters were removed.[23] In spite of this recognition, however, Nikolajeva's consideration of secondary characters continues to function as only a small piece of the greater whole in her study of characters.

Other scholars who write about characters, archetypes, and modern myths have given even less consideration to the sidekick. For instance, in their text *The Myth of the American Superhero*, John Lawrence and Robert Jewett offer an understanding of a culturally specific adaptation of a hero's journey: reinterpreting the hero as a Christ-figure. But where is Peter in their scheme? Lawrence and Jewett make no room for such vital secondary characters in their American monomyth: "a community in a harmonious paradise is threatened by evil; normal institutions fail to contend with this threat; a selfless superhero emerges to renounce temptations and carry out the redemptive task; aided by fate, his decisive victory restores the community to its paradisiacal condition: the superhero then recedes into obscurity."[24] Absent from the nucleus of this monomyth is the sidekick, even though Lawrence and Jewett apply their American monomyth to a variety of genres including comic books, where sidekicks appear regularly.[25] In fact, the American monomyth's premium on selflessness, as well as placing the good of society over the glory of a single hero, has placed a strong foothold in the world of comic book superheroes—as the archetypal Superman mythos undoubtedly reads like a monomythic primer in all things selfless, American, and Edenic. Lawrence and Jewett rightly focus on comic books in exploring their American monomyth, but, as I would stress, sidekicks may be just as important to a literary monomyth as they are in comic books themselves.

Although comic books will not be my primary focus, they are worth a short digression, since I believe that comics, along with YA, form the two most productive loci for the sidekick in all of literary history. Comic books themselves are currently experiencing exposure and legitimacy like never before, if only as measured on screen. In particular, big-budget comic-book–based-movies are blazing an unmistakable trail through the American—and global—box office. In doing so, they also blaze their way into public awareness. As of late 2018, no fewer than nineteen films and eleven spin-off television shows have been released as part of an effort by Marvel Comics (and Disney) to bring proprietary titles to the realm of movies and television.[26] Several of these films have eclipsed the $1 billion mark in box-office sales worldwide. At least two more films plan to be released in the next year, not counting the four animated television series currently also under production.[27] This does not even take into consideration the highly successful Batman trilogy directed by Christopher Nolan, the DC Cinematic Universe, the five Sony Spider-Man films not in the Marvel Cinematic Universe, the three Fantastic Four films, the nine (depending on how you count them) X-Men films, among others. Even those who have never seen any of these films could have scarcely missed the titanic efforts behind merchandizing.

While not quite as wellknown as the movies based on comic books, literary criticism of comics has consistently recognized the importance of sidekicks, as superheroes almost universally have sidekicks, a fact that cannot be ignored by comic book scholars. Research that stems from sociocultural subjects other than comic books, per se, naturally tends to subsume the sidekick into a larger context, rather than exploring it as a unique literary facet of its own. For instance, to what extent are there homosexual overtones in the relationships between superheroes and sidekicks? Or, how does a sidekick serve to entice a certain readership, whether women, minorities, or someone younger than the typical hero? While sidekicks exist as staples in comic books and graphic novels, they are often disregarded when a desire for "legitimacy" arises. This is often seen in film adaptations of comics, most notably Robin's absence from Christopher Nolan's *Batman* trilogy. Exceptions occur, of course, and contemporary television shows like *Titans* (2018–) have begun to challenge this notion. It should still be noted, however, that *Titans* (or the animated television shows *Teen Titans* [2003–2006], *Teen Titans Go!* [2013–], or the film, *Teen Titans Go! To the Movies* [2018]) focuses on sidekicks that band together, rather than sidekicks in traditional hero/sidekick scenarios.

Comic book scholarship offers many avenues of sidekick research. For instance, Richard Reynolds suggests Frank Miller's use of Carrie Kelly as the thirteen-year-old female Robin in *The Dark Knight Returns* radically changes the meaning of Batman's sidekick.[28] Studies such as Reynolds's underscore how sidekicks are a viable and compelling part of the superhero genre. Beyond this, Coogan's influential study, *Superhero: The Secret Origin of a Genre* argues that sidekicks are not just generic conventions, but are in fact an inherent part of the mythological heritage of comics. Coogan writes, "The surface similarities between superheroes and mythological heroes are several."[29] Among these similarities are "the crossing of heroes and gods into each other's stories," something Coogan ties to the "crossovers, guest stars, and team-ups" often found in comic book continuities.[30] Additionally, Coogan suggests the exemplary Batman mythos is "brimming with the conventions" of heroic literature, including "the helpful authority figure—Police Commissioner Gordon; the sidekick—Robin . . . and so forth."[31] As he touts the debt comic books owe to ancient mythologies, Coogan suggests that comic book sidekicks mirror those found of old: "Enkidu serves as Gilgamesh's sidekick just as Patroclus did for Achilles, Iolaus and Hylas for Hercules, and Robin for Batman."[32]

Coogan's choice to focus on Batman as mythic hero and Robin as his sidekick is a logical one; Robin is one of the oldest recognized sidekicks in comic book history. Moreover, and more to the point, Robin also provides a connection to young adults. Bradford W. Wright calls Robin's introduction in 1940 the creation of a character "with whom young readers could supposedly identify."[33] In their cultural study, *Enter the Superheroes*, Alex Romagnoli and Gian Pagnucci describe this further: "Robin perfectly fit with the age of the young boys buying Batman comic books at the time, and sales reportedly doubled as a result of his introduction."[34] Romagnoli and Pagnucci suggest Robin was a conduit through which young readers could invest themselves in Batman. Because they were younger than Batman, "comic book readers could imagine themselves as a kid sidekick, and comic books quickly filled with them."[35] Robin's introduction, then, very nicely brings the young adult reader into the conversation about sidekicks.

While Robin (in each of his or her iterations) begins as a young teenager (or younger), comic book writers recognized how their readers aged with the passage of time and allowed Robin to age alongside them. This process slowed down around the end of the 1970s, keeping the first Robin, Dick Grayson, in his "mid-twenties at the oldest."[36] The 1980s, then, saw the introduction of newer—and younger—Robins as a neat and tidy way to re-entice younger readership to pick up Batman comics. The need to relate to a youthful character (in this case, the sidekick) is a phenomenon readily recognized in YA. Yet as Robin's exact age posed a problem, so too does the definition of what constitutes a "young adult." From the beginning of criticism on children's literature, defining YA has been an ongoing problem. Definitions based on the age of the intended audience have often restricted certain works to the continuum of "juvenile literature," placing YA works alongside children's chapter books, illustrated storybooks, and read-to-me editions. However, YA texts also consistently exhibit adult themes and storylines, which makes establishing an easy definition all the more problematic. While we can easily differentiate between the gang clashes of *The Outsiders* and the depiction of second grade in *The Beast in Ms. Rooney's Room*, it is more difficult to make that distinction between books intended for fifth- through eighth-grade reading levels. On the other end of the teenaged spectrum, texts dance along the line dividing YA from traditional "adult" fiction. Ursula K. Le Guin's *Earthsea* cycles ask significant questions regarding life, death, power, and gender—but are not always considered adult fare. Which is which, and does it matter? The issue of whether or not it matters how a book is categorized is something of a passing concern (although I would eagerly enter into that debate elsewhere). What is necessary is choosing and moving forward with a working definition of YA texts.

However, many scholars of YA themselves have found defining YA to be difficult or nearly impossible. Michael Cart chronicles this historical growth of YA (and adolescence itself, for that matter), and Cart equates offering a definition for "young adult" to something "migraine inducing."[37] One of his many examples of attempted definitions (of both "young adult" and "young adult literature") comes from the writings of Isabelle Holland: "I am coming more and more to the conclusion that adolescent literature is whatever any adolescent happens to be reading at any given time."[38] Betty Carter offers this opinion: "Books are designated adult or young adult merely to distinguish the publishing divisions they come from, not to set absolute boundaries which define readership."[39] Carter's purpose in finding a definition lies in her need to make "appropriate selections"[40] from both camps when the need arises, arguing that marketing is one of the biggest sources of the differentiation between adult and young adult texts. The overriding aim of book marketing is to "spend the advertising dollar where it has the potential of drawing the most sales," which, according to Carter, is the schools and libraries acquiring YA—those institutions more likely to "purchase more copies of a hardcover book than [will] individual young adults."[41] Carter, while clearly demarcating the publication differences, is careful not to malign the literary status of either: "Maya Angelou, Harper Lee, Olive Ann Burns, David Halberstam, and Michael Dorris, adult authors favored by many young adults, are all well respected literary figures whose mastery of craft both challenges and captivates their readers."[42]

But surely a suitable definition of YA need not cover all possibilities, nor rely solely on the convenience of publishers. I will turn here to Nilsen and Donelson's *Literature for Today's Young Adults,* an excellent resource in choosing a definition for this study. Longtime students of pioneering scholar G. Robert Carlsen, Nilsen and Donelson have studied YA over the course of an over forty-year partnership in scholarship and publishing. Their definition of YA begins with "anything that readers between the approximate ages of twelve and eighteen choose to read either for leisure reading or to fill school assignments."[43] Even as they offer such a fluid range of ages from which to define a genre, they acknowledge subcategories like "Tweener fiction" that further splinter the "young adult" spectrum.[44] Perhaps most fittingly, and most helpful here, Nilsen and Donelson quote the highly respected, longtime YA critic and advocate Patty Campbell in an attempt to define YA thematically:

> The central theme of most YA fiction is becoming an adult, finding the answer to the question "Who am I and what am I going to do about it?" No matter what events are going on in the book, accomplishing that task is really what the book is about, and in the climactic moment the resolution of the external conflict is linked to a realization for the protagonist that helps shape an adult identity.[45]

If YA's core theme is "Who am I and what am I going to do about it?," this sounds much like the historical coming-of-age novel, the *Bildungsroman*. Although YA has no exclusive claim on the genre, YA has undoubtedly reappropriated the *Bildungsroman* as its own throughout its emergence and development as a separate genre over the past fifty years. In this vein, and for my purposes, if a text struggles with this central question of how adult identity should be shaped, it will be considered part of YA. This definition, coupled with Nilsen and Donelson's point that "puberty is a universal experience but adolescence is not,"[46] opens the door for even more supposedly "adult" texts to be considered part of YA—as it is certainly possible for "adults" older than eighteen to need to shape their maturing identities through internal or external conflict.

Before diving in to YA literature's treatment of sidekicks, it is important and worthwhile to explore the general nature of sidekicks. The purpose of chapter 1 is to explore the four foundational roles of narrative gateway, devil's advocate, comic relief, and foil. Ron Buchanan's "'Side by Side': The Role of the Sidekick" helps frame this chapter, as it has performed a similar study, albeit on a smaller, more limited scale. Buchanan explores the sidekick as a "confidant," a "sounding board," and a way to "bring the audience into the story."[47] These examples augment my own study, bolstering what I see as the narrative gateway role. I use two sidekick examples to illustrate each role: one from literature written for adult audiences, and one from a YA text. The intention here is to show how YA texts stretch the traditional parameters of sidekick use. Major texts analyzed in this chapter include Sir Arthur Conan Doyle's *A Study in Scarlet*, Harper Lee's *To Kill a Mockingbird*, Ben Edlund's *The Tick*, and Mark Twain's *The Adventures of Tom Sawyer*, among others.

Chapter 2 explores in greater depth how YA uses and adapts established dynamics of heroes and sidekicks by viewing the possible combinations of males and females in either role. Family dynamics give this chapter its framework, as I explore possibilities like mother-daughter, father-son, father-daughter, mother-son, and so forth. Some of these pairings naturally share overlapping characteristics, so some examples will be studied at greater length than others. Included in these different possible hero-sidekick pairings are two exceptions to the duo dynamic: heroes with two sidekicks, and heroes who eventually develop romantic feelings for their sidekicks. Examples in this chapter come from some texts already introduced in chapter 1, as well as Frank Miller's *The Dark Knight Returns*, the *Nancy Drew* series, Tamora Pierce's *Alanna*, Suzanne Collins's *The Hunger Games*, Jasper Fforde's *The Last Dragonslayer*, and more.

Chapters 3, 4, and 5 examine the ways YA elevates the sidekick beyond the conventions defined by the family dynamics of chapter 2. I argue that there are three such patterns in which YA sidekicks get elevated: the "secondary hero" (explored in chapter 3), the "sidekick sequel" (the focus of chapter 4), and the "self-aware sidekick" novel (the purpose of chapter 5). I distinguish between the second and third kinds of sidekick elevation by the original intent of the character in question. In the former, the sidekick has appeared as a secondary character in a previous novel, and has now become the main character in a later work. The latter, the "self-aware sidekick novel," begins with an original character in an original story. Chapter 3's "secondary hero" is illustrated through close analysis of Neville Longbottom from J. K. Rowling's *Harry Potter* series and Tenar from Le Guin's *Earthsea* series. Neville shows a form of elevation that comes from a gradual maturation over the course of books four through seven. Tenar, on the other hand, shows how this maturation can occur in a much more condensed manner. The "sidekick sequel" in chapter 4 focuses on a close reading of Shay from Scott Westerfeld's *Uglies* series, as well as Bean from Orson Scott Card's *Ender's Game* and *Ender's Shadow*. Shay and Bean offer the opportunity to study what happens when sidekicks become the protagonists in their own novels. The fact that these novels occur simultaneously with the original novels increases the complexity inherent with this kind of elevation. Chapter 5 looks at "self-aware sidekick novels," including Jack Ferraiolo's *Sidekicks* and John David Anderson's *Sidekicked*. The sidekicks in these examples, Scott Hutchinson and Andrew Bean, are two case studies revealing the increasingly complicated nature of heroes and sidekicks in these kinds of texts.

The Conclusion offers final thoughts regarding sidekick elevation, particularly in an attempt to succinctly express the ultimate findings of this analysis as a whole. It furthermore posits a few questions that arose as a result of performing this study, offering suggested avenues through which one might attempt to find answers.

NOTES

1. Johnathon Culler, *Structuralist Poetics: Structuralism, Linguistics and the Study of Literature* (London: Routledge, 1975), 230.
2. Seymour Chatman, *Story and Discourse: Narrative Structure in Fiction and Film* (Ithaca, NY: Cornell University Press, 1989), 107.
3. Alex Woloch, *One vs. the Many: Minor Characters and the Space of the Protagonist in the Novel* (Princeton: Princeton University Press, 2003), 15.
4. Aristotle, *The Rhetoric and the Poetics of Aristotle*, trans. W. Rhys Roberts and Ingram Bywater (New York: McGraw, 1984), 228.
5. Plato, *Phaedrus*, trans. W. C. Helmbold and W. G. Rabinowitz (New Jersey: Prentice, 1956), 3.
6. Maria Puente, "Always Someone Right by Superheroes' Side," *USA Today*, January 13, 2011, 2D, Academic Search Complete.
7. Northrop Frye, *Anatomy of Criticism: Four Essays* (Princeton: Princeton University Press, 1957), 136.
8. Dan Jurgens et al., *The Death of Superman* (New York: DC Comics, 1993), 138+.
9. Mark Waid and Alex Ross, *Kingdom Come* (New York: DC Comics, 2008), 129.
10. Joseph Campbell, *The Hero with a Thousand Faces* (New Jersey: Princeton University Press, 1972), 36.
11. Ibid., 69.
12. Ibid., 246.
13. C. G. Jung, *The Archetypes and the Collective Unconscious*, trans. R. F. C. Hull (New Jersey: Princeton University Press, 1981), 43.
14. Ibid.
15. Ibid.
16. Claude Levi-Strauss, *Structural Anthropology*, trans. by Claire Jacobson and Brooke G. Schoepf (New York: Basic, 1963), 218.
17. Ibid., 208.
18. Ibid., 210.
19. Ibid., 211.
20. Ibid.
21. Maria Nikolajeva, *The Rhetoric of Character in Children's Literature* (Lanham: Scarecrow, 2002), 112.
22. Ibid.
23. Ibid.
24. John Shelton Lawrence and Robert Jewett, *The Myth of the American Superhero* (Grand Rapids: Eerdmans, 2002), 6.
25. William G. Doty, *Mythography: The Study of Myths and Rituals*, 2nd ed. (Tuscaloosa: University of Alabama Press, 2000), 244.
26. "Marvel Movies: Marvel Cinematic Universe (MCU)," Marvel, accessed December 28, 2018, https://www.marvel.com/movies.
27. Ibid.
28. Richard Reynolds, *Super Heroes: A Modern Mythology* (Jackson: University Press of Mississippi, 1994), 100.
29. Peter Coogan, *Superhero: The Secret Origin of a Genre* (Austin: MonkeyBrain, 2006), 117.
30. Ibid.
31. Ibid., 41.
32. Ibid., 118.
33. Bradford W. Wright, *Comic Book Nation: The Transformation of Youth Culture in America* (Baltimore: Johns Hopkins University Press, 2001), 17.
34. Alex S. Romagnoli and Gian S. Pagnucci, *Enter the Superheroes: American Values, Culture, and the Canon of Superhero Literature* (Lanham: Scarecrow, 2013), 172.
35. Ibid.
36. Coogan, *Superhero*, 213.

37. Michael Cart, *Young Adult Literature: From Romance to Realism* (Chicago: ALA, 2010), 8.
38. Qtd. in Cart, *Young Adult*, 8.
39. Betty Carter, "Adult Books for Young Adults," *The English Journal* 86, no. 3 (1997): 63.
40. Ibid.
41. Ibid., 64.
42. Ibid.
43. Alleen Pace Nilsen and Kenneth L. Donelson, *Literature for Today's Young Adults*, 8th ed. (Boston: Pearson, 2009), 3.
44. Ibid., 4.
45. Qtd. in Nilsen and Donelson, *Literature*, 4.
46. Cart, *Young Adult*, 7.
47. Ron Buchanan, "'Side by Side': The Role of the Sidekick," *Studies in Popular Culture* 26, no. 1 (2003): 17.

Chapter One

Four Classic Sidekick Roles

Exploring Sidekicks as Narrative Gateways, Devil's Advocates, Comic Relief, and Foils

This chapter, in conjunction with chapter 2, serves as the literary, historical, and critical foundation for chapters 3 through 5, where I will discuss how YA stretches the very definition of sidekick. Before showing how the sidekick has changed, it is necessary to recognize how the sidekick has historically been established in the literary realm, with particular attention to the areas of criticism outlined in the introduction: archetypal, comic book, and YA. As I use these critical areas to help frame the evaluation, I consider sidekicks in the four foundational (or classic) sidekick roles: narrative gateway, devil's advocate, comic relief, and foil.

Recognizing these roles also allows me to highlight how they have been prolifically adapted in YA in particular. For each role, I will analyze an example from a text traditionally defined as "adult fiction" and from YA. These pairings will also continue to underscore the complicated definitional relationship between adult fiction and YA, which was begun in the introduction. Moreover, even before delving into the overt changes to sidekicks, there are significant differences in how adult texts and YA texts use or treat the sidekicks within their stories. Discussing these differences not only allows me to lay some groundwork for the further YA considerations in future chapters, but also shows how YA has tended to employ sidekicks carefully and creatively, in due consideration of its core readership.

Before proceeding, I should also make an observation about the selection of the literary examples cited in this chapter. While a hero/sidekick pairing can occur almost anywhere, certain genres lend themselves more easily to a hero/sidekick relationship: those requiring the fulfillment of a quest or the solving of a problem. Fantasy's preoccupation with the quest almost always demands a supporting cast for its hero. Mystery novels often have sidekicks as well, no doubt taking after the memorable detecting sidekicks created by Sir Arthur Conan Doyle and Edgar Allan Poe. Comic book superheroes fall into both of these categories—they are typically crime/mystery tales, with a touch (or a ton) of the fantastic or supernatural. Many of the texts I examine come from fantasy texts, mystery texts, or comic books for this very reason. It is also imperative to recognize the rationale behind choosing specific texts for this chapter—fantasy, mystery, or otherwise: texts were chosen based on the extent to which a sidekick exemplified one of the four classic sidekick roles. For this reason, certain textual comparisons become understandably problematic. For example, if I were to compare a comic book to a work of classical Spanish literature, drawing meaningful parallels would be difficult. The primary concern of the analysis is to define, explain, and illustrate these roles as completely as possible from a character standpoint. Therefore, the embodiment of the role supersedes any issues regarding cross-genre issues, and I give further explanation for a text's inclusion where genres do not match as ideally as possible. It is also important to point out that three of the four YA texts used in this chapter represent texts from an older generation of YA texts: all three were published well before 1967. This date is a watershed regarding YA, as it is largely recognized that the "Young Adult" moniker was not widely used until the publication of S. E. Hinton's *The Outsiders* and Robert Lipsyte's *The Contender* in 1967. Other important authors writing during this time period include Paul Zindel, M. E. Kerr, Robert Cormier, Judy Blume, Richard Peck, Anne McCaffrey, Lois Duncan, and Ursula K. Le Guin.[1] (The fourth YA text in this chapter, Le Guin's *A Wizard of Earthsea*, was published in 1968, putting it in the same historical moment as *The Outsiders* and *The Contender*.) Regardless of the recent categorization of literature as YA, there have always been texts that "appeal" to an adolescent reading audience. I have intentionally chosen older texts in this chapter for two reasons. First, as this chapter is meant to establish the ways sidekicks have traditionally been used, texts taken from an older selection of YA help historicize these uses. Second, the later chapters of this book deal specifically with significantly more recent YA texts. Using older texts here further exemplifies the contrast between how sidekicks have been used and how that use is now being challenged, stretched, and redefined.

The first role, the one I consider the easiest to define, is a sidekick as a "narrative gateway" through which the reader can better understand or sympathize with an enigmatic hero. Ron Buchanan, in "Side by Side: The Role of the Sidekick," refers to this role as a "confidant" or as "a sounding board for the main character."[2] This sounding board "represents the audience and through the interplay with the main character brings the audience into the story."[3] For instance, nearly all of the "assistants" from the vast *Dr. Who* continuum (1963–1989; 2005–present) have worked to help explain the ins and outs of the Time Lord's complexities. Another notable science-fiction example reverses the roles: how *Star Trek's* hero Captain Kirk helps illustrate the humanity of the supremely logical Mr. Spock, the Vulcan sidekick. In fact, nearly every incarnation of *Star Trek* has followed this pattern of the hero serving as the narrative gateway for the sidekick: Picard and Data (*The Next Generation*), Sisko and Odo (*Deep Space Nine*), Janeway and Seven of Nine (*Voyager*), and Archer and T'Pol (*Enterprise*). Regardless, it is much more common for a given narrative's hero to need the illumination provided by a sidekick. Richard Castle, from ABC's *Castle,* helped introduce the viewer to the procedural methods of the emotionally-distant homicide detective Kate Beckett—the hero from the NYPD. Dr. Leonard Hofstadter from CBS's *The Big Bang Theory* helps the viewer understand the socially impaired Dr. Sheldon Cooper. (As a hero/sidekick pairing, Hofstadter and Cooper are so necessary to each other that they are de facto co-protagonists.) However, the quintessential literary example of the sidekick as a narrative gateway is Dr. Watson, as nearly all of the reader's impressions of Sherlock Holmes come from the good doctor's point of view. For this reason, I use Watson to introduce the narrative gateway in detail. From YA literature, I cite Scout and Jem from *To Kill a Mockingbird*, as they also help the reader better understand the greater narrative as a whole.

Sherlock Holmes's sidekick Dr. John Hamish Watson has seen something of a renaissance in recent years. As Pulitzer Prize–winning journalist Michael Dirda puts it, "Nigel Bruce portrayed Watson as a bumbling idiot, but more recently actors such as Edward Hardwicke, Jude Law and Martin Freeman have shown that he is, in his own way, as admirable as his better-known friend."[4] Let us not forget to mention the portrayal of Joan Watson by Lucy Liu in CBS's television show *Elementary* (2012–present), nor John C. Reilly's turn as Watson in the Will Ferrell vehicle *Holmes & Watson* (2018). Reexamining the source material suggests that Watson has always deserved more than the memorably blustering portrayal of Nigel Bruce. *A Study in Scarlet* is the first case Dr. Watson "writes down" regarding his partnership with consulting detective Sherlock Holmes. Although Doyle would go on to more fully develop the relationship between the two, the dynamic of Watson's deference and disbelief in light of Holmes's observations and "deductions" is firmly established even at this early venture. Watson is an obvious narrative gateway through which "the great thinking machine" was "gradually humanised [*sic*]."[5] Obviously, all of Doyle's descriptions and considerations of Holmes are imagined as coming from Dr. Watson's pen. Consider his physical description of Holmes during their first days together: "In height he was rather over six feet, and so excessively lean that he seemed to be considerably taller. His eyes were sharp and piercing . . . and his thin, hawk-like nose gave his whole expression an air of alertness and decision."[6] Also included is Watson's initial checklist regarding Holmes's knowledge: "Knowledge of Literature.—Nil . . . Knows nothing of practical gardening . . . Knowledge of Chemistry.—Profound."[7] The inward tendencies of this hero would be lost without the first-person narration provided by this sidekick.

The second way in which Watson is the narrative gateway is his meticulous recording and recounting of the varied deductions Holmes gives. Here is Watson recording, in Holmes's own stream of consciousness, how Holmes deduces that Watson is a military doctor who has been wounded in Afghanistan:

> Here is a gentleman of a medical type, but with the air of a military man. Clearly an army doctor then. He has just come from the tropics, for his face is dark, and that is not the natural tint of his skin, for his wrists are fair. He has undergone hardship and sickness, as his haggard face says clearly. His left arm has been injured. He holds it in a stiff and unnatural manner. Where in the tropics could an English army doctor have seen much hardship and got his arm wounded? Clearly in Afghanistan.[8]

Such passages of Holmes piecing together seemingly innocuous details create the bread and butter of the Sherlock Holmes mythos—and it is thanks to Watson's diligent efforts in narrative "note-taking." Similar narrations of deduction appear throughout the *Sherlock Holmes* stories, and are unquestionably characteristic of the detective and the detective genre itself.

The third and final way Watson is a narrative gateway is found in Watson's musing as to Holmes's perceptiveness in unraveling a case. As Holmes gathers evidence upon his arrival at the crime scene in *A Study in Scarlet*, Watson remarks, "I was unable to see how my companion could hope to learn anything from it. Still, I had had such extraordinary evidence of the quickness of his perceptive faculties, that I had no doubt that he could see a great deal which was hidden from me."[9] Watson's impression that a great deal has been hidden from him turns out, as it always does, to be true. In this instance, the particulars gleaned from the crime scene include the height of the murderer, the type of his footwear, his choice in cigar, and the length of his fingernails.[10] When Holmes tells Watson how he came to these conclusions, Watson replies quite assuredly, "you have brought detection as near an exact science as it ever will be brought in this world."[11]

Watson's assertion that Holmes has taken detection to a scientific level summarizes, at least at the superficial level, an insight into the way Holmes's mind operates. A more focused study of Watson would undoubtedly reveal how completely he shows "his" readers the mind of the consulting detective—as well as his own, for it is his pen that supposedly produces the stories. In praise of Watson's narrative ability, Owen Edwards recognizes that although "naturally" bundled with other "secondary personalities, there to interpret great but unfathomable heroes," Watson belongs to a more revered archetype.[12] That archetype, according to Edwards, includes various protagonists who serve as narrative gateways: Everyman, Bunyan's Christian, and the protagonist of Langland's *Piers Plowman*—they are all the "eternal seeker . . . crossed with the eternal disciple."[13] When the protagonist is unable to fill that seeker-disciple role, enter Dr. Watson: the sidekick as narrative gateway.

As the focal duo in an early YA novel, Scout and Jem Finch form an excellent example of how a sidekick can function as a narrative gateway for the protagonist. That Scout narrates the text further aligns it with the already discussed first-person narration of Watson.

I consider *To Kill a Mockingbird* as a YA text, based not only on the youthfulness of Scout and Jem, but also in its ubiquity in secondary-school reading curricula and the greater cultural understanding of its influence on younger readers (at least in the United States). Nilsen and Donelson call it an adult book that "set the stage for contemporary YA novels."[14] (See also its inclusion in *Time* magazine's article on "The 100 Best Young Adult Books of All Time," where it is listed twelfth.[15]) As a YA text, then, it is notable that what Scout and Jem express differently is their youthfulness as the story is retold. Dean Shackleford points to this element of the novel as well, stating that "part of the novel's success has to do with the adult-as-child perspective."[16] Scout is a young girl during the events (when the story begins, she is age six), but is certainly older in its retelling. Scout has not put her thoughts down on paper while still a youth—indeed, a good amount of time has passed since the experiences recounted and the actual narration. Part of the difference between Scout and Watson, for example, is in Scout's somewhat limited ability in understanding what happens during the narration, as opposed to Watson's more learned and practiced writing (regardless of his own admission of ignorance regarding Holmes's actions). However, as is the case with all stories told after a long passage of time, both Scout and Watson give their ruminations from a more experienced vantage. It is this similarity in narration that makes these examples fit together so well, regardless of the difference in genre. For example, when the major conflict of *To Kill a Mockingbird* is introduced, Scout finds herself eavesdropping on her father's conversation with his brother, Uncle Jack:

> "You know what's going to happen as well as I do, Jack, and I hope and pray I can get Jem and Scout through it without bitterness, and most of all, without catching Maycomb's usual disease. Why reasonable people go stark raving mad when anything involving a Negro comes up, is something I do not pretend to understand. . . . I just hope that Jem and Scout come to me for their answers instead of listening to the town. I hope they trust me enough."[17]

Scout does not reveal the deeper meaning of Atticus's words, in part because the details of the case brought against Tom Robinson have yet to be disclosed to the reader, but also in part because as a girl of seven or eight (time has passed since the book began), the full implications of what was said are understandably lost. However, as she leaves to go back to bed, having been told by Atticus to do so, she states, "It was not until many years later that I realized he wanted me to hear every word he said."[18] The narrative dichotomy exists, then, between the youthful Scout describing events as she saw them at age seven or eight, and the adult Scout explaining their significance some years later. Shackleford suggests Lee gives this "image of an adult reflecting on her past" as a recollection of "her own childhood."[19]

The literary theory used to study autobiography further underscores the complexity we see here in Scout's narrative. Sidonie Smith and Julia Watson theorize that "the narrated memory is an interpretation of a past that can never be fully recovered."[20] Granted, Scout's memory must be perfect in the fictional sense—she remembers whatever Lee wants her to remember. At the same time, however, her narrative (and Lee's own attempts at fictionalizing this experience) lends itself to this active reinterpretation of events from an older perspective. Keeping in mind the pervasive influence of Jim Crow laws in *To Kill a Mockingbird*, it becomes clear that Scout's memories of the racially torn South makes her use of memory an act of political record-making. As Smith and Watson argue, "what is recollected and what is obscured . . . is central to the cultural production of knowledge about the past."[21] Lee's writing about race relations in the early part of the twentieth century makes Scout "authorized to remember . . . both personally and collectively" the political ramifications of her youth.[22] Scout moves beyond Watson's primary narrative role as a reporter in this sense, as she offers another kind of narrative gateway, namely a collective memory of major events of her time.

Another significant move beyond Watson's reporting role is Scout serving as a narrative gateway to reveal how Jem grows. Scout is certainly Jem's sidekick, regardless of the fact that one of the novel's major themes is the distance in their relationship created by their growing older. Scout spends a considerable amount of time studying the changes occurring in her older brother, as well as how he reacts to the events Atticus finds himself involved in. In this way, Scout serves as the observant eye capturing and translating the events that are bringing Jem into manhood—many of which come from Atticus in one form or another. Not only does Scout's role as narrative gateway allow a look into Jem's maturation, but this theme is also fundamental to the literary dynamic of YA. Granted, this theme of growing up is not exclusive to YA, but it is certainly a pillar of the genre and occurs with much more frequency than in others. Roberta Seelinger Trites makes this clear in her study *Disturbing the Universe: Power and Repression in Adolescent*

Literature. Trites asks, "What children's book *is not* about growth?"[23] Trites draws a distinction between books of growth (*Entwicklungsromane*—"virtually all children's and adolescent novels") and books where an adolescent emerges into adulthood (*Bildungsromane*—"the protagonist comes of age as an adult").[24] In light of this distinction, Scout's gateway into Jem's growth stays within the broader genre of the *Entwicklungsroman*, as Jem is decidedly not an adult at the novel's end. However, as an older Scout narrates recollections from her past, her own experience becomes part of the *Bildungsroman* tradition. This complex interplay in *To Kill a Mockingbird* between the two fundamental thematic forms of YA is driven by the narrative gatekeeping of the sidekick, and in this regard is far more interesting than the static window of adulthood of Watson in *A Study in Scarlet*.

The very nature of the sidekick as narrative gateway helps us see one of the most basic ways that a sidekick can function: in this instance, to better introduce the hero. Dr. Watson asks the questions of Holmes that allows the detective to showcase his observant and "deductive" prowess. Scout's position as an older voice retelling the events she witnessed as a young girl brings a very specific lens through which to view Atticus, Jem, and the sociopolitical tensions of their era.

Just as the narrative gateway role allows a sidekick to reveal a hero's nature, the devil's advocate role also reveals elements of the hero; in this case, the role shows (in part) how a sidekick can challenge, hone, and improve a hero's decision-making. This role seems partially nestled within the narrative gateway role, but they do exist independently. "Devil's advocate" could be alternatively titled "the voice of reason," a distinction that helps introduce how the role works. Penny from the *Inspector Gadget* cartoon series (and two theatrical films) is a good beginning example, as her uncle Gadget is clearly oblivious to what needs to happen to get the job done. To borrow once again from *Star Trek*, Dr. McCoy, with his cool medical professionalism, is the devil's advocate for Captain Kirk and his headstrong optimism and recklessness. A somewhat quirky, but fitting example could be made of Wilson the volleyball from Robert Zemeckis's film *Cast Away* (2000). While never actually speaking, Wilson offers "advice" that Tom Hanks's character Chuck Noland argues with . . . until realizing that Wilson was right all along.

From more traditional literature, a good place to ground this examination is Cervantes's *Don Quixote*, highlighting how Sancho acts as the voice of reason (pathetic as it may be) to the unrealistic actions of Quixote. Perhaps the quintessential moment of Sancho's action as the voice of reason is his very first: his exhortation for Don Quixote to not attack the windmills. In reply to Don Quixote's desire for "righteous warfare" against the "thirty or so wild giants" with "huge arms," Sancho states that the windmills "aren't giants . . . and what seem to be arms are just their sails, that go around in the wind and turn the millstone."²⁵ Nevertheless, and in spite of Sancho's continued shouts that "without any question it was windmills,"²⁶ Don Quixote attacks. While this instance places Sancho in the role of reason, it is hard to forget he willingly leaves his farm, his wife, and his children all in the hope of becoming governor of his very own island—promised to him by Don Quixote. If this is the mental state of one who "virtually encapsulates . . . every one of the squirely virtues to be found anywhere,"²⁷ then someone like Arthur from Ben Edlund's *The Tick*, follows perfectly in this tradition.

Like Don Quixote, The Tick is a hero exceedingly oblivious to much of reality. (The capitalization of the definitive article "The" in The Tick's name reinforces the parody/superhero-spoof nature of this series.) The Tick's sidekick, Arthur, works tirelessly to help The Tick survive, and as *The Tick* exists in various media, there are a number of versions of Arthur to consider. (*The Tick* originated as a comic book series, was adapted into an animated cartoon, and has since been adapted into two live-action television shows: one for Fox in 2001, one for streaming through Amazon in 2017.) Recognizing the somewhat limited existence of Arthur in different formats and versions of *The Tick* also presents an opportunity for a methodological digression on character studies—do we look at this triple (or quadruple) Arthur as a unified whole, or as three (or four) different and distinct characters? *The Tick* is also my first example from a comic book, which brings into play the history and criticism of that medium.

Arthur does more than simply follow in the Sancho Panza/Quixotic tradition—he also falls into the tradition of comic book/superhero parody. (Coupled with the number of times *Don Quixote* has been parodied, or viewed as metaparody, the connection deepens even further.) According to Thomas Schatz, in order for a parody to be successful, the audience must have a proper "saturation" of the original genre. Unsuccessful parody falls on deaf ears without such saturation—it simply does not work.²⁸ The success of *The Tick*—and of Arthur—stems back to the readily accepted conventions of a superhero and his or her sidekick. Peter Coogan, while studying the superhero-genre as a whole, believes such acceptance happens in "mini-cycles within each stage" of comic book development.²⁹ By the time Arthur arrives as The Tick's sidekick, the genre has reached the end of another mini-cycle. Arthur, like The Tick for that matter, falls far outside the normative superhero expectation; he too is clearly a parody. A memorable example of the extent to which *The Tick* uses parody (and even metaparody in this case) comes from the cartoon episode titled, "The Tick vs. The Tick," in which Arthur is denied access to a superhero club and is forced to go to "the Sidekick's Lounge," a run-down shack located behind the club. The parody inherent in *The Tick* brings the devil's advocate role into sharper focus. It is the conventions of parody that allow the sidekick to so completely occupy the "brains department" of the superhero/sidekick duo. I focus next on the original comic book series of *The Tick* to show this element of Arthur as the devil's advocate.

Considering how integral his intellect makes him, it is a wonder that it takes Arthur four issues to arrive. In the fifth issue, "Early Morning of a Million Zillion Ninjas," we learn that Arthur is a former clerk who bought a mechanical flying moth suit and decided to fight crime. At this point in the comic's story arc, it is clear that The Tick is mentally unstable, evidenced by nearly all of his inner thoughts ("Last night I almost had a lucid moment"),[30] clueless interactions with other characters ("I saw you on TV, Clark! I came to Team-up with you! You can be the sidekick, okay?"),[31] and the fact that the first frame of the first issue shows him straight-jacketed inside a mental institution.[32] Arthur, on the other hand, quickly shows himself to be on the ball and adept in fighting crime—at least intellectually—when he advises The Tick and Paul the Samurai (a sword-wielding ally) on how to properly proceed. Moreover, and in keeping with the devil's advocate/voice of reason role, Arthur successfully opposes this agenda proposed by Paul the Samurai: "We want to swim in the hot, flowing river of our foe's blood," followed enthusiastically by The Tick's "Yeah!"[33] Arthur wisely advises to simply allow the enemy to come to them, which is what happens.[34]

Arthur also offers an intriguing look into the nature of literary character, which I believe is beneficial to consider here. Because Arthur exists in three different media, he exists as three slightly different, yet still interconnected personas (or four, again considering the Amazon series). In fact, because of Arthur's limited, and very recent, existence, it becomes essential to consider all three. (Something similar could be performed with virtually any character from the intentionally altered versions of Douglas Adams's *The Hitchhiker's Guide to the Galaxy* as it appears in text, radio, stage, and film. Ford Prefect, sidekick to protagonist Arthur Dent, would be a good starting point.) As Edlund was instrumental in the creation of *The Tick* cartoon, Fox Network's live action adaptation, and Amazon's most recent version of the characters, many of the same scenes showing the early interactions between Arthur and The Tick are found in all versions.

What is most compelling here are the differing amounts of crime fighting prowess Arthur possesses in each. In the comic, he is well-informed, confident, and has a decent muscular physique despite his self-description as "chubby." It is also suggested that he has been unsuccessfully trying to involve himself in superhero intrigue for some time. The cartoon version of Arthur, on the other hand, embraces the influence of parody even more fully. He is introduced while still working as an accountant—fresh and naïve to the world of superheroes and often frightened to boot.[35] Arthur, from the live-action series, closely mimics his cartoon counterpart. The role Arthur plays as the voice of reason is not diminished in any way, but his authority to do so lessens in correlation to his experience. In fact, the comic book Arthur is better equipped to play the hero role than The Tick, the only exceptions being The Tick's nigh-invulnerability and his penchant for finding trouble; Arthur's only power is self-powered flight, and he can't find intrigue despite his best efforts. (This kind of cross-medium character study is also developed and utilized in chapter 3.)

For the early YA example of a devil's advocate, I argue Huckleberry Finn plays this role in Mark Twain's *The Adventures of Tom Sawyer*. Much has been written about whether or not *Tom Sawyer* is a children's book, YA book, or not meant for children at all. Beverly Lyon Clark weighs in, acknowledging how *Tom Sawyer* was "generally relegated to children's literature" and *Huckleberry Finn* was "considered suitable for adults" for much of the twentieth-century.[36] She further confirms that both "straddled the two readerships," especially as "initial critics rarely mentioned one book without the other."[37] Finally, Lyon Clark suggests that in the light of "the Harry Potter phenomenon," *Tom Sawyer* finds itself in an act of "repositioning itself" in regard to its audience.[38] Furthermore, while understanding that the post–*Harry Potter* world "erodes the boundaries between child and adult reading publics," *Tom Sawyer* can clearly be considered a YA text.[39] Within the novel, Twain creates verbal interplay between Tom and Huck which makes their hero/sidekick relationship inherently complex. While it is certainly possible to perform a similar, cross-medium study of Huckleberry Finn (considering the myriad ways he has been characterized over 140 years), it is not quite as necessary as it was with Arthur. Instead, all that is needed are a few examples of Huck's moments as the voice of reason in Twain's *Tom Sawyer*. Indeed, they are each other's voices of reason, and alternate as sidekicks in each other's respective titular novels. Their occasional falling out as friends also creates situations where *neither* is the voice of reason, as they take turns ignoring each other or take turns projecting responsibility for the situation onto the other. The most telling of these situations is their discussion after witnessing Injun Joe murder Dr. Robinson and frame Potter.[40] Their dialogue deals mostly with whether or not to tell the authorities of the murder:

[Tom]: "Who'll tell? We?"

[Huck]: "What are you talking about? S'pose something happened and Injun Joe *didn't* hang? Why he'd kill us some time or other, just as dead sure as we're a-laying here."

[Tom]: "That's just what I was thinking to myself, Huck."[41]

In this first instance, Huck offers his decidedly forceful opinion on what to do, convincing Tom, who not only quickly acquiesces, but also suggests that

Huck's opinion was his own from the start. Tom asks if Huck can keep the information to himself, making an effort to ensure the plan is possible. Huck replies in the affirmative.[42] In this case, as before, Tom is the initiator—he asks for Huck's opinion. Huck, while adamant in giving it, also seems to wait for Tom's choice to listen to the advice. It is possible that Tom would have reached the same conclusions without Huck's influence, but the knowledge does indeed lie with Huck in this instance.

Coupling this conversation with another previously had by Tom and Huck (about whether or not a dead cat can help rid oneself of a wart),[43] the line between who is hero and who is sidekick blurs: the roles the boys play could be swapped. This relative interchangeability is further problematized with the text of *Huckleberry Finn*. In this case, Huck is the narrator of his own tale, as opposed to merely a player in Tom's. In a Bakhtinian analysis of the two texts, Paul Lynch suggests the most pivotal change comes from Twain's choice to narrate *Huckleberry Finn* from Huck's first-person point of view, allowing "Huck to be a different kind of hero, and one that is ultimately more compelling."[44] While I develop this idea further in chapter 4, Lynch's drawing of similarities between Tom and Huck help inform the idea of interchangeability—both are "able" to take the lead position. At the same time, Lynch recognizes Huck's role in *Tom Sawyer*. Huck "only" has the authority to rehash what has been stated, what Lynch recognizes as Michael Holquists's description of "internally-persuasive discourse."[45] Within the confines of *Tom Sawyer*, then, Tom is the clear hero. Furthering the notion of interchangeability is Huck's choice to listen to Tom's questionable advice late in the narrative of *Huckleberry Finn*, an act Daniel Davis Wood calls "heartless" and "reckless."[46] Most interesting is the fact that Tom and Huck serve each other interchangeably as the devil's advocate over the courses of their respective novels. This intellectual codependence fits firmly inside YA: part of growing up involves learning from one another, listening to counsel and choosing whom to listen to. In this way, Huck exhibits an element of the voice of reason not found with Sancho or Arthur. Sancho's character is complex in the scope of the entirety of *Don Quixote*, but his role alongside Quixote is firmly situated. Quixote's haughty treatment of Sancho is typical of their static, one-way relationship. Arthur and The Tick have the same dynamic—regardless of Arthur's repeated wisdom or help, The Tick remains clueless. Conversely, Tom and Huck trade back and forth with each other.

The devil's advocate/voice of reason sidekick role works in conjunction with the narrative gateway to reveal select complexities in the hero's character. In this case, the sidekick is able to engage on the same plane as the hero as he or she challenges a possible course of action, or proposes a more advisable one. Arthur is The Tick's voice of reason, offering sound advice when The Tick's intuition and intentions seem ill-conceived (which they often are). Huckleberry Finn and Tom Sawyer take that role even further as they trade back and forth, effectively taking turns offering contrary, engaging opinions.

The sidekick as comic relief differs from the narrative gateway and devil's advocate sidekicks in that its function is not contingent to revealing part of the hero's character. Instead, it lives up to the expectations triggered by the obvious definition: the comic relief sidekick is present to give the reader something humorous. This is a role very familiar to the modern consciousness, thanks to any number of famous straight-man/comic duos: Laurel and Hardy, Abbott and Costello, Martin and Lewis, Ball and Ricardo, among many others. A more recent example of the straight-man/comic, hero/sidekick pairing can be found in the comedic partnership of Tina Fey and Amy Poehler—who often trade the two roles back and forth. Perhaps most notable are their memorable portrayals of Sarah Palin and Hilary Clinton, respectively, during *Saturday Night Live*'s lampooning of the 2008 presidential election campaign (not to mention their two-year hosting of the Golden Globe awards). This straight-man/comic pairing occurs often in literature. For instance, Grumio in *The Taming of the Shrew* gives a hilarious performance as Petruchio's servant, mishearing direction and abusing his fellow servants according to what he believes is his master's whim. Another interesting version of this role is P. G. Wodehouse's Jeeves. The quintessential valet embodies all things English while acting in stark contrast to (and often in disbelief of) his foppish master, Bertie Wooster. In this case, it seems that the roles of comic and "straight man" are reversed: the hero is the comic figure. After analyzing Jeeves here in more depth, I will next explore a notable YA example of the sidekick as comic relief: twelve of the thirteen dwarves (as well as Bilbo Baggins) from J. R. R. Tolkien's *The Hobbit*. Published in 1937, *The Hobbit* is also widely recognized as either children's literature or YA as it bridges the two readerships in the same way as *The Adventures of Tom Sawyer*. (Like *To Kill A Mockingbird*, *The Hobbit* is also included in *Time*'s "100 Best Young Adult Books of All Time," where it is listed twenty-ninth.[47]) Because the twelve dwarves that accompany Thorin in *The Hobbit* are almost narratively indistinguishable, I treat them collectively as a single sidekick.

The instance of Jeeves as comic relief is remarkable in that he is, as described by John Mortimer, the servant in a "master-servant relationship in which the servant is, inevitably, the master."[48] Jeeves is the straight man in their comic duo; Wooster is the comic. In many ways, this almost disqualifies Jeeves as a sidekick, except that he would, in his impeccable devotion to duty and diligence, balk at such a suggestion. Additionally, while Wooster is the inherently more comic figure, he still commands the narrative and the social standing. The comedy, indeed, comes from Jeeves, but not from his figure of hilarity, rather from the exact opposite. As is the case in so many narratives, the reader sees Jeeves through the perspective of Wooster, disallowing an initially unbiased opinion of the valet. Yet it is through this ongoing bias that the comedy emerges, as so much of it is based in Wooster's amazement at Jeeves' ability to fix nearly everything, from a nasty hangover[49] to unwanted marital engagements.[50] Mortimer likens the Wooster-Jeeves duo to the inspiration provided by the Don Quixote-Sancho Panza pairing, in that the servant shows more sense than the master.[51] In this way, it becomes clear that Jeeves also fulfills the "voice of reason" sidekick duties. "The Birth of Jeeves," from the *Virginia Quarterly Review*, presents an interesting (and compelling) argument for Wodehouse's choices regarding the creation of the master/servant scenario: a boarding school "ethos" that Wodehouse may have retained long after adulthood.[52] When comparing the master-servant dynamic of Wooster and Jeeves to similar stories (Watson offers both *Don Quixote* and *The Pickwick Papers*), Wodehouse's works are "schoolboying in a way [the others] are not: all sunny afternoons, famous poems flippantly quoted out of context, as boys do, practical jokes and late-night tuck."[53] This is what makes Jeeves such a great example of comic relief: the very nature of Wodehouse's writing was meant to bring levity and humor to readers perhaps unaccustomed to finding it in similarly-themed stories.

More than anything, it often seems that Wodehouse's comedy comes from Jeeves's near-perfect prescience, as well as Wooster's consistent inability to see his valet's wisdom. In "Jeeves Takes Charge," the short story chronicling Jeeves's first few days on the job, Wooster must dispose of his uncle's memoirs or else suffer the end of his marital engagement. That his uncle is also his benefactor complicates matters significantly. Jeeves (as he almost always does) provides the solution, protecting Wooster from his uncle, ensuring the memoir gets published, and guaranteeing that the ill-advised engagement is called off.[54] The best comedic note of the story comes from a suit Wooster initially insists on keeping, despite Jeeves's advice to the contrary.[55] Wooster begins to harbor some animosity toward Jeeves, citing his particular attachment to the suit, as well as his understanding that one should not give too much power to one's valet.[56] After Jeeves extricates Wooster from the debacle concerning the manuscript, as well as the engagement, Wooster awakes the next day to allow Jeeves, regarding the suit, to "give the bally thing away."[57] Jeeves responds that he had given it to "the under-gardener last night."[58] The delayed revelation of the punch line is a classic piece of comedic timing, and Wodehouse lets Jeeves perfectly anticipate the preferred and eventual outcome to the scenario. Jeeves as comic relief is as complete as the thoroughness he takes in watching over Wooster.

The comic relief found in *The Hobbit* does not come from the timing of a single, in-control sidekick, as is the case with Jeeves. Rather, it comes from the timing of twelve largely interchangeable dwarves. It is this commonality in timing that links these two rather disparate texts together in this analysis.

As I delve into *The Hobbit*, it is worth noting that within the novel, the tone of high fantasy, of which Tolkien was certainly a master, is not uniformly dignified and serious in this instance and subsequently sets the stage for occasional comic turns of playfulness and joviality. One of the more marked of such instances occurs early in the text, in a narrative retelling of how the famous hobbit Bullroarer cut off the head of a great goblin, sending it sailing "a hundred yards through the air" and into a rabbit hole: "In this way the battle was won and the game of Golf invented at the same moment."[59] This is also one of the few times Tolkien mentions something as out of place with Middle-earth as golf. Even the game of riddles between Bilbo and Gollum serves as a moment of lightness—regardless of the fact that those riddles are told "in the dark."[60] The sometimes subtle, and yet significant role of comedy in *The Hobbit* plays into Tolkien's views on what he called the "eucatastrophe." In his study on catastrophe versus eucatastrophe, Christopher Toner defines Tolkien's term as the "sudden turn in the story that, perhaps just for a moment, lets a gleam of final victory shine on a history of long defeat."[61] Much of the catharses found in reading Tolkien's texts rely heavily upon this hope of overcoming certain defeat, especially in the more heavy-hearted narrative of *The Lord of the Rings*. On a much smaller scale, the presence of comedy in *The Hobbit* helps support the "gleam of final victory" that occurs after the book's final battle. According to Christopher Garbowski, Tolkien believed that "joy is the proper end of the fairy tale, or fantasy."[62] This certainly pertains to both *The Hobbit* and *The Lord of the Rings*.

As the titular protagonist, Bilbo does not need/warrant a sidekick. However, a strong case can be made that Bilbo is not the hero of the adventure. Instead, he is incorporated into Thorin's company of thirteen dwarves. In many ways, then, Bilbo and Thorin's company serve as sidekicks to Thorin. Yet considering Thorin's repeated and ongoing disdain for Bilbo, it is hard to call Bilbo his sidekick. Crafted to embody so much of what it meant to be English in the early twentieth century, Bilbo's personality creates the opportunity for comedic tension when the dwarves disturb the meticulous balance of his everyday life. The dwarves as a group are a core comic element in *The Hobbit*. Without the inherent chaos stemming from fourteen strong-minded characters embarking on a quest (fifteen, when Gandalf is with them), there would be considerably fewer opportunities for comedy. Also, without the dwarves, the presence of eucatastrophe would surely be lessened, eucatastrophe being so necessary to balance their tragic fates: it is Bilbo's return home after the death of so many dwarves (including Thorin) that brings the proper, joyful end. Any number of passages would serve to illustrate this comic relief, but I intentionally focus on the dwarves' introductions to Bilbo and Beorn, as these two instances draw their comedy from timing—again, to strengthen the comparison (and ultimate contrast) with Jeeves as comic relief.

The first introduction, to Bilbo, acts doubly as comic relief as it upsets Bilbo's pleasant, simple existence as well as showcases the behavior of the twelve "sidekick" dwarves. The first dwarf to knock on the unsuspecting hobbit's door is Dwalin, who enters "uninvited" and "without a word of explanation."[63] Bilbo's notice of Dwalin's omission of social convention speaks to his incredulity regarding such behavior. Balin, who comes next, acts similarly to his brother Dwalin: "he too hopped inside as soon as the door was open, just as if he had been invited."[64] Bilbo recovers himself enough to provide the brothers proper tea and refreshments. His next thought proves to be one of the best setups for a joke in the novel: "He had a horrible thought that the cakes might run short, and then he—as the host: he knew his duty and stuck to it however painful—he might have to go without."[65] That Bilbo might run out of cakes to serve his guests, and subsequently leave him with none, compounds the nature of hospitality with the dietary habits of average hobbits: they eat a lot, and often. The tension and ultimate punch line comes with the timing of three more waves of arrival: first by Kili and Fili, then by Dori, Nori, Ori, Oin, and Gloin, and finally with Bifur, Bofur, Bombur, Thorin, and Gandalf. If two dwarves threatened the supply of cake, what then would six times as many houseguests do to the precious larder?

The narration helps establish the level of incredulity felt by Bilbo. When Dori, Nori, Ori, Oin, and Gloin arrive, the narrative states, "It was not four after all, it was FIVE."[66] The font change denotes both a feeling of surprise and a feeling of dread—what would Bilbo do with nine dwarves? This, of course, heightens even further with the arrival of the remaining four dwarves and Gandalf. This final group enters by falling inside, "one on top of the other" due to Bilbo's abrupt and unexpected opening of the door.[67] This is part of the way Tolkien uses comedy to cleverly address the needs of a YA audience. If such readers do not pick up on the social ridiculousness of over a dozen unexpected dinner guests, then they would certainly react to a moment of physical comedy. This coincides with Cart's analysis of first-person adolescent narrators. Michael Cart calls it "zany, wisecracking, adolescent humor."[68] The physical comedy of the dwarves exists in the same vein—even more so if one remembers that the true original audience for the book was Tolkien's own children. The *Lord of the Rings* trilogy, by contrast, was intended from the start for an adult reading public. This difference can be seen even more clearly when looking at the Peter Jackson–directed film versions of Tolkien's novels. *The Hobbit* films have a significant amount of slapstick humor, where *The Lord of the Rings* films have but a few instances.

The dwarves' introduction to Beorn, occurring some one hundred pages later in the novel, is another one of these moments of physical humor, and is a clear parallel with the introduction to Bilbo. Much of the lightness of this scene comes from Gandalf's sly handling of the situation rather than from the dwarves themselves. Gandalf forebodingly tells the dwarves ahead of time about Beorn's temperament, that they should be "careful not to annoy him," and that he "can be appalling when he is angry."[69] He introduces his plan to slowly introduce them two at a time. During the introduction, Gandalf tells Beorn of their recent exploits with the goblins of the mountains as pair after pair of dwarves arrives. The arrival of Dwalin and Balin strike him as funny, causing Beorn to stop "frowning" and to "burst into a chuckling laugh; they looked so comical."[70] Beorn even vocalizes his opinion of their appearance, calling them "a fine comic [troop]."[71] Tolkien also remarks on Bombur's physical appearance, citing the fact that he was fat as a reason for his shortness of breath during his arrival. The frequent interruptions caused by the comic dwarves make Beorn "more interested in the story," a gambit that "kept him from sending the dwarves off at once like suspicious beggars."[72]

In the end, the question is not whether or not the dwarves are comedic—it is clear that they are. The questions are, then, what is the connection between their comedy and their roles as sidekicks, and how do they differ from Jeeves? The first question finds its answer in the actions and treatment of Thorin, the leader of the company, and the novel's tragic hero. Thorin is not allowed to be funny—at least, not in the same way as his kinsmen. Thorin arrives at Bilbo's door at the bottom of the dog pile of dwarves, a situation less than ideal for a celebrated leader, especially considering how Bifur, Bofur, and the "immensely fat and heavy" Bombur sprawled on top of him.[73] Tolkien's introductory description of Thorin calls him "enormously important" and "great," as well as "not at all pleased" and "very haughty."[74] The other twelve get nearly nothing in the way of an initial personality description (the exception being Dwalin and Balin, the brothers, who talk "like old friends").[75] In fact, there is very little to differentiate the twelve followers of Thorin, except perhaps Bombur.

As Thorin does not have occasion to be humorous, the sidekicks do it for him and provide levity where it might not otherwise occur. The comic actions that help gain Beorn's assistance come from the troop of dwarves, not from Thorin. Thorin arrives first, after Gandalf and Bilbo. There is nothing markedly comic about his introduction to Beorn. In fact, another thing setting Thorin apart from his sidekicks is Beorn's knowledge of his parentage: "Thorin (son of Thrain, son of Thror, I believe)."[76] This moment of recognition builds the case for Thorin's importance even more, considering Beorn claimed never to have heard of Gandalf only moments before. (Such a remark means little in the context of *The Hobbit*, but in the greater context of Middle-earth's mythology, it is certainly notable to have heard of a dwarf and not to have heard of a higher-level being of immense power and immortality like Gandalf.) The other dwarves' fealty to Thorin also mimics Jeeves's commitment to Wooster: both the dwarves and Wooster exist in a hierarchical society where their service and/or allegiance is inherent in one's place inside that society (although serving as one's valet is significantly different than serving one's king). Furthermore, and more to the point regarding Tolkien, Thorin's somber nature finds itself felt all the more potently by its contrast to the joviality of the twelve, again in line with Tolkien's application of eucatastrophe.

Were it not for the comedy provided by the company (Bilbo included, when and where the story allows), *The Hobbit* would hold much more serious overtones. As it stands, regardless of the inclusions of mortal danger, death, and war, *The Hobbit* comes across tamely when compared to its sequel(s), *The Lord of the Rings*. Much of this strong tonal dichotomy can be attributed to the lightness brought into the story by the physical comedy of the sidekick dwarves—a comedy very much removed from the always-in-control seriousness of Wodehouse's Jeeves. In his own way, however, Jeeves brings relief through the resolution to the absurd social complications Wooster continually finds himself embroiled in. This physical comedy, then, is one of the major differences between Wooster and the dwarves. The inclusion of physical comedy represents significant tonal distance, and is a demarcation between the two texts. Considering something like the inclusion of physical comedy might come too close to the high-brow/low-brow debate, but such a distinction actually plays very well into these two examples. Jeeves represents everything high-brow, while the dwarves are, quite literally, of the earth.

In both Tolkien and Wodehouse, the sidekick exhibits significant comic relief by highlighting the seriousness inherent in the hero's more elevated social status, and both do so by utilizing moments of comedic timing. In one sense, the seriousness of the hero suggests further denigration on the part of the sidekick, and some of that is indeed true. In chapter 3, this issue of relative social denigration comes up again when I analyze the character Neville Longbottom from J. K. Rowling's *Harry Potter* series: Neville, I will argue, begins as a definitive example of comic relief, but grows into a very different role by the end of the series.

Sidekicks can often also function as a foil for the protagonist, but I have found that the difference between a foil and a sidekick can often blur, leading me to question how long a sidekick can act as a foil before he or she can no longer be considered a sidekick (a consideration I further develop in chapter 5). The sidekick as foil presents a difficulty, almost a paradox, in definition: to be considered a foil, the character must show a recognizable contrast to the protagonist, so as to better highlight the strengths, failings, and/or intrigue of the hero. (The use of "foil" in this sense hearkens back to the practice of using foil as a contrasting backing for precious gems, setting off the brilliance of the stone.) This contrast is often within the context of an equal playing field, "characteristically" speaking. The sidekick, on the other hand, often languishes in a subsidiary capacity (as established in the introduction)—hence the paradox at play here. An excellent example of such a pairing is Hal Foster's Prince Valiant and Sir Gawain, from his long-running comic strip *Prince Valiant in the Days of King Arthur*. Over the course of the strip's eighty-plus year history, Valiant and Gawain often alternate between the roles, beginning with Valiant serving as Gawain's squire. A more recent pop-culture example comes from the American version of *The Office*, as everyman-hero Jim Halpert puts up with the absurdities of his counterpart Dwight Schrute.

From literature, Horatio in *Hamlet* is a classic introductory example of this foil/sidekick quandary. Horatio is the closest thing Hamlet has to a sidekick, mainly because of their "intimate" friendship, but also because of their differences.[77] Buchanan even considers Horatio a "surrogate" for Hamlet.[78] Fortinbras and Laertes, the other readily identifiable foils to Hamlet, lack the necessary relationship with the protagonist to be considered sidekicks—not to mention their antagonistic tendencies.[79] Moreover, given how the entire play revolves around whether and how the melancholy Hamlet can and will define his own character, almost every other character in *Hamlet* can be read as a humoral foil, even the choleric Fortinbras, who only lurks offstage. A character like Samwise Gamgee of *The Lord of the Rings* similarly falls into this Horatio-like pattern of the foil/sidekick.

While YA has often claimed J. R. R. Tolkien's *The Lord of the Rings* as its own (and will continue to do so), I consider it here as a work of adult fiction, for if anything it bridges the gap nicely between YA and more "standard" adult novels. Betty Carter cites the phenomenon of middle-school–aged boys often reading adult "quest fantasy" in preference over more pointedly YA fare.[80] Considering *The Hobbit*'s position as prelude to *The Lord of the Rings*, the transition from one to the other by young adults is simply a logical one. The four major hobbits of the *Lord of the Rings* help bridge this gap further, as they represent a young demographic of hobbits. Frodo Baggins comes of age in the opening chapters of the saga. When he leaves on his quest, he is accompanied by Meriadoc Brandybuck, Peregrin Took, and Samwise Gamgee—all of whom are (for all intents and purposes) the same approximate age. Samwise, or Sam, is clearly Frodo's sidekick, as he dutifully follows him through the perils they face to destroy the One Ring. Sam offers moments of both disagreement and clarity in his back-and-forth with Frodo, but never quite falls into a devil's advocate role—his position in the social hierarchy of hobbits is far too entrenched to allow him the status to question Frodo in this manner. Robin Robertson describes Sam's status as "a simple gardener, born into this lower strata of society as generations before him had been."[81] Furthermore, Robertson thinks it "unthinkable for Sam to consider himself Frodo's equal."[82] Sam's inability, or refusal, to consider himself Frodo's peer comes up again and again. Any comedic moments involving Sam do not add up to enough comic relief to define him as such—there is far too much drama involved in the later parts of their quest. Therefore, although Sam exhibits fluidity between sidekick roles, the role that he illustrates most completely might be the fourth and final role of foil.

Sam proves his worth as a foil near the end of *The Two Towers*, book two of the trilogy. Believing Frodo has been killed by the immense spider Shelob, Sam faces a dilemma. Part of him wants to end his own life and travel with Frodo wherever he may now be going. Another part desires to stay and wait until the two of them are discovered, and thus end it all. But a third part wins out over all: to act as the final remaining member of the Fellowship and finish the job with which they were entrusted. In the face of this knowledge, Sam's inner turmoil is revealed, "You are the last of all the Company. . . . Why am I left all alone to make up my mind? I am sure to go wrong."[83] Regardless of his own misgivings concerning his judgment or decision-making, Sam takes the One Ring from Frodo's neck. Putting it on his own neck, he feels both the responsibility of the mission and the physical manifestation of the Ring's influence upon him: "His head was bowed to the ground with the weight of the Ring, as if a great stone had been strung on him. But slowly . . . he could walk and bear his burden."[84]

It is the placing of the Ring on his own neck and subsequently placing himself under its influence that moves Sam into a position of similarity with Frodo. While he carries the Ring for only a short time (he soon finds the revived Frodo and returns it), carrying it qualifies him as a ring-bearer. Robertson describes Sam's actions as "stepping beyond the limits of his class, of what someone like him is capable of being."[85] Sam, therefore, eclipses his gardener status and shows fortitude comparable to Frodo's as a ring-bearer. Sam-as-foil comes into play as he, a lowly gardener, can exhibit similar traits to the "master of the finest house in Hobbiton."[86] All ring-bearers are given the option to leave Middle-earth and sail across the sea, as Frodo explains: "You too were a Ring-bearer, if only for a little while. Your time may come."[87]

In this way also, Sam proves himself to be the true fulfillment of the quest. Carrying the Ring has damaged Frodo too completely for him to find rest and peace in Middle-earth. Sam, on the other hand, finds himself able to embrace the life they once led—he marries and has children. His progeny are the innocents for whom the Fellowship embarked upon their mission to destroy the ancient evil of Sauron once and for all. The wish was once for all five hobbits connected to the Ring to return and live their lives normally once more. The two non-ring-bearers, Merry and Pippin, move into this life easily. Bilbo and Frodo, each carriers of the Ring for a significant time and significant purpose, cannot forget it, nor its influence. Sam bridges both possibilities and brings the overarching story to completion. He carried the Ring, but falls back into life in the Shire with love and enthusiasm. It is not for many years that the decision falls to Sam. At the age of 102, after his wife passes away, Sam settles his affairs and travels west, where according to tradition, he "went to the Grey Havens, and passed over Sea, last of the Ring-Bearers."[88] In this way, Sam's fate shows "the brilliance" of what Frodo's fate could not bring. Frodo, as the hero, needed to remove himself from a world no longer able to sustain him. Sam embraces that possibility, finding solace in the soil, his family, and the world he helped save.

Within YA, I look at Vetch from *A Wizard of Earthsea*, as an even clearer example of a sidekick who serves as a foil to the hero.[89] Most of the adventures Ged experiences throughout Le Guin's *A Wizard of Earthsea* are undertaken on his own. He encounters other people, certainly, but none travel with him throughout the story's arc. It is the book's major theme, what Peter Hollindale describes as its "preoccupation with death," that at last elicits Ged's need for something more than a passing companion.[90] As he sets out to encounter what seems to be his certain end, fittingly near the end of the novel, Ged brings Vetch with him. Vetch is the only logical choice considering their long-established friendship. The older of the two, Vetch begins that friendship with Ged while they were still students in the wizarding school on the island of Roke: "Vetch had been three years at the School, and soon would be made Sorcerer. . . . He offered and gave Ged friendship, a sure and open friendship which Ged could not help but return."[91] The fact that Vetch was older, and was already on his way to achieving the next class of magic mastery, makes little difference in their friendship, neither at first nor later on. After Ged spends the required year studying the true names of things (without which no true magic could be woven),[92] he returns to the main school to find Vetch a full sorcerer, "but that set no barrier between them."[93] Ged's ambition allows him to lead Vetch, if it can be called leading, when they interact with the other students during their time on Roke. This dynamic, like all other relationships in Ged's life, changes when he calls forth the shadow: it puts him in a coma-like state for weeks, undermines his confidence for years, and eventuates the great quest he undertakes.

After Ged wakes from his first encounter with the shadow, Vetch comes to him to say good-bye; Vetch has gained his wizard's staff and must go out in to the world. Vetch restores Ged's confidence, telling him, "I see before you, not rooms and books, but far seas, and the fire of dragons, and the towers of cities, and all such things a hawk sees when he flies far and high."[94] When he leaves, Vetch entreats Ged to visit him in the East, to "send for [him]" by his true name: Estarriol. Vetch's revelation of his true name gives Ged also "the proof of unshaken, unshakeable trust."[95] Without this revelation, it is possible Ged's sense of self would not have recovered enough to accomplish anything. In their analysis of Le Guin's use of names, naming, and Jungian psychology in the *Earthsea* books, Craig and Diana Barrow call this gift the "provisional independence" necessary to overcome the shadow, the "darker part of himself."[96]

In many ways, then, Vetch is more of an older brother, a helper in the way of the archetypal wizened old man.[97] In this manner, he also can be considered a foil. Where Ged was once headstrong, Vetch was always patient. Where Ged was foolhardy and proud, Vetch was kind and good at listening. While Ged released the shadow through a dangerous act of uncontrolled magic, Vetch studied diligently. Ged spent the better part of a year recuperating from his foolishness; Vetch graduated and moved on. They do share some similarities beyond their ability to use magic, however: they are both from poor villages, both from islands from the eastern part of the known world, and both represent a younger demographic within the students at Roke. However, when Ged nears the end of his quest to confront his shadow, the older brother dynamic changes. Vetch recognizes that it is Ged's quest, and offers, nay insists, that he accompany him. Ged accepts. While on the quest together, Ged is the hero (almost by default, considering only he can confront the shadow, as the two are linked). Vetch accompanies in a support position, both to bolster Ged's morale as well as to know the outcome of the quest—good or bad—in order to either immortalize the deed in song or to warn the world of the shadow's evil.[98]

While Vetch is not as powerful a wizard as Ged, he is also not reliant upon him for saving him from enemies—he has his own formidable skills. Again, Vetch is older than Ged—there is no need for him to look to Ged for guidance or protection. It is also important to note how Vetch does not qualify as a sidekick in any of the other three typical roles: he is absent from too much of the story to help a reader understand Ged, he does not try to dissuade Ged from his quest or challenge him in any fashion, and there is almost nothing comical about the text at all. What sets Vetch apart, in the YA fashion, is when he embodies (as foil) a fully neutral position where he neither questions nor condemns Ged—he accepts him based on the friendship they forged during their boyhood, during their teenage years. He is what Horatio should have been to Hamlet, the friend and confidant that so many adolescents yearn for—and many never find. Ged, well past his adolescence in one way (he is a full wizard having faced dragons,[99] ancient evil,[100] and his own shadow[101]), is still a young man in others: he is only nineteen at the end of his quest.[102] Furthermore, according to Jeanne Murray Walker, "Adolescents who read Ursula Le Guin's fantasy *A Wizard of Earthsea*, participate in Ged's symbolic transformation from childhood to adult status."[103] In the same sense, adolescents participating in Ged's transformation vicariously enjoy being in Vetch's confidence.

As someone so close to Ged, Vetch has insight into how Ged uses power—and really, has insight into him as a person. He was there when Ged released the shadow, an act Hollindale accurately calls opening "the door between life and death."[104] He saw the scars inflicted onto Ged's face that night, and was the only student who tried to help when Ged was attacked.[105]

Similarly, Vetch alone cared enough to come back to say good-bye when he was permitted to finally see Ged.[106] In a word, Vetch is devoted. This devotion does not come lightly, nor does it leave lightly. If Ged were a wizard, mighty and powerful, and Vetch were his non-wizard follower, it would be easy for Vetch to cleave to the majesty put forth in front of him. However, because Vetch is always ahead of Ged in their studies (perhaps not in power, but certainly in years and experience), there is no awe to blind him with—he knows the darkness within Ged as well as he knows the darkness within himself. As Le Guin's novel explores the idea of inner darkness battling against inner lightness, it is not surprising that Vetch unassumingly assists Ged on his journey to confront his shadow-self, and this shows a devotion of a higher sort.

As the fourth, final, and most complex sidekick role, the sidekick as foil presents a challenge: the sidekick needs to provide contrast to the hero in order to better illuminate him or her. In doing so, however, the sidekick often comes close to becoming something more, something greater than a subservient companion. If a sidekick were to cross that line, he or she would cease to be a sidekick—hence the difficulty. This is perhaps why Sam holds himself unquestionably to be Frodo's servant. Part of this is his nature; part of this is his place in the hobbit social hierarchy. Vetch allows himself to become Ged's sidekick because he honors their friendship and recognizes the importance of the quest. Recognizing this delicate balance between sidekick and "something more" comes into fruition in chapter 5, when I examine a number of texts told from a superhero sidekick's point of view (this makes the sidekicks the protagonists and narrators, and in these examples, almost all question the integrity of the superheroes they follow).

It is not difficult to recognize, as this chapter has tried to show, that sidekicks are very numerous in adult literature, both early and contemporary; in comic books, among other popular forms; and in YA, and that sidekicks can be usefully differentiated into several discrete types. In turn, these sidekick character types relate in critically relevant ways to the wider purposes of the narratives in which they occur. Chapter 2 complements the literary-historical and critical orientations of chapter 1 by exploring, in a more thematic vein, two other essential ways in which heroes and sidekicks must interact: both within the duologies of gender-specific standpoints, and also in the light of specific family relationships. Subsequently, chapters 3 through 5 will delineate how the canon of YA texts in particular seems especially adept at challenging and complicating these various critical and thematic characteristics of the sidekick.

NOTES

1. Alleen Pace Nilsen and Kenneth L. Donelson, *Literature for Today's Young Adults*, 8th ed. (Boston: Pearson, 2009), 70.
2. Ron Buchanan, "'Side by Side': The Role of the Sidekick," *Studies in Popular Culture* 26, no. 1 (2003): 17.
3. Ibid.
4. Michael Dirda, "Holmes and Away," *New Statesman*, November 7, 2011, 42.
5. Ibid.
6. Arthur Conan Doyle, *A Study in Scarlet*, ed. Owen Edwards (Oxford: Oxford University Press, 1999), 14.
7. Ibid., 16.
8. Ibid., 20–21.
9. Ibid., 26.
10. Ibid., 33.
11. Ibid., 36.
12. Owen Edwards, "Introduction" to *A Study in Scarlet*, by Arthur Conan Doyle, ed. Owen Edwards (Oxford: Oxford University Press, 1999), xxxiv.
13. Ibid., xxxv.
14. Nilsen and Donelson, *Literature*, 62.
15. "The 100 Best Young Adult Books of All Time," *Time*, accessed December 18, 2018, http://time.com/100-best-young-adult-books/.
16. Dean Shackleford, "The Female Voice in *To Kill a Mockingbird*: Narrative Strategies in Film and Novel," *Mississippi Quarterly* 50, no. 1 (1996): par. 3, Academic Search Complete.
17. Harper Lee, *To Kill a Mockingbird* (New York: Warner, 1982), 88.
18. Ibid., 89.
19. Shackleford, "The Female Voice," par. 3.
20. Sidonie Smith and Julia Watson, *Reading Autobiography: A Guide for Interpreting Life Narratives*, 2nd ed. (Minneapolis: University of Minnesota Press, 2010), 22.
21. Ibid., 25.
22. Ibid.
23. Roberta Seelinger Trites, *Disturbing the Universe: Power and Repression in Adolescent Literature* (Iowa City: University of Iowa Press, 2000), 10.
24. Ibid.
25. Miguel de Cervantes, *Don Quixote*, ed. Diana de Armas Wilson, trans. Burton Raffel (New York: Norton, 1999), 43.
26. Ibid., 44.
27. Ibid., 11.
28. Thomas Schatz, *Hollywood Genres: Formulas, Filmmaking, and the Studio System* (New York: McGraw, 1981), 39.
29. Peter Coogan, *Superhero: The Secret Origin of a Genre* (Austin: MonkeyBrain, 2006), 197.
30. Ben Edlund, "Early Morning of a Million Zillion Ninjas," in *The Tick: Omnibus: Sunday through Wednesday* (Quincy: New England Comics, 1995), 6.
31. Ben Edlund, "High Rise Hijinx," in *The Tick: Omnibus: Sunday through Wednesday* (Quincy: New England Comics, 1995), 8.
32. Ben Edlund, "The Tick," in *The Tick: Omnibus: Sunday through Wednesday* (Quincy: New England Comics, 1995), 1.
33. Edlund, "Early Morning," 15.
34. Ibid.
35. "The Tick vs. the Idea Men," YouTube, accessed August 23, 2017, https://www.youtube.com/watch?v=EJ9EroNcHe8 (page deleted).
36. Beverly Lyon Clark, ed. *The Adventures of Tom Sawyer: A Norton Critical Edition*, by Mark Twain (New York: Norton, 2007), vii.
37. Ibid.
38. Ibid.

39. Ibid.
40. Mark Twain, *The Adventures of Tom Sawyer*, ed. Lee Clark Mitchell (Oxford: Oxford University Press, 1998), 78.
41. Ibid., 80-81.
42. Ibid., 81.
43. Ibid., 54.
44. Paul Lynch, "Not Trying to Talk Alike and Succeeding: The Authoritative Word and Internally-Persuasive Word in *Tom Sawyer* and *Huckleberry Finn*," *Studies in the Novel* 38, no. 2 (2006): 173.
45. Ibid., 173–74.
46. Daniel Davis Wood, "Character Synthesis in *The Adventures of Huckleberry Finn*," *The Explicator* 70, no. 2 (2012): 83.
47. See note 15 above.
48. John Mortimer, "Introduction" to *The Best of Wodehouse: An Anthology*, by P. G. Wodehouse (New York: Random, 2007), x.
49. P. G. Wodehouse, *The Best of Wodehouse: An Anthology* (New York: Random, 2007), 222.
50. Ibid., 240.
51. Mortimer, "Introduction" to *The Best of Wodehouse*, x.
52. George Watson, "The Birth of Jeeves," *Virginia Quarterly Review* 73, no. 4 (1997): 641–52. Academic Search Complete.
53. Ibid.
54. Wodehouse, *Best of Wodehouse*, 239.
55. Ibid., 225.
56. Ibid., 224, 225.
57. Ibid., 241.
58. Ibid.
59. J. R. R. Tolkien, *The Hobbit* (New York: Ballantine, 1974), 17.
60. Ibid., 68.
61. Christopher Toner, "Catastrophe and Eucatastrophe: Russell and Tolkien on the True Form of Fiction," *New Blackfriars* 89, no. 1019 (2008): 81.
62. Christopher Garbowski, "The Comedy of Enchantment in *The Lord of the Rings*," *Christianity and Literature* 60, no. 2 (2011): 275
63. Tolkien, *Hobbit*, 7.
64. Ibid.
65. Ibid., 8.
66. Ibid., 9.
67. Ibid., 10.
68. Michael Cart, *Young Adult Literature: From Romance to Realism* (Chicago: ALA, 2010), 60.
69. Tolkien, *Hobbit*, 114.
70. Ibid., 121.
71. Ibid.
72. Ibid., 123.
73. Ibid., 10.
74. Ibid.
75. Ibid., 8.
76. Ibid., 119.
77. Stephen Greenblatt, ed. *The Norton Shakespeare*, 2nd ed. (New York: Norton, 2008), 1687.
78. Buchanan, "Side by Side," 17.
79. Greenblatt, *Norton Shakespeare*, 1688–89.
80. Betty Carter, "Adult Books for Young Adults," *The English Journal* 86, no. 3 (1997): 63.
81. Robin Robertson, "Seven Paths of the Hero in *Lord of the Rings*: The Path of Love," *Psychological Perspectives* 52, no. 2 (2009): 227.

82. Ibid.
83. J. R. R. Tolkien, *The Two Towers* (New York: Ballantine, 1974), 433.
84. Ibid., 434.
85. Robertson, "Seven Paths," 239.
86. Ibid., 227.
87. J. R. R. Tolkien, *The Return of the King* (New York: Ballantine, 1974), 382.
88. Ibid., 472.
89. Most of the remaining portion of chapter 1 has appeared in a different form as "Finding Balance through Friendship: Reading *A Wizard of Earthsea*," in *The Explicator* 76, no. 1 (2018): 8-10, doi: 10.1080/00144940.2018.1430676, rights courtesy of Taylor & Francis Publishing, https://www.tandfonline.com.
90. Peter Hollindale, "The Last Dragon of Earthsea," *Children's Literature in Education* 34, no. 3 (2003): 184.
91. Ursula K. Le Guin, *A Wizard of Earthsea* (New York: Houghton, 1968), 54.
92. Ibid., 61.
93. Ibid., 62.
94. Ibid., 83.
95. Ibid., 84.
96. Craig Barrow and Diana Barrow, "Le Guin's *Earthsea*: Voyages in Consciousness," *Extrapolation* 32, no.1 (1991): 28.
97. Joseph Campbell, *The Hero with a Thousand Faces* (New Jersey: Princeton University Press, 1972), 72.
98. Le Guin, *Wizard of Earthsea*, 178.
99. Ibid., 102–9.
100. Ibid., 133.
101. Ibid., 201.
102. Ibid., 182.
103. Jeanne Murray Walker, "Rites of Passage Today: The Cultural Significance of *A Wizard of Earthsea*," *Mosaic* 13, no. 3–4 (1980): 190. JSTOR.
104. Hollindale, "Last Dragon of Earthsea," 184.
105. Le Guin, *Wizard of Earthsea*, 76.
106. Ibid., 82.

Chapter Two

Family Ties

An Investigation into the Potential Familial Relationships between Heroes and Sidekicks

While a sidekick can embody a certain role in terms of how he or she interacts with his or her hero, the relationship does not entirely rely upon whether or not a sidekick is a narrative gateway, devil's advocate, comic relief, or foil. Complicating these roles is another foundational component of the hero/sidekick pairing: the particular nature of the bond that forms between the two as characters within the story itself. This chapter explores how that relationship is quite often established to mimic a kind of family. Just as there are innumerable ways any two people can interact within a binary relationship, so too are the relational possibilities between a hero and his or her sidekick. Nevertheless, hero/sidekick bonds more often than not resemble familial relations; they tend to simulate those of parents and children or those of two siblings.

It is interesting—and indeed prototypical—that many YA sidekicks come from an unstable, broken, or nonexistent family situation. Walter Hogan notes that "separation from parents and family is a major theme of adolescence."[1] Furthermore, Hogan makes the case that perhaps "families in which one parent has died prematurely may be overrepresented in YA literature," and that there are "literally thousands of YA novels in which the protagonist's parents are divorced."[2] Hogan continues by citing title after title of YA novels in which one or both parents are absent for one reason or another. In light of this foundational element of YA, I believe a YA sidekick often aligns him- or herself with a hero—or vice versa, notably—in order to fulfill a need for family. I agree with the contention that using a broken family unit as a starting place allows a YA author to tap into a reader's recognition that adulthood requires independence, typically apart from (or in spite of) one's parental units. Trites offers a psychoanalytical approach to understanding how YA uses parental figures: *in parentis*, *in loco parentis*, and *in logo parentis*.[3] Nikolajeva applies Trites's work by using these three possibilities in her book chapter on secondary characters.[4] Nikolajeva states that the first, *in parentis*, or the presence of biological parents, is "a rare case in children's fiction."[5] She furthermore agrees with Trites that the fact of whether or not a character has biological parents is a way to differentiate between children's literature and young adult literature.[6] The third, *in logo parentis*, or "parents made out of words," governs a scenario when characters create "a substitute parent in their imagination."[7] The second, *in loco parentis*, or "instead of parents," is the "most common" scenario and is the one that applies here.[8] Moreover, the way a hero and sidekick develop their surrogate relationship, *in loco parentis*, almost always culminates in an ironic *reinforcement* of the gap left by missing parents. There are two basic archetypal possibilities for YA heroes and sidekicks to fill that breach of family: by mimicking the bonds between parents and children or mimicking the bonds between siblings.

To illustrate how *in loco parentis* or this "need for family" occurs, I will first offer examples of these familial categorizations from eight specific possibilities. I begin by showing how Bruce Wayne (Batman) and Dick Grayson (Robin) embody the father-son relationship. Batman and Robin can also illustrate the father-daughter relationship when considering Carrie Kelly as Robin in Frank Miller's *The Dark Knight Returns*. Helen and Violet Parr from Pixar's *The Incredibles* embody the mother-daughter, while Lady Jessica and Paul Atreides from Frank Herbert's science fiction classic *Dune* are the mother-son (literally, in these cases). To show how heroes and sidekicks create brotherly bonds, I briefly revisit Ged and Vetch. I use Nancy Drew and George Fayne/Bess Marvin as a sister-sister sidekick relationship.

The sister-brother (or brother-sister) relationship can become more complicated, depending on the ages of those involved, and whether or not the relationship remains platonic or moves into romance. For instance, I use Jennifer Strange and Tiger Prawns from Jasper Fforde's *The Chronicles of Kazam* series as the illustration for the older sister hero and younger brother sidekick scenario. However, if both hero and sidekick are of a similar age, or both nearing adolescence, as in the case of Alanna and Jonathan from Tamora Pierce's *Song of the Lioness* series, the relationship lends itself to romantic tension. Romantic or sexual tension is often not resolved in the first book of a continuing series. In fact, it is usually only just introduced or hinted at. For the purposes of this chapter, focusing only on the introduction, recognition, and consideration of romantic/sexual tension will suffice. However, as nascent sexual tension is an important part of the adolescent experience—and therefore plays an important part in YA fiction—additional analysis of the development and repercussions of such a relationship as it affects the hero/ sidekick duology presents rich possibilities for future research.

A ninth intriguing scenario occurs when the presence of two sidekicks complicates matters even further by creating what I call the hero/sidekick triad, similar in some respects to what Nikolajeva calls the "collective protagonist."[9] The triad does some interesting things to the family dynamic, especially when it involves either the ever-popular love triangle or a shifting definition of who are heroes and who are sidekicks. Harry Potter, Hermione Granger, and Ron Weasley are an easily recognizable example to showcase both instances: readers waited in anticipation to see whom Hermione would choose romantically, and the three friends' evolving friendship over seven books supplants the typical hero/sidekick pairing. For reasons I explain later, I instead use Percy Jackson, Annabeth Chase, and Grover Underwood from Rick Riordan's *Percy Jackson and the Olympians* series to show the possibilities of the triad. (I disqualify George Fayne and Bess Marvin from consideration as part of a hero triad because they are essentially two interchangeable halves of a single sidekick, or occupying what Nikolajeva calls "identical actantial positions."[10] These identical positions create, essentially, a "mere duplication of a character, perhaps primarily for didactic purposes." In all fairness to George and Bess, I am oversimplifying Nikolajeva, who introduces this duplication of character by a clear example of two sisters who have "no individual traits," and are contrasted by brothers who have "radically different roles."[11] However, while George and Bess have their own individuality, the way in which they act as Nancy Drew's sidekicks show two halves of what might be easily carried out by one sidekick. These halves are different, hence George's and Bess's individuality, but as the two are so readily defined by their status as cousins and Nancy's companions, that considering them as one sidekick makes sense.)

Recognizing the establishment of a family dynamic between a hero and sidekick lets me begin to break that dynamic apart in later chapters. Part of how YA portrays the maturation of its characters is the acknowledgment that they must stand alone someday, without the aid of their parent or parents. This is especially true when the hero has an established familial relationship, whether actual or metaphorical, with his or her sidekick. If and when sidekicks evolve beyond the need for—or the influence of—their heroes, the familial relationships also change. Outside of the YA arena, sidekicks often function without need for change or independence. Even Watson, who eventually marries and moves out of Baker Street, still pines for and cavorts with Holmes to solve cases—yet his role as narrative gateway hardly changes. When the adolescent sidekick comes into his or her own, however, the connection between sidekick and hero must change accordingly.

As I stated in the introduction, Batman and Robin might just qualify as the indisputable comic book hero/sidekick pairing, since they have been a perennial influence in popular culture almost since their creation and currently stand well-fixed atop the podium, as it were. However, in fairness, it should be recognized that Batman and Robin were not the first detective hero and his sidekick—not by a long shot. Much could be said about late nineteenth-century or early twentieth-century detective characters like Nick Carter and his adopted son Chick, or Nelson Lee and his assistant Nipper; boy detectives Barney Cook from Harvey J. O'Higgins's *The Adventures of Detective Barney* (1915), Dan Mordaunt from Horatio Alger's *Dan the Detective* (1884), or even Mark Twain's Tom Sawyer in *Tom Sawyer, Detective* (1896)[12]; and countless others from dime novel detective stories (Cap Collier, Old Sleuth, or Bob Brooks, to name a few).[13] By the time Batman was developed in 1939, the detective story in America had been developing for nearly a century if one marks Edgar Allen Poe's Auguste Dupin as the "first ever fictional detective," who first appeared in print in the 1840s.[14] Batman was intentionally designed to take advantage of the success of Superman, giving DC another costumed superhero.[15] On his own, Robin is less directly derivative as he "stands as the first sidekick and can also be considered the first kid superhero."[16] Robin looks to Batman for guidance, education, and livelihood. As a father figure to Robin, Batman fulfills his latent need to procreate, especially given Bruce Wayne's famous status as an orphan and the sole heir to the family fortune. Batman eventually *does* procreate, allowing for a father-as-hero/son-as-sidekick situation where Bruce Wayne's son Damian takes on the role of Robin. The ongoing relationship between Bruce Wayne/Batman and Damian Wayne/Robin is tumultuous, to say the least. First introduced to "normal" Batman continuity in Grant Morrison's "Batman and Son" story arc [Batman #655+], Damian is the illegitimate child of Bruce Wayne and Talia al Ghul, and was raised by his mother and trained by the League of Assassins. Upon arriving in Gotham under Batman's care, Damian proceeds to overwhelm Alfred, seriously injure Tim Drake/Robin, and decapitate the villain "The Spook," all before finally helping Batman find and foil Talia's current maniacal plan. Damian ultimately disappears with his mother at the end of the story arc. After this introduction, Damian's role as son to Batman plays out in at least two significant ways over the ongoing continuity of Batman comics: he is Robin during Dick Grayson's tenure as Batman, and ultimately becomes Batman himself.[17]

Long before Damian existed (in either comic book continuity or real-world years), Robin "the Boy Wonder," was created in 1940 as a "character with whom young readers could supposedly identify,"[18] and there have been at least ten distinct characters acting as Batman's sidekick.[19] Dick Grayson is the first and most famous. Dick initially existed as a narrative gateway for younger readers to identify with Batman's adventures, which essentially pigeon-holed him for nearly thirty years. J. L. Bell calls this period Dick's "success in stasis."[20] Writers of the series kept him at age thirteen (at most) until the formation of The Teen Titans in 1965.[21] He was allowed to age in real time for the next five years until he started college in 1969—when he should have been well over forty years old, if not pushing fifty. Coogan points out that Dick stopped aging somewhere in his mid-twenties, adhering to the maxim that "no superhero or major supporting cast member seems to have aged since about 1978."[22] There are exceptions to this rule, however, as specialized titles, story lines, and single shot comics are released regularly, although they often exist outside of the canonical comic book "continuity."

The nearly eighty-year history of Robin (as Dick Grayson or otherwise) offers any number of opportunities for study. For instance, there are the original, relatively unchanging "Batman and Robin stories" intended for "younger readers . . . the main market for superhero comics."[23] Bell notes that these comics, published from the 1940s through the early 1960s, were largely unconcerned with Batman's or Robin's origin stories; readers were more "excited by what they saw Batman and Robin doing on the page, not by their past."[24] An interesting element of the earliest stories is how the writers were hesitant to firmly establish Dick's age, ostensibly to allow "all young boys" to relate to him, to "let young readers of any age identify with him."[25] The young Robin often served as a Watsonesque character to Batman's Holmes, serving as both confidant for Batman's crime deductions and "readers' baffled but curious stand-in," as he would comment on Batman's unrevealed plan.[26] Another version of Dick Grayson's Robin that is ripe for study can be found in the twenty-issue *Batman Family* comic, published in the mid- to late 1970s. Some consider this series a "seminal" text in the Batman canon, as it problematizes Dick's Robin costume in regard to his identity, and introduces a romance between Dick and Barbara Gordon/Batgirl.[27] Of particular interest with this often "overlooked" series is the anthology approach for the stories within each issue, particularly how they are mostly told from "people connected with Batman's world," and not Batman himself.[28] A third notable opportunity to delve into Dick Grayson is his decision to become Nightwing. Kristen L. Geaman notes that there are at least two versions of Nightwing's genesis. The first version occurs before the watershed *Crisis on Infinite Earths* (the 1985 series that ultimately allowed for the rebooting of any and all titles involved); the second occurs post-*Crisis*.[29] The first Nightwing (first appearing in print in 1984) is the culmination of Dick involving himself with the Teen Titans, dropping out of college, and drawing Bruce Wayne's disapproval.[30] The post-*Crisis* reboot involves a significantly darker turn of events, all of which begin with Bruce's decidedly different decision to fire Dick—essentially casting him out without his consent.[31]

In light of all of these possible moments (or versions) of Dick Grayson to study, I have chosen to study Dick as he appears in *Batman: The Animated Series* from 1992. This series has been hailed as one of the more successful and influential chapters of the Batman mythos. Mark Waid, author of the celebrated graphic novel *Kingdom Come*, called the series "electrifying . . . unlike anything else we'd ever seen on TV before, and that's what made it so compelling."[32] Waid calls "Heart of Ice," one of the series' stories, "easily one of the best Batman stories ever told."[33] Devin Grayson, author of *Nightwing*, *Batman*, *Catwoman*, and *Titans* comics during the late 1990s through early 2000s, admits that the series was "unusually good at distilling the Batman mythos into a pure, clean story world. I still hear Kevin Conroy's voice when I think of Bruce."[34] The series showcases a clean and strong animation design intended to bring Batman back to his roots: dark, brooding (dare I say, gothic) amidst a clear 1930s/1940s Hollywood-gangster motif. (The creators/producers called it "dark-deco.") It is never stated that the series takes place in the years before World War II, and this would be clearly anachronistic given the kinds of technology used throughout the series. However, the architecture, automobiles, firearms, and fashion sense are clearly nostalgic. Waid calls *Batman: The Animated Series* an "important marker in Batman's history" because it influenced much of the Batman stories that came after it, which becomes all the more apparent when contrasting previous television Batman series like the 1960s "Batman," starring Adam West and Burt Ward, or the continued campiness of Hanna-Barbera's cartoon *Superfriends*, ca. 1973.[35] Nevertheless, even though the series is continually praised, and its influence marked, it is also largely absent from academic studies of Dick Grayson.

Despite not being in every episode of *Batman: The Animated Series*, Dick Grayson gets considerable screen time and backstory regardless of existing in only a handful of episodes as opposed to nearly eighty years in print. As a consequence, his relationship with Batman grows and develops in a relatively condensed period. In the documentary-featurette "Robin Rising," the creative team behind the series explains the decision-making process behind their particular portrayal of Dick Grayson—part of which took its cue from the work of Batman writer/artist Neal Adams. The choice to make Bruce a father-figure is quite deliberate, and makes sense; Dick, like Bruce, loses his parents at the hand of a lowly gangster. Another important choice is to place Dick in college. Several reasons went into this choice, including explaining Dick's absence in some episodes and moving away from the childlike behavior of a younger Robin: "it was a hard and fast effort to toughen him up a bit . . . a strength of his own."[36] Putting Dick in college strongly connects to the YA mentality, even though he might be older than some YA readers/viewers. Dick is at a crossroads in the series: he comes into his own and begins to question Bruce—he's "on an emotional journey."[37] Dick leaves Bruce in the same way that a college graduate is expected to strike out on his or her own after graduation. The series also eventually sees Dick "growing" into Nightwing. Dick arrives at a moment of independence when he becomes Nightwing, and also returns to the basic YA structural characterization, namely a position of parentless-ness. This return includes an emboldened questioning of Batman's methods and ethics in his crusade on crime, a shift in perspective that I develop further in chapter 5.

If Dick Grayson shows how a surrogate child can eventually leave a father, then studying Batman's relationship with Carrie Kelly shows how a child can stay. Reynolds's take on Frank Miller's *The Dark Knight Returns* states that Miller takes the "familiar and received ingredients" of what makes a Batman story and "radically restructures their meaning."[38] Nathan Tipton similarly views Carrie as "an interesting, if ultimately failed, experiment," in this case as a way for Miller to explore a "gender troubling of Robin."[39] In Miller's text, Robin becomes a thirteen-year-old girl—a far cry from an angst-ridden college-aged Dick Grayson. Carrie certainly fits the mold of a Robin. Her parents are still alive, but are so concerned about reliving the glory days of the 1960s—and doing drugs—that they hardly notice Carrie at all. At one point, while Carrie clings to the back of the Batmobile mowing down crowds of rowdy "mutants," her parents have this conversation: "great dinner, hon." "thanks, babe." "hey . . . . . .didn't we have a kid?"[40] That night, Carrie is brought into the fold as the new Robin, and her parents are never mentioned or shown again. Another requirement Carrie fulfills is a background with gymnastics, which she mentions twice.[41] The father-daughter relationship between Bruce Wayne and Carrie is significantly different than Bruce's father-son relationship with Dick. Firstly, Bruce is pushing fifty at this point, virtually old enough to be Carrie's biological grandfather. Secondly, Carrie proactively joins Batman by putting herself in harm's way for his sake before even knowing him. Thirdly, Miller's text only covers a matter of weeks, at most. The relationship is forged during a baptism of fire when Batman fights the leader of the mutant gang in the city dump.

Throughout the fight, Batman holds an inner monologue addressed to Dick, reminiscing about their past, and about how Dick is not in the seat next to him. Batman finds himself physically outmatched. As he begins to pass out from his injuries, he silently asks, "Where . . . are you . . . Dick . . . you were always . . . my little monkey wrench."[42] Carrie leaps forward to stop the mutant leader from using a crowbar on Batman's head. Delirious, Batman sees her as Robin (she is in costume) and saves them both by throwing a smoke bomb in the leader's face. Before passing out, he says softly, "Dick. . . ."[43] Considering he is in shock, Batman possibly believes this Robin *is* Dick Grayson, come back to save him or to be saved, depending on which point of view is taken. Batman's inner thoughts regarding Dick (and later Carrie) place Carrie in an odd devil's advocate role: he sees danger differently when she accompanies him. Carrie, like Dick before her, fulfills Batman's well-recognized latent desire for a child.

Joining Batman is the end of Carrie's search for a father figure. She introduces herself as "Carrie. Carrie Kelly" in one frame, only to revise herself in the next: "Robin," with a determined and somewhat pleading look in her expression.[44] The connection is cemented a few pages later when Bruce puts his hand on her shoulder and she joyfully leaps into his arms.[45] Part of this connection can be attributed to a kind of Florence-Nightingale syndrome, stemming from how Batman saved Carrie earlier in the text.[46] He saved her life, and she feels involved with his fate, which is why she decided to suit up as Robin in the first place. Batman sees her skills, "young," "smart," "brave," proven beyond doubt in the coming pages.[47]

Carrie's motivation for "adopting" Batman as her father figure is love—there is not another or better word for it. An interesting moment illustrating this love occurs when Alfred picks Carrie up from school. She looks his way with an expectant smile on her face and runs to the car like an impatient lover, or in this case, a giddy daughter.[48] When Dick joined Bruce, he did so with a desire to avenge his parents' murder—very akin to the philosophical impetus of Bruce's own mission. Carrie, however, owes her life to *the Batman*. Whether her motivation comes more from inspiration or from seeing him as a protective father-figure does not matter, as both are present. Batman further provides that protection through two life-or-death situations: pulling her away from an exploding building,[49] and catching her when she could have fallen to her death.[50] Love is perhaps the most powerful of sidekick motivations. What else would bring a thirteen-year-old to put herself in way of this kind of harm? The gravest instance of danger comes with the final showdown with the Joker. Batman and Robin arrive at the county fair to find the Joker has already killed dozens. Batman's inner voice talks to him: "Somewhere a woman calls out for her son . . . somewhere a calliope plays the same tune, again and again . . . a tiny hand tightens its grip on my arm . . . a girl of thirteen breathes in sharply, suddenly, her innocence lost . . . it ends tonight, Joker."[51] The "girl of thirteen" is obviously Carrie, seeing dead peers for the first time. Furthermore, Carrie ends up very nearly choked to death by the Joker's henchman. After she is saved by a fortuitously placed piece of roller coaster track, Carrie is shown with a blank wide-eyed stare, tears streaming down her face, and snot from her nose.[52]

From the hero's standpoint, Batman could not protect Carrie's innocence in the same way that parents cannot protect their children from growing up. (Similar themes appear throughout various Batman story arcs, notably the much-maligned [or revered, depending] *All-Star Batman & Robin, the Boy Wonder* series—also written by Frank Miller.) Part of the shock present in Carrie's face almost certainly comes from her disbelief that Batman was not there to save her personally. The adopted father-figure failed her. Tipton believes this can partially be attributed to a lack of "a certain emotional connection between Bruce/Batman and Carrie/Robin."[53] From Batman's perspective, that might well be the case considering the brief time he has known Carrie. However, Tipton's thesis focuses on Robin as Miller's "connection to heteronomativity, and her appearances ... coincide more and more frequently within scenes of overt homoeroticism."[54] Carrie's emotional devotion to Batman is obvious, whether or not Batman feels more connected to a male Robin (which, as I stated in the introduction, is a question to be examined in more depth later on). That Batman had been accused of child endangerment is appropriate and true—and he would not disagree, as he considers Carrie as a soldier taking part in a war.[55] It is possible that Batman could have worked harder to make Carrie's loss of innocence less traumatic, but what part of growing up is not traumatic? The pivotal moment in their father-daughter relationship comes when Batman calls for aid after dealing with the Joker—the panel shows the same Carrie, blank-faced and in shock.[56] She comes out of it and answers, saving *him* in the end. The moment of disillusionment could have easily gone differently, with Carrie choosing to walk away.

Their partnership is re-established as the graphic novel ends: Carrie is with Bruce in what was once the Batcave, helping him set up what comes next. They are the only two left of the "old guard," which, of course, she is not really a part of as she is the link between the old and the new. Batman must rely upon her in his old age in ways he would not have needed to with Dick. Carrie is young enough to be his granddaughter, but she is the daughter of his old age—a fact further explored in the sequel, *The Dark Knight Strikes Again* (2001–2002), as well as scrutinized by Tipton.[57] Batman will always be an intriguing figure to study because of the way he willingly brings his surrogate children into harm's way (not to mention the never-ending potential to study him through a psychoanalytical lens). The absence of a second parental figure makes the nurturing of youth a difficult task for any single parent, much less one bent on stopping criminals or supervillains. Batman's task-oriented approach shows substantial differences when viewed against some hero-as-mother scenarios.

In direct contrast to Batman's surrogate children, the mother-child pairings I study here include two examples of mothers and their biological offspring. In keeping with the search for familial stability, both examples are products of family instability or brokenness, and understandably add to the narrative already established in this chapter by the father-son, father-daughter examples. The mother-daughter example is Helen and Violet Parr from Pixar Studio's *The Incredibles* (2004) and *Incredibles 2* (2018). Pixar's cinematic record shows a collection of multilayered films appealing to children, young adults, and adults alike, earning accolades as a "legendary studio" with an unprecedented series of "amazing movies" (as of 2013).[58] *The Incredibles* is no exception. Furthermore, it makes sense to categorize *The Incredibles* as a YA text based on this multilayered storytelling approach. While children undoubtedly find the film entertaining and engaging, the story itself resonates with those mature enough to understand and comprehend marital issues, distrust, discontent, and the steps needed to reconcile family. The start of the film shows the Parr family at a time of unrest: each member of the family struggles in such a way as to parallel his or her powers. As a whole, it is largely understood that the powers of the Parr family are a remixing of those of Fantastic Four. Bob Parr, as Mr. Incredible, has super strength and invulnerability (i.e., The Thing). Helen, as Elastigirl, can stretch her limbs and body (i.e., Mr. Fantastic). Daughter Violet can turn invisible and project shields (i.e., The Invisible Woman). Baby Jack Jack is shown with the ability to change himself with a variety of powers, among them being covered in flames (i.e., Johnny Storm). Middle child Dash stands outside of the Fantastic Four model, but still has a classic superpower as he can run impossibly fast (i.e., The Flash). The plot of the film essentially begins with a series of escalating lawsuits that sparks the systematic retirement of the superhero community, forcing them all into a form of witness protection. Bob is depressed as he has been rendered impotent in an insurance-claim job where his boss consistently demeans him. He largely ignores his family as a result, only finding solace in secretly reliving "the glory days" while Helen thinks he goes bowling. Helen struggles to maintain the family's precarious status quo, but Bob constantly undermines her efforts. Violet's self-confidence issues make her socially invisible. A junior-high-school student, Violet's thoughts remain on a popular boy at school—who presumably does not know she exists. He looks in her direction, but she turns invisible and he walks away. Nonetheless, she is thrilled he "looked at her." Conversely, Dash wants to stand out and compete in track-and-field, but his parents will not allow it because of their need to remain anonymous. Although I focus on Helen and Violet, the Parr family's struggles are not exclusive to a hero/sidekick scenario. It is a story of a family with strong conflicting dynamics of individualism. Bob's gallivanting causes Helen to suspect an affair, which brings all but Jack Jack into a situation where they must gel as both a family and a superhero team.[59]

My focal point is how Violet acts as her mother's sidekick. Violet and her mother have their first sidekick/hero moment when Helen, Violet, and Dash fly to the island where Bob has been locked up. When the movie's villain shoots missiles at the jet, Helen asks Violet to surround the jet with a force field. Violet fails out of confusion at being asked to use the powers she has always been required to hide. Helen manages to save them, and they make it to the island. When they talk about it later, Helen tells Violet that it "wasn't fair of her to ask so much [of Violet]."[60] Helen also leaves her with this thought: when the time comes for Violet to use her powers, "you'll know what to do, it's in your blood."[61] As Helen runs off to Bob, Violet considers her mother's words, puts on a superhero mask, and stands a little straighter. Helen's words come true later on, as Violet dives between Dash and a machine gun, saving them both by creating a force field. As Dash asks her how she is doing that, she responds with "I do not know."[62] Just as her mother predicted, Violet's instincts took over and she acted without thinking. Her powers end up being some of the most valuable: she saves Dash's life a number of times, frees the entire family from captivity, and participates in a significant way in the climactic battle.

Violet is the only member of the family who exists in a sidekick capacity—and that capacity is intimately linked to her relationship with her mother. Dash does not require affirmation—he is raring to go from the start and has to be reined in. Helen likewise does not need anyone's words of encouragement, although her marriage is reinforced by Bob's opening up about his feelings. In turn, Bob finds support in Helen's response to his confessions of love. As a junior-high-school student, Violet represents any and all adolescents in a similar place in life. She is not Carrie Kelly, the self-assured, already-game-for-anything sidekick. She is timid, shy, and unsure about using her invisibility and shielding powers, which themselves embody adolescent wishes. The confidence to do so comes from long-awaited affirmation from her mother. This appears to be in conflict with what Frances A. Nadeau cites as the "bond between mother and daughter as one inhibiting the daughter from establishing her own identity."[63] However, considering Helen's lack of attention is what inhibits her daughter's development, it makes sense that the inhibition is lifted once that attention is given. Helen's instinct to protect Violet from harm initially aggravates her daughter's consternation, but it is that same nurturing outlook (unlike Batman's warrior or soldierly outlook) that eventually enables Violet to come into her own.

While Helen and Violet Parr showcase a somewhat straightforward mother-daughter relationship, my example for the mother-son presents a more complicated study (perhaps even overcomplicated). My choice comes from Frank Herbert's science fiction opus, *Dune*. (*Dune* falls into that YA definition that comes from the nebulous category of adult books-read-by-teens: NPR ranked it as number forty-one in its 2012 list of "100 Best-Ever Teen Novels.") The complication that comes from looking at such a relatively unusual example is a welcome issue. While I could have potentially reused Helen Parr from *The Incredibles* by studying her relationship with her son Dash (in a way similar to how I reused Batman for the father-son, father-daughter), using a less straightforward example shows a different element to this kind of hero/sidekick pairing. In fact, looking at *Dune* for any kind of study presents its own challenges, as Herbert's sweeping book is not easily taken apart; it is a loosely allegorical text of vast political intrigue, ecological responsibility, religious and philosophical questioning, and genetic manipulation, among other things. In an article studying the ambivalent hero of contemporary science fiction, Juan Prieto-Pablos calls *Dune* "the most elaborate science fiction since Tolkien's saga of the Middle-World."[64] The focus of the novel is Paul Atreides, a.k.a. Paul-Muad'Dib, a messianic prophet. Paul is destined to set off a universe-wide holy war redistributing the balance of power and beginning a new galactic regime that will last for thousands of years. Before he can do this, however, he is nothing more than the gifted fifteen-year-old son of Duke Leto Atreides and the Lady Jessica. Political events lead to Duke Leto's death and Jessica and Paul's exile into the desert. This focus on political move and countermove requires Herbert to tell the tale from multiple vantages, using an omniscient third-person point of view to reveal "plans within plans within plans," "a feint within a feint within a feint."[65] As a member of a matriarchal religious powerhouse called the Bene Gesserits, Jessica provides many of these revelations. Perhaps most importantly of all, Jessica explains the deeply religious nature of her training and her son's potential as a messiah figure. In this way, she fosters her son's development to surpass her someday as the one destined to be the hero. Broadly speaking, Jessica's ongoing protection for Paul and her dedication to seeing him develop in his ability represent typical mother-son dynamics often present in YA literature. More to the point for my purposes here, however, is the distance these developmental steps naturally create between mother and son (especially when that son begins to move beyond his mother's protection or support), prompting questions regarding Jessica's inability to create relationship *in loco parentis* after Paul matures.

The continued uniqueness of Jessica and Paul's situation stems from Paul's eventual rise to hero, and *Dune* scholarship studying this rise to hero is extensive.[66] In light of this, my focus is both on Paul as sidekick and Jessica as hero. For two-thirds of the book, over the course of their tale of survival and revenge (as a dynamic duo), Jessica is the one who acts, and Paul follows her lead. The knowledge of Paul's eventual supremacy makes him the eventual hero regardless of his youthfulness, which complicates the way Jessica approaches her role as mother. In this sense, Jessica is the hero-destined-to-be-sidekick. While this role becomes apparent throughout the text, there are at least three notable cases where her knowledge and protectiveness explicitly force her to take the lead. The first comes after they are ambushed by a group of Fremen, the native people of the desert planet Arrakis (a.k.a. Dune). Jessica takes the leader by surprise, showcasing her superior fighting skills. During the same episode, she uses her Bene Gesserit knowledge to align herself and Paul with long-held Fremen beliefs and prophesies.[67] The second comes when she truly and completely integrates the two of them into Fremen culture by assuming the role of Reverend Mother to all of their peoples.[68] The third takes place at the very end of the novel. Paul has overcome the forces of the Emperor, defeating all who joined him in his conspiracy. As a final act of proving himself, Paul defeats his cousin in single combat. Before the battle, Jessica gives Paul a code word that would render his opponent paralyzed. Paul does not use this knowledge, per se. Afterwards, Jessica, along with Paul's mate Chani, finalize the conditions of Paul's ascension to the throne.[69] The exceedingly political nature behind Jessica's relationship with Paul brings them closer together to achieve their vengeance, but distances them as mother and son. Paul's role through all of this is to act as the dutiful son, deferring to his mother's instruction. In the end, both are subsequently left with a feeling of distance, making *loco parentis* all the more necessary.

The concept of *in loco parentis* takes a significantly different turn when an overtly parental position is not a possible factor in the equation. For instance, Jessica and Paul are complicated because it is not always clear who is the parent and who is the child (from an actantial sense). Subsequently, one questions who holds the power within their relationship. When it comes to filling parental positions with a surrogate sibling, however, the dynamic inherently changes to something more resembling an equality of action. This change is the most important to note when evaluating surrogate parental relationships versus surrogate sibling relationships, because it impacts who holds the authority (or power) within the relationship.

The idea of a sidekick and hero forging a brotherly connection can be nicely fleshed out by building upon the previous use of Le Guin's Ged/Vetch and Tolkien's Frodo/Sam (even though I consider *The Lord of the Rings* adult fare, the illustration it provides is useful). Frodo and Sam show what is possible when the heroes/sidekicks are willing to lay down their lives for one another. Sam very nearly does so. As the less-capable (in the sense that Frodo was chosen to carry the Ring, and not him), Sam is committed to the point of death when he carries the invalid Frodo near the end of their quest. Ged and Vetch share a similar kinship, albeit on a smaller scale (from a plot standpoint). Building upon their aforementioned relationship, it is important to recall how young both Ged and Vetch are in *A Wizard of Earthsea*. Ged is nineteen, the same age as Vetch's younger brother. The brotherly connection, then, is not lost on Vetch, as he undoubtedly sees Ged as his wizardly "little brother." Vetch is the less powerful wizard, but goes with Ged to see the journey through, just as Sam is the "less powerful" hobbit. This issue of differential power brings Paul and Jessica back to mind, as defining their respective literary roles depends upon the evolving power relationship between the two.

Analyzing these various character sets also implies the need for an accurate understanding of their natures: Frodo and Sam's quest is quite different than Ged and Vetch's. Briefly contextualizing Tolkien and Le Guin helps reveal how their heroes and sidekicks embodied specific historical needs and responses—which further the connection between brothers. This is particularly evident in regard to the influence World War I had on *The Lord of the Rings*. Tolkien, a British survivor of the Battle of the Somme, published *The Hobbit* between the wars and *The Lord of the Rings* in the 1950s, following World War II. What more evident need for heroes and sidekicks than warfare? Le Guin, publishing in 1968 America, offers a much more "gray" understanding of the nature of good and evil. Many of her works, *A Wizard of Earthsea* among them, place great value on interpersonal relationships in the face of ambiguous large-scale power struggles.

Understanding at least part of the moral contexts surrounding these issues is important because it lets us see how these heroes and sidekicks are utilized differently and how they have been adapted to help their audiences deal with (or at least consider) these important questions. For Ged and Vetch, the YA audience needs to determine what is good and what is evil: can we see the world in only white and black, and if not, how do we handle what is shaded in gray? Frodo and Sam help their readers problematize that understanding even in the face of the classic characterizations of good versus evil found in high fantasy. Frodo's descent into the One Ring's control brings to mind the ideas of falling, "grayness," and redemption. Other YA texts can move entirely away from the philosophical, bringing the reader into a harsh, inescapable, and very real-world context: how do we bridge the distance separating us from those who would kill us? In this case of heroes and sidekicks, I would suggest that the answer lies in the brotherly connection formed both in the texts and potentially in a reader's own situation. Frodo leans on Sam for help through the fires of Mordor. Ged needed Vetch to help him face a dark doppelganger.

Such reliance on the brother-brother connection is mirrored by the sister-sister connection, as Nancy Drew for instance relies on the support given to her by her sidekicks. Although to be fair, Nancy never shies from her call of responsibility and protection—she easily assumes her role in the relationship. Part of this comes from the nature of the *Nancy Drew* series in general, which is an interesting microcosm unto itself, considering its extensive publication history. For this study, I have used the revised 1950s–1960s versions due to their easy availability and mass market saturation. Because much has already been written about the revisions and their effect,[70] I will not delve into that conversation here, except to note Nancy's age change: in the originally published books, she was sixteen, which was revised in later editions to age eighteen. The age change is important here regarding classifying *Nancy Drew* books as YA. Adding two years to Nancy's age reflects the cultural necessity of Nancy's independence: what was once considered common place for a sixteen-year-old in the 1930s no longer held true for the 1950s. Nancy's pseudo-adulthood at eighteen, while perhaps intended for a somewhat "younger" audience, demands the consideration whether or not the series should be considered YA. Granted, from a historical standpoint, YA was still years away from being recognized as its own subset of literature, and *Nancy Drew* lacks some of the emotional or situational depth typical of YA of the 1970s or 1980s. Nevertheless, when it comes to studying cousins Georgia "George" Fayne and Bess Marvin as Nancy's sidekick(s), the series works well.

The sidekick cousins first appear in the fifth novel of the series, *The Secret of Shadow Ranch*. George and Bess bring Nancy to their uncle and aunt's horse ranch in hopes that she can help them solve why mysterious and destructive things have been occurring on the ranch.[71] The mystery grows to include George and Bess's cousin Alice and her search for her missing father.[72] The relationship Nancy has with George and Bess exists under the conspicuous fact that Nancy has been without a mother since the age of three.[73] While this is never commented on in this volume of the series, it certainly places their partnership into the aforementioned pantheon of broken-family beginnings. Nancy's single-parent starting point quite strongly influences her assumption of the hero role. George and Bess's personal characteristics are quickly described and set the stage for how they interact as Nancy's sidekicks in the mystery-solving process. George is an "attractive tomboyish girl with short dark hair," while Bess is a "pretty, slightly plump blonde."[74] The two do very little in *The Secret of Shadow Ranch* to distance themselves from these basic and constrictive descriptions. As the tomboy of the group, George ends up performing many of the physical endeavors called for during their investigation and foiling of the villains.[75] Bess, as the slightly plump blonde, has her fair share of "blonde" or "girly" moments[76] as well as supposedly "plump" moments where she wonders what she is going to eat next.[77] In collating these descriptions and their actions, it is easy to see how George exhibits the stereotypical male actions, Bess exhibits the stereotypical female actions (while also playing the comic relief role), and Nancy exhibits a mixture of both. This would become even more interesting if viewed through a gender-role/gender-study lens, especially considering how the three interact in any given scenario. I am certainly not the first to make mention of this.[78]

What is it, then, about Nancy Drew and the sister-sister relationship that is different than what we saw in the brother-brother relationships? Perhaps not much, as we see a similar camaraderie and willingness to put one's self in harm's way for the other as was found in the brother-brother examples.[79] We also see the codependence on facing the issues at hand, especially in the absence of strong parental figures. However, because of the nature of mystery novels, George and Bess must give Nancy support in ways specific to this genre. This obviously hearkens back to my consideration of Watson's back-and-forth with Holmes. Unlike Watson however, George and Bess actively participate in piecing together the clues needed to solve the mystery. In a move quite unlike the self-involved Holmes, Nancy recognizes the value of the given support, and capitalizes on it by sharing her thoughts about each part of the mystery. While George and Bess are sometimes just the Watson-esque sounding board Nancy needs to figure out a clue, they do have some moments of individual insight. For example, while initially disappointed in an apparent chance to find Alice's father, George sensibly suggests that they keep looking around the area in hope of spotting him.[80] In response, "the others agreed that George had a point."[81] It tells much about all three that there exists a commonsense dialogue of ideas and possibilities: the cousins are levelheaded and trustworthy enough for Nancy to share her workings-out of the mystery, and Nancy is not too prideful to keep the logic hidden from her sidekicks, as Holmes often tends to do.

George and Bess do inevitably fill Watson's shoes as they give Nancy some physical backup. Watson carries the pistol when Holmes needs a firearm; George and Bess watch out for Nancy when she is threatened. Near the end of *Shadow Ranch*, the villains attempt to kidnap Nancy: "Before Nancy could say anything to the two men, Bess's voice rang out. 'She is *not* going with you!' 'Let her go!' George ordered. . . . The two [men] ran away fast, disappearing under the grandstand."[82] But one thing that George and Bess cannot do (that Watson, interestingly, did to some degree), is take on the role of parent for Nancy. Consequently, Nancy does not parent them either, regardless of Nancy's assuming the lead position as hero. To locate a situation where the adolescent hero becomes an obvious parental figure, I turn to the nonromantic, mixed-gender hero/sidekick paring.

These pairings show some expected similarities to the brother-brother or sister-sister pairings, as the nature of sibling care and protection runs true in these cases as well. One instance that does create a different scenario is when there is a marked age difference between the siblings—whether of the same sex or mixed. In Jasper Fforde's fantasy tale, *The Last Dragonslayer*, first-person protagonist Jennifer Strange finds herself leading the much younger Tiger Prawns. Jennifer's fostering of Tiger's development is unlike the other relationships I have covered so far in that the (almost) sixteen-year-old Jennifer *must* take on the role of Tiger's guardian/parent. There is no ambiguity or reluctance. While this mirrors Batman's fostering the growth of Robin, I make the differentiation here based on Jennifer's age and situation. She is a scant four years older than Tiger and they are both foundlings—a tried-and-true fantasy trope. Jennifer is an orphan with no knowledge whatsoever of her parentage. Foundlings in *The Last Dragonslayer* typically find themselves in an orphanage, and eventually enter into indentured servitude until age eighteen.[83] As she unravels the complications inherent to the plot, Jennifer soon discovers she is the last Dragonslayer, foreseen four hundred years ago.[84] Tiger does not fulfill any prophecies, but is similarly caught up in life as a foundling.

Foundlings fit exceedingly well into scenarios where the creation of a surrogate family takes precedence. Furthermore, a foundling is a symbol of infinite possibility in the world of fantastic literature, which is, perhaps, why the character type is so prevalent. A few other notable uses of the foundling in YA fantasy include Shasta from C. S. Lewis's *The Horse and His Boy*, Taran from Lloyd Alexander's *The Chronicles of Prydain*, Matthias from

Brian Jacques' *Redwall*, Lyra from Philip Pullman's *The Golden Compass*, and Rossamünd from D. M. Cornish's *Monster Blood Tattoo*. Michele S. Ware gives a brief account of the foundling myth: "[It] is the complex working out and revelation of the main character's parentage, along with the concurrent restoration to his rightful place in society. The foundling moves through the novel (and this movement *is* the plot) from illegitimacy and exclusion to self-knowledge and inclusion."[85] If a foundling appears in an important role in a text, then, the nature of "being found" drives the focus of the narrative. In the case of *Bleak House*, the foundling is Esther Summerson—a character Ware calls "Dickens' fully realized foundling myth."[86] The quintessential foundling in English literature might just be the title character from Henry Fielding's *The History of Tom Jones: A Foundling*.[87] Jennifer Strange and Tiger Prawns, then, belong to a very specific subset of characterization. This subset can become even more complicated depending on the circumstances of a foundling's birth. Many are assumed to be bastards—a terminological "slippage" that leaves children "open to the stigma" that resides therein.[88]

While Jennifer, as a foundling, must move toward legitimacy and inclusion, she must also act as the surrogate parent helping Tiger do the same. The act of placing an adolescent in the role of parent is one that has cropped up in YA or children's novels time and again: *The Boxcar Children* (clearly a children's literature series), *The Hunger Games*, *The Outsiders*, *Homecoming*, *A Series of Unfortunate Events* (also a children's series), to name but a few. YA author and critic Nancy Werlin states, "The truth is that parents and parental authority figures are usually of great importance in YA novels, even, and perhaps especially when they are not present in the story at all."[89] Typically, a foundling begins his or her quest in a lowly social position, as a servant or ward of some fashion. However, this circumstance is often thrust upon foundlings because the cloudy circumstances of their discovery position them as harbingers of change. Jennifer and Tiger share this possibility. Jennifer, as the hero, has already been established as the acting manager of the Kazam House of Magic, and a litany of astounding things have happened (and will continue to happen) to her.[90] Tiger's arrival, aside from allowing some explication regarding their world, also suggests the further possibility of greatness. Tiger, as the sidekick, does what a good sidekick would do: enables his hero to act.

There are many such interactions between Tiger and Jennifer. Most of them serve as moments of respite before Jennifer needs to rush away again. One in particular, however, shows Tiger's value as a sidekick. In this case, Jennifer turns down an offer of freedom for herself and Tiger. After she apologizes to Tiger (who had overheard her side of the phone conversation), he replies with "No apology necessary." He continues: "'Sister Assumpta bet me a moolah I wouldn't last a week at Kazam, but aside from that, I would only be back where I started.' He was taking it quite well, all things considered."[91] Tiger exemplifies the perfect sidekick for a character like Jennifer. His background as a foundling brings them instant solidarity. His unquestionable support for her decisions allows her to act with impunity. Finally, his choice to side with her against the moody and cranky employees of Kazam reinforces her role as a capable and beloved guardian.[92]

Although Tiger is a dutiful sidekick/foster younger brother, there are two things he cannot do that make him a specific kind of sidekick. The first is that he cannot take Jennifer's place. Many of the other sidekicks mentioned up until this point have had moments of opportunity to take up the mantle of hero. Robin has many adventures in which he takes the point position in front of Batman. Jessica and Paul fit into the "dual protagonist" scenario first described with Tom and Huck. Sam picks up the One Ring when Frodo cannot. Tiger, on the one hand, does rise to the occasion to run Kazam when Jennifer goes gallivanting as the last dragonslayer. On the other hand, Tiger never accompanies her on these quests until the beginning of book two, *The Song of the Quarkbeast*. By book three, *The Eye of Zoltar*, Tiger is back to running the business while Jennifer leaves for destinations unknown. The second thing Tiger cannot do is begin a romantic relationship with Jennifer. This is mostly due to their obvious age difference, which would make such a romance socially and ethically inappropriate. When romance *is* brought into the equation, however, all sorts of questions arise regarding parental roles, protection of the less powerful, and interdependence.

While it would be inappropriate for Jennifer Strange to begin a physical relationship with Tiger Prawns, the same is not true for Alanna of Trebond in Tamora Pierce's *Song of the Lioness* quartet. In the first novel, *Alanna: The First Adventure*, Alanna complicates any easy reading of her story: she trades places with her twin brother and presents herself as a young man seeking to become a knight. As was the case with George and Bess, Alanna's identity-hiding and cross-dressing present a rich mine of potential application and research. It certainly brings to mind any number of works and similar themes, including Shakespeare's *Twelfth Night* and its many versions, re-tellings, and adaptations. Additionally, *Alanna* aligns itself with *Twelfth Night*'s "tendency to destabilize understandings of the human subject in general and the masculine-feminine dyad in particular."[93] This destabilization is apparent throughout *Alanna*. The boys she befriends know her as a boy, even as she struggles to hide the signs of her physical development: she wraps her breasts flat and surreptitiously hides her period. Although she begins her time in study as the weakest of the entry-level pages (she is ten when the novel opens), her tenacity brings her respect. At the beginning of the saga, only three people besides Alanna know her secret: her brother Thom, their nursemaid Maude, and Coram, the soldier assigned to accompany Alanna to the palace for her training. By the end of the first book, an additional three others know as well. Two become love interests for Alanna: Prince Jonathan and George, the Thief King. The third is George's mother, who helped Alanna understand her body's changes during puberty. An awareness of Alanna's cross-dressing is essential when considering her sidekick, Jon, as it is an omnipresent factor in the first two books of the series.

The hero/sidekick relationship between Alanna and Jon is complicated by their ranks. Because Jon is four years older, he becomes a knight at eighteen when Alanna is becoming a squire at fourteen. Alanna's successes as a page make her the most desirable squire: Jon plans to take her on as his squire even before he discovers she is a girl. The book's climax comes in the final pages, as Jon and Alanna encounter and defeat several ancient beings of magical power, the Ysandir.[94] During the battle, Alanna's clothes are magically—and literally—stripped off of her, leaving her clad only in her "belt and scabbard."[95] Jon, despite "openly staring," chooses to focus on defeating the Ysandir and waiting for a subsequent explanation.[96] Alanna learns in the aftermath that Jon had intended her as his squire—and still does.[97] Alanna then becomes his squire, which takes the tale into the second novel, *In the Hand of the Goddess*, where romance becomes much more important.

Consequently, as a squire to a knight, Alanna would be expected to fit more naturally in the ranks of sidekicks. Two factors, however, keep her firmly situated in the role of hero while Jon remains the sidekick. The first is the narrative focus and nature of the quartet: it is Alanna's story. Throughout *Alanna: The First Adventure*, life as a page is one of an equal playing field. It is only during her time as a squire that Alanna could be considered a sidekick. But this is short lived: by the end of *In the Hand of the Goddess*, Alanna is a knight herself and no longer serves in a subservient status. The second factor is Alanna's abilities. It is clear to the reader that she is gifted beyond her peers, squires or otherwise, so much so that Deirdre F. Baker describes Alanna as being able to accomplish the "appropriation of the magic and fighting skills of various cultures."[98] Conversely, much of Jon's narrative is spent keeping him in droll court settings or throwing him in peril only to be saved by Alanna—which she does several times. Any intrigue is uncovered by Alanna; she is squire in name only.

In the Hand of the Goddess also brings romance and sex to the forefront. Alanna finds herself drawn to develop her skills as a woman-at-court, complete with the expected dress, posture, and the like.[99] This desire comes partly from her general thirst for knowledge, but also partly from jealousy over Jon's romantic conquests. Alanna finds herself in a love triangle: George professes his desire for her, and even makes a marriage proposal.[100] Jon similarly shows his interest in Alanna,[101] but succeeds where George does not: he and Alanna become lovers.[102] The movement from friends to lovers is a quantum leap in filling the role of absent parents. Alanna, essentially abandoned by her only parent and separated from her only sibling, creates her own family. Jon, as the prince, holds the political authority in their union, and Alanna, as his squire, is dedicated to protecting him when he cannot do so for himself. Alanna, at least by the end of *In the Hand of the Goddess*, eschews her relationship with Jon to strike out on her own as a knight of the realm. By leaving to go adventuring, Alanna chooses to place her surrogate family on hold—indeed, putting on hold the very possibility of creating her own family with herself as mother. In fact, it is Alanna's intention to never procreate (although she eventually does).

Another female hero with intentions to never have children—but who eventually does—is Katniss Everdeen from Suzanne Collins's *The Hunger Games*. Like Alanna, protagonist Katniss finds herself in a love triangle between two potential sidekicks. Unlike Alanna, however, Katniss fights the need for a sidekick even as she keeps being paired with them, one after another. She is the first hero studied here who is truly reluctant to have a sidekick. This reluctance makes her a fitting co-example along with Alanna for this section of my study. In many ways, the only sidekick Katniss readily accepts comes from outside of her love triangle: Rue, the tribute from District 11. Rue is a surrogate little sister for Katniss (reminding Katniss of her younger sister Primrose),[103] and actively helps her by providing medicinal knowledge,[104] information about their competition,[105] and a second pair of hands in a scheme to sabotage their competition.[106] This sister-sister relationship is a limited one, however, as Rue dies shortly after their alliance.[107] The focus on sidekicks must then turn to the love triangle involving Katniss with Gale Hawthorne and Peeta Mellark.

Katniss describes Gale as "the only person with whom I can be myself."[108] Along with this familiarity, Gale is also Katniss's hunting partner and the closest thing she has to a romantic relationship at the series's outset. He is also the closest male figure in her life, as her father died in a mining accident years earlier. While Katniss maintains that "there's never been anything romantic between [us]," she clearly denies romantic feelings regarding Gale.[109] Katniss also rationalizes the jealousy she feels when other girls give Gale attention, explaining that it would be difficult to replace him as a hunting partner. Later on, she does begin to recognize the depth of their relationship, citing "friend" as "too casual a word" to describe what he means to her.[110] However, over the course of the novel, Gale becomes a nonplayer in the plot. He simply is not there. When Katniss goes to the Hunger Games, he becomes the hope she leaves behind. She considers him the one who will help provide for her sister and mother if she fails to survive. As a result, Gale's memory complicates Katniss's romantic feelings toward her second in-game sidekick: Peeta. This complication could stem from Katniss's reluctance to accept any male figure in her life, perhaps in fear that he would leave her as well. (In the tyrannical political atmosphere in which they live, this is a likely scenario.) Gale, while initially the obvious romantic match for Katniss, becomes a nonfactor by the middle of book two, *Catching Fire*.

Peeta, on the other hand, only grows in his romantic possibility. Because Peeta is the male tribute from Katniss's district, the two of them share a great deal of time together during the pre-Hunger Games happenings. It is interesting that although Peeta has above average strength,[111] he depends on Katniss to keep him safe for a good portion of the Games. This might be unfair to Peeta, as it is his idea to present the two of them as star-crossed lovers: helping secure the hearts and pocketbooks of an adoring public.[112] Additionally, his actions within the arena help keep the most of the vicious tributes away from Katniss for the early portion of the contest.[113] However, Katniss is always seen as the greater threat. Similarly, she always holds the power in their relationship. This is especially true once Peeta's festering leg injury requires him to rely completely on Katniss.

Peeta becomes the obvious romantic winner for a number of reasons. The attention he gives Katniss before the Games is marked by an intellectual and emotional gravity. While Gale shared in Katniss's pre-Games responsibilities, Peeta fills Katniss's emotional needs within the Games; he is the emotion to her strength. Furthermore, they survive the death- and sickness-filled Hunger Games together—twice. Ultimately, Peeta retains his purity throughout the series while Gale eventually sacrifices his. In terms of family, Peeta and Katniss marry and have children after the overthrow of the government. Peeta becomes the other half of Katniss's physical family, a move made all the more meaningful after Prim's death. Gale, on the other hand, ceases to function in any meaningful way in Katniss's life. It is not terribly surprising that Katniss (and Alanna, for that matter) finds herself in a love triangle. Katniss's and Alanna's love interests also function as sidekicks in adventuring, however, which moves all involved beyond mere romance and into an alternate hero/sidekick pairing. It is important to note that Alanna and Katniss never go adventuring with both sidekicks at the same time, because that situation creates something substantially different: the hero/sidekick triad.

A fascinating take on the mixed gender pairing is the hero/sidekick triad: where a hero has two sidekicks instead of just one. For instance, Taran, the hero of Lloyd Alexander's *The Chronicles of Prydain*, has the Princess Eilonwy and the creature Gurgi as sidekicks. Meg from Madeleine L'Engle's *A Wrinkle in Time* has her brother Charles Wallace and their friend Calvin. J. K. Rowling's Harry Potter has Hermione Granger and Ron Weasley. The trio from *The Hunger Games* does not qualify, as Katniss, Peeta, and Gale never adventure together as a unified group. Likewise, Alanna, Jon, and George maintain strict lines of separation. My triad of choice comes from Rick Riordan's *Percy Jackson and the Olympians* series. The hero is Percy Jackson, his female sidekick is Annabeth Chase, and his male sidekick is the satyr Grover Underwood. Percy's origin story is similar to Harry Potter's: he has a less-than-ideal living situation at home (his stepfather is a lowlife), he discovers that he has inherent supernatural abilities (he is the son of the Greek god Poseidon), and he goes away to a special school for kids like him, "Camp Half-blood." Riordan makes the special school a summer vacation camp, instead of the school year institution of Rowling's Hogwarts, flip-flopping the series' respective calendar of events. There is also an air of mysterious promise around Percy: while Harry was "the boy who lived," Percy is the apparent fulfillment of a far-reaching prophecy with far-reaching implications. Percy, again like Harry, interacts with an intelligent and gifted female sidekick (Annabeth is the daughter of Athena) and an awkward but loyal male sidekick (Grover is trying to prove his worth as a satyr).

What makes the Percy/Annabeth/Grover triad different from the Harry/Hermione/Ron triad, in part, are the dual quests of books two and three. Book two, *The Sea of Monsters*, has Percy try to recover the Golden Fleece, as well as the imprisoned Grover. Book three, *The Titan's Curse*, sends out a tracking team to find the missing goddess Artemis, and also the kidnapped Annabeth. In these books, then, Percy supplements his original triad with other supporting characters in an effort to restore his original group. The sidekick status quo, as it were, needs to be restored in both of these instances. The divine prizes are not the quest, however, as the "real" quests are to recover the hero's sidekicks (a quest very familiar within the Batman comics). Because this part of the study is not about Percy but about Annabeth and Grover, the implications of removing one of them from the triad equation is what makes it so compelling.

At the beginning of *The Sea of Monsters*, Percy dreams that Grover is in trouble. At the end of *The Lightning Thief* (book one), Grover left to search for the missing god Pan, and Percy has not heard from him in the intervening months.[114] Percy begins his quest to retrieve Grover, who happens to be in the same place as the Golden Fleece needed to save the camp's magical boundaries.[115] What makes this quest different, in part, is that it includes Tyson, Percy's newfound half brother Cyclops. Tyson is the ad hoc Grover, taking the place of the male sidekick, complete with magical/mythical powers based in nature. Tyson's inclusion as a new character also allows for any requisite exposition for new readers who may have missed the first book.

Making Grover part of the quest's purpose places his role as sidekick in an external locus: his well-being becomes the driving force behind the actions of the hero. Furthermore, Grover has used his nature-based magic to forge an "empathy link" between himself and Percy, allowing them to communicate over long distances.[116] Grover simultaneously exists as sidekick and not-sidekick. The triad remains complete, however, as Percy and Annabeth travel to reunite themselves with Grover. Tyson is not the only additional character in the questing process, as Clarisse (daughter of Ares) also joins in. With only one new addition, Grover may have been displaced by Tyson.

Adding in two characters creates a tension that disallows for such a structural substitution. Grover retains his place.

In a very similar setup, *The Titan's Curse* takes Annabeth and places her as the object of the quest. Percy and Grover join with newcomers Thalia, Zoe, and Bianca to rescue Artemis and Annabeth. Percy and Annabeth are now in the eighth grade, and their age and absence create the first real notions of a potential romance, shifting their one-time brother/sister role. In this instance, romantic feelings further compound Percy's perception of Annabeth's peril, making his concern for her all the more palpable.

Directly contrasting with how Riordan separates his major characters, Rowling never parts the three members of Harry Potter's hero/sidekick triad for long. With the minor exception of the Tri-Wizard Tournament, Harry hardly ever needs "to quest" to save his sidekicks. Riordan's books, on the other hand, are based on the premise of questing—the influence of Greek mythology and Heracles's tasks are apparent throughout. Making a sidekick the object of the quest places him or her as the central focus for the novel and the hero. This scenario is not a new one, recalling Campbell's explications of the reception of the ultimate boon[117] or the need for rescue.[118] Granted, his descriptions suggest different connotations than Percy Jackson's situation, but as Campbell notes, "the changes rung on the simple scale of the monomyth defy description."[119] YA also has its fair share of questing for one's sidekick/companion. Take, for example, Lloyd Alexander's third *Chronicles of Prydain* book, *The Castle of Llyr*. Taran's newly flourishing feelings for Eilonwy dominate the text, culminating in his attempt to rescue her from an evil kidnapper.[120] In an empowering plot development, Eilonwy is the one who holds the power to free herself, and it is she who does so in the end, regardless of the efforts put forth by Taran and others to free her.[121]

There is one thing, however, that problematizes Riordan's repeated "save the sidekick" scenario. In both cases, there is a graver reason for the quest: finding the Golden Fleece and finding Artemis. If Grover and/or Annabeth were not Percy's sidekicks, he would have no compelling, personal impetus to save them, and the quests would only be thinly veiled repetitions of classical models/myths. In fact, in both cases, Percy uses the universally more pressing quest as a front in order to gain permission to save his friends. From the standpoint of the YA hero, then, the choice is clear: saving the sidekick is the biggest concern.

YA's precondition of a "broken" family dynamic for partnering a sidekick with a hero needs further analysis, which I will undertake in the next chapters, in those cases where the new "family" dynamic of hero/sidekick subsequently breaks down. Given the nature of a YA sidekick, the relationship will likely break or evolve as the sidekick matures and changes. In other genres, a sidekick can exist with relatively little development over any number of novels or adventures. When a YA sidekick does leave his or her hero, it is not always a negative break, as a YA character's maturation is often based on the realization that one must stand alone someday, without the aid of a parent, parents, or hero. However, it certainly can be a painful process, especially when the hero and sidekick part ways under negative or destructive circumstances.

Although this chapter has showcased how heroes and sidekicks come together *in loco parentis*, the literary examples also give some hints of the aforementioned eventual (and perhaps inevitable) separation between hero/sidekick. Dick Grayson finds himself at odds with Batman and strikes out on his own (or is fired, depending on whether one considers pre-*Crisis* or post-*Crisis* texts).[122] While Carrie Kelly continues as Batman's new Robin through the conclusion of Frank Miller's take on the Dark Knight, her role shifts as she gains confidence and experience. Violet Parr remains a junior high student at the end of *The Incredibles*, although it would be interesting to see what her relationship with her mother would be like when she hits her later teenage years (a question still only hinted at in *Incredibles 2*, as the direct sequel does not show any passage of time between films). Jessica remains Paul's mother, but Paul's role as galaxy messiah (or antichrist, depending on one's viewpoint) keeps their relationship at arm's length in many ways. Frodo could not stay with Sam in the Shire, leaving to travel to the peace offered across the sea. George and Bess, on the other hand, continue to solve mysteries with Nancy Drew to this day . . . and continue to stay essentially the same.

More substantial examples of separations exist, and studying a few of them in-depth forms the basis of the coming three chapters, which show three distinct ways YA enables these separations to occur when a sidekick comes into his or her own. Chapter 3 explores what happens when a sidekick is given enough narrative opportunity to grow outside of the sidekick role, emerging into the role of hero: I study Neville Longbottom from Rowling's *Harry Potter* series and Tenar from Le Guin's *Earthsea* series.

NOTES

1. Walter Hogan, *Humor in Young Adult Literature: A Time to Laugh* (Lanham: Scarecrow, 2005), 1.
2. Ibid., 2.
3. Roberta Seelinger Trites, *Disturbing the Universe: Power and Repression in Adolescent Literature* (Iowa City: University of Iowa Press, 2000), 58–69.
4. Maria Nikolajeva, *The Rhetoric of Character in Children's Literature* (Lanham: Scarecrow, 2002), 110–27.
5. Ibid., 117.
6. Ibid., 119.
7. Ibid., 118.
8. Ibid.
9. Ibid., 67.

10. Ibid., 84.
11. Ibid.
12. Leroy Lad Panek, *The Origins of the American Detective Story* (Jefferson: McFarland, 2006), 138, 192.
13. Gary Hoppenstand, ed. *The Dime Novel Detective* (Bowling Green: Bowling Green University Press, 1982), 71, 136, 182.
14. Panek, *Origins*, 7.
15. Bradford W. Wright, *Comic Book Nation: The Transformation of Youth Culture in America* (Baltimore: Johns Hopkins University Press, 2001), 16.
16. Peter Coogan, *Superhero: The Secret Origin of a Genre* (Austin: MonkeyBrain, 2006), 200.
17. Grant Morrison, Andy Kubert, and Jesse Delperdang, *Batman and Son* (New York: DC Comics, 2007).
18. Wright, *Comic Book Nation*, 17.
19. Jim McLauchlin, "Batman's 10 Greatest Robins, Ranked." Newsarama, last modified March 23, 2018. https://www.newsarama.com/15683-ranking-the-robins-from-10-to-1-yes-there-are-10.html.
20. J. L. Bell, "Success in Stasis: Dick Grayson's Thirty Years as a Boy Wonder," in *Dick Grayson, Boy Wonder: Scholars and Creators on 75 Years of Robin, Nightwing and Batman*, ed. Kristen Geaman (Jefferson: McFarland, 2015), 8.
21. Coogan, *Superhero*, 213.
22. Ibid., 214.
23. Bell, "Success in Stasis," 9.
24. Ibid.
25. Ibid., 11.
26. Ibid., 10.
27. Fernando Gabriel Pagnoni Berns and César Alfonso Marino, "Outlining the Future Robin: The Seventies in the *Batman Family*," in *Dick Grayson, Boy Wonder: Scholars and Creators on 75 Years of Robin, Nightwing and Batman*, ed. Kristen Geaman (Jefferson: McFarland, 2015), 28.
28. Ibid., 29.
29. Kristen Geaman, ed. *Dick Grayson, Boy Wonder: Scholars and Creators on 75 Years of Robin, Nightwing and Batman* (Jefferson: McFarland, 2015), 112.
30. Ibid., 113.
31. Ibid., 118–19.
32. "Batman: The Legacy Continues," in *Batman: The Animated Series. Vol. 1* (1991; Burbank, CA: Warner Home Video, 2004), DVD.
33. Ibid.
34. Geaman, *Dick Grayson*, 284.
35. "Batman: The Legacy Continues."
36. "Robin Rising," in *Batman: The Animated Series. Vol. 1* (1991; Burbank, CA: Warner Home Video, 2004), DVD.
37. Ibid.
38. Richard Reynolds, *Super Heroes: A Modern Mythology* (Jackson: University Press of Mississippi, 1994), 100.
39. Nathan G. Tipton, "Gender Trouble: Frank Miller's Revision of Robin in the *Batman: Dark Knight* Series," *The Journal of Popular Culture* 41, no. 2 (2008): 334.
40. Frank Miller, *The Dark Knight Returns* (New York: DC Comics, 2002), 76.
41. Ibid., 60, 145; Tipton, "Gender Trouble," 330.
42. Miller, *The Dark Knight Returns*, 82.
43. Ibid., 83.
44. Ibid., 85.
45. Ibid., 92.
46. Ibid., 30, 31, 34.
47. Ibid., 92.
48. Ibid., 121.

49. Ibid., 116.
50. Ibid., 138.
51. Ibid., 140.
52. Ibid., 149.
53. Tipton, "Gender Trouble," 333.
54. Ibid., 331.
55. Miller, *The Dark Knight Returns*, 138, 93.
56. Ibid., 155.
57. Tipton, "Gender Trouble," 327.
58. Richard Corliss, "Can Pixar Still Go Up?" *Time*, vol. 181, no. 24 (June 24, 2013): 56.
59. *The Incredibles*, Brad Bird, dir.2004 (Walt Disney Home Entertainment, 2005), DVD.
60. Bird, *The Incredibles*.
61. Ibid.
62. Ibid.
63. Frances A. Nadeau, "The Mother/Daughter Relationship in Young Adult Fiction," *The ALAN Review* 22, no. 2 (1995): 14.
64. Juan A. Prieto-Pablos, "The Ambivalent Hero of Contemporary Fantasy and Science Fiction," *Extrapolation* 32, no. 1 (1991): 66.
65. Frank Herbert, *Dune* (New York: Penguin, 1990), 18, 43.
66. Including (but certainly not limited to): Norman Spinrad, *Science Fiction in the Real World* (Carbondale: Southern Illinois University Press, 1990); Michael R. Collings, "The Epic of *Dune*: Epic Traditions in Modern Science Fiction," in *Aspects of Fantasy: Selected Essays from the Second International Conference on the Fantastic in the Arts*, ed. William Coyle (Westport: Greenwood, 1981), 131–39; Donald Palumbo, "The Monomyth as Fractal Pattern in Frank Herbert's *Dune* Novels," *Science-Fiction Studies* 25, no. 3 (1998): 433–58.
67. Herbert, *Dune*, 281, 294.
68. Ibid., 351–59.
69. Ibid., 481–87.
70. See Sara Paretsky, "Introduction" to *The Secret of the Old Clock*, by Carolyn Keene (Bedford: Applewood, 1991); Melanie Rehak, *Girl Sleuth: Nancy Drew and the Women Who Created Her* (Orlando: Harcourt, 2005); Phil Zuckerman, "Publishing the Applewood Reprints," in *Rediscovering Nancy Drew*, eds. Carolyn Stewart Dyer and Nancy Tillman Romalov (Iowa City: University of Iowa Press, 1995), 41–46.
71. Carolyn Keene, *Nancy Drew Mystery Series: The Secret of Shadow Ranch* (New York: Grosset, 2002), 4–6.
72. Ibid., 13–14.
73. Ibid., 7.
74. Ibid., 1.
75. Ibid., 6, 10, 66, 91, 100, 116, 173.
76. Ibid., 27, 46, 56, 65, 72, 75, 112, 119.
77. Ibid., 4, 17, 113, 116-17, 134, 138.
78. See Sherrie A. Inness, "Is Nancy Drew Queer? Popular Reading Strategies for the Lesbian Reader," *Women's Studies* 26, no. 3–4 (1997): 361; Stephanie Foote, "Bookish Women: Reading Girls' Fiction: A Response to Julia Mickenberg," *American Literary History* 19, no. 2 (2007): 525; Carolyn Stewart Dyer and Nancy Tillman Romalov, eds. *Rediscovering Nancy Drew* (Iowa City: University of Iowa Press, 1995), 17, 35.
79. Keene, *Nancy Drew*, 140.
80. Ibid., 116.
81. Ibid.
82. Ibid., 140.
83. Jasper Fford, *The Last Dragonslayer* (New York: Houghton, 2012), 16.
84. Ibid., 123.
85. Michele S. Ware, "'True Legitimacy': The Myth of the Foundling in *Bleak House*," *Studies in the Novel* 22, no. 1 (1990): 2.
86. Ibid., 4.
87. Ibid., 2.

88. Marilyn Francus, "Virtuous Foundlings and Excessive Bastards," *The Eighteenth Century* 49, no. 1 (2008): 87.
89. Nancy Werlin, "Get Rid of the Parents?," *Booklist* 95, no. 21 (1995), 1934–35.
90. Fford, *The Last Dragonslayer*, x, 2.
91. Ibid., 201.
92. Ibid., 134, 163, 249.
93. L. Monique Pittman, "Dressing the Girl/Playing the Boy: *Twelfth Night* Learns Soccer on the Set of *She Is The Man*," *Literature Film Quarterly* 36, no. 2 (2008): 123.
94. Tamora Pierce, *Alanna: The First Adventure* (New York: Simon, 2005), 250–62.
95. Ibid., 253.
96. Ibid., 254.
97. Ibid., 273–74.
98. Deirdre F. Baker, "Reader at Large: Musings on Diverse Worlds," *Horn Book Magazine* 83, no. 1 (2007): 45.
99. Tamora Pierce, *In the Hand of the Goddess* (New York: Simon, 2005), 156.
100. Ibid., 90.
101. Ibid., 127.
102. Ibid., 178–79.
103. Suzanne Collins, *The Hunger Games* (New York: Scholastic, 2008), 201.
104. Ibid., 200.
105. Ibid., 206.
106. Ibid., 208.
107. Ibid., 236.
108. Ibid., 6.
109. Ibid., 10.
110. Ibid., 112.
111. Ibid., 108.
112. Ibid., 135.
113. Ibid., 162.
114. Rick Riordan, *Percy Jackson and the Olympians: The Lightning Thief* (New York: Hyperion, 2005), 356; Rick Riordan, *Percy Jackson and the Olympians: The Sea of Monsters* (New York: Hyperion, 2006), 73.
115. Riordan, *Sea of Monsters*, 87.
116. Ibid., 74.
117. Joseph Campbell, *The Hero with a Thousand Faces* (New Jersey: Princeton University Press, 1972), 172.
118. Ibid., 201.
119. Ibid., 246.
120. Lloyd Alexander, *The Castle of Lyre* (New York: Random, 1990), 57.
121. Ibid., 188–89.
122. Geaman, *Dick Grayson*, 113, 117.

Chapter Three

The Secondary Hero

*Neville Longbottom and Tenar as
Sidekicks-Turned-Heroes*

In the first chapter, I argued that sidekicks can be usefully categorized into a number of distinct types directly and critically relating to the wider purposes of the narratives in which they exist. The second chapter explored the ways in which heroes and sidekicks might interact within specific family role standpoints in the re-creation of those relationships. This stems from a sidekick's desire to create a surrogate family, a point strongly distinguishing YA heroes/sidekicks from those found in other literatures. This establishment of the surrogate family allows the sidekick to begin growing, either transforming their corelationships with heroes into something entirely new or fracturing them entirely.

For the remaining chapters, I will examine this growth pattern, what I call "sidekick separation." In YA, and especially in series of multiple volumes with extended chronologies, this "sidekick separation" seems almost always to move the sidekick narratively upward, becoming a kind of "sidekick elevation." In light of the YA audience, "sidekick elevation" makes both aesthetic and logical sense. Just as the YA reader, who can naturally relate most closely to younger and more subsidiary sidekicks, will grow and enter adolescence, so too will the sidekicks tend to grow and be "elevated" in significant ways if they remain part of those stories. This is especially apparent when these readers concurrently experience adolescence alongside characters from a publication history of longer stories like *Harry Potter*.

I argue that "sidekick elevation" often takes one of three distinct trajectories. I call the first the "secondary hero," which will be the focus of this chapter. This occurs when sidekicks are given narrative space ample enough for them to emerge in their own heroic roles. Sometimes, sidekicks become the main focus of story lines already traversed, or what I call "sidekick sequels" (examples of this second trajectory will be analyzed in chapter 4). Finally, as I will delineate in chapter 5, trajectory three is the "self-aware sidekick novel," that is, where the primary narrative point of view is that of the sidekick, not that of the hero.

Since "deutero-protagonists" are fairly common throughout literature, and since this trajectory of sidekick elevation seems to involve the least narrative displacement of the hero, I begin with the "secondary hero." Previous allusions to this scenario include Dick Grayson as Robin, as his many decades as the Boy Wonder eventually bring him to strike out on his own as Nightwing. This emergence is particularly felt in the realm of YA, as it brings to mind the *Bildungsroman* or *Entwicklungsroman* yet again. The difference here, and perhaps a new element in understanding elements of these genres, is the eventual ending point for the sidekick: does he or she grow, emerging as an indisputable "adult," or is the ending point something else entirely? In this direction, Roberta Trites categorizes YA as "probably the only genre in the world designed to propel the reader out of his or her own subject position."[1] Trites uses the first four Harry Potter novels to illustrate how YA sets up its readership to eventually grasp that "the only way for adolescents to empower themselves is to quit being so adolescent. Grow up. Get over yourselves."[2] While Trites makes a compelling argument (and one that is difficult to dispute, given the nature of YA), my investigation of the sidekick asks whether or not there are other ways toward empowerment beyond simply "growing up," or perhaps whether or not the analysis changes with differing definitions for "growing up." Considering that my focus is the sidekick and not the hero also counters Trites's claims to a certain extent. To introduce this idea of the secondary hero, I use an extended case study investigating sidekick elevation that comes from J. K. Rowling's sizable *Harry Potter* universe: Neville Longbottom. A second case study, and perhaps the one that pushes the understanding of this emergence even farther, is Tenar from Ursula Le Guin's *Earthsea* novels.

Initially, Neville does not play a role significant enough to function as Harry's sidekick in any fashion. The more obvious choices for Harry's sidekick are Hermione and/or Ron. In this case, however, I consider Hermione and Ron ineligible as they are as much the "hero" as Harry by the end of the series, a by-product of the hero/sidekick triad over the course of seven novels. Harry's triad with Hermione and Ron remakes the roles of hero and sidekick. In this case, the triad begins with the young male hero, paired with a young female and young male of similar ages. In many regards, throughout the series, Harry is even something of an underdog in his relationship with Hermione: she is more studious, she knows about her magical heritage for much longer than Harry, and she is a stronger witch than Harry is a wizard.

Hermione is already very outspoken and confident—traits still developing in the orphaned, neglected, and emotionally abused Harry. Harry makes his surrogate family with Hermione and Ron, both of whom come from stable family environments.

Neville, however, generally remains subservient to the hero from books one through four. This becomes complicated in the fifth book of the series, *Harry Potter and the Order of the Phoenix*. It is in this book that Harry learns of the prophecy foretelling Voldemort's downfall, and that both he and Neville were capable of fulfilling it. The prophecy is, in many ways, the impetus for the entire series: it prompted Voldemort's attack on the infant Harry, which resulted in the death of Harry's parents, Voldemort's initial defeat, and Harry's infamous lightning-bolt scar. In this case then, Neville becomes the "could-have-been" Harry. His leadership status in Harry's absence during book seven even grants him his own sidekick of sorts in Luna Lovegood, not to mention the support of the rest of Dumbledore's Army. While serious scholarly work focusing solely on Neville is exceedingly limited (although I doubt that will remain the case for long), a considerable amount of growing interest for Neville comes from nonliterary sources, including the ever-expanding fan base dedicated to singing Neville's praise.[3] For one instance, Emily Asher-Perrin claims Neville is the "one person who determines the course of the Harry Potter series."[4] Aside from calling Neville "what most Gryffindors would be like in the real world,"[5] Asher-Perrin bases her argument for Neville's importance on a series of parallels between Harry's generation and his father's generation: Neville succeeds where his predecessor, Peter Pettigrew, failed. Peter's betrayal of those closest to him is the lynchpin allowing Voldemort to triumph over the first Order of the Phoenix. If Neville occupies the same social position within Harry's cadre of friends (and Asher-Perrin goes to great lengths in making her case), then the fact that he "makes all the hard choices that Pettigrew refused the first time around"[6] certainly cements both his importance and his role as sidekick to the hero triad of Harry, Hermione, and Ron.

Neville, like Arthur from *The Tick*, allows for an interesting study regarding characters appearing in novels and their film adaptations. Considering the success and popularity of the Harry Potter films in conjunction with the novels, the actions taken by a character like Neville may become blurred in the mind of the reader/viewer: the differences between the textual and the filmic character become less clear. As I did with Arthur, I analyze both the cinematic and the textual versions of Neville. I believe this to be a necessary and beneficial course given the way fans of the books have so heartily embraced the films.

Neville's first significant cinematic appearance is in the movie version of book four, *Harry Potter and the Goblet of Fire*. In the previous three films, he is relatively static: a wallflower called upon for the punch line of a physical gag. In the fourth film, (arguably the first of the series to be considered YA), Harry's need of Neville's knowledge of herbs and plants lays the groundwork for Neville's eventual move into the sidekick role. As Harry is forced to compete in the Triwizard Tournament, he must overcome a series of obstacles. Obstacle two is the rescue of a loved one from his or her bonds underneath the Hogwarts' lake. In the novel, Harry despairs in not finding a way to accomplish such a task until Dobby the house-elf provides him with gillyweed: "Right before you go into the lake, sir—gillyweed! . . . It will make Harry Potter breathe underwater, sir!"[7] The gillyweed transforms Harry: complete with gills, webbed hands, and "elongated" feet with webbed toes that "looked as though he had sprouted flippers."[8] Because of his new ability to breathe and maneuver underwater, he subsequently finishes his task with a flourish—rescuing Ron as well as Gabrielle Delacour, sister to failed champion Fleur Delacour. Dobby's gift of the gillyweed is the talisman or magical aid given to Harry (à la Campbell's "other helpers") to complete this cycle of heroism, limited or brief as it may be.

In the film version, however, it is Neville who acts as helpful other and provider of the gillyweed. As was the case in the novel, Harry receives his answer at something of the eleventh hour. Harry, Ron, and Hermione are trying to determine how Harry might spend an hour underwater. When Ron and Hermione get summoned to Professor McGonagall's office (where they will be taken as the captives for the next day's trial), Neville gets propositioned to give Harry a hand with his books. Neville, somewhat nervously, tries to make small talk involving his significant love of plants. Harry impatiently replies, "Neville, no offense, but I really do not care about plants. Now, if there's a Tibetan turnip that will allow me to breathe underwater for an hour, then great. But otherwise . . . ."[9] Neville's response comes right before the scene change, allowing for simultaneous suspense and relief on the part of the viewer: "I don't know about a turnip, but you can always use gillyweed."[10] The next scene shows Neville handing the gillyweed to Harry on their way to the tournament's trial. After Harry seems upset over Neville's uncertainty about the duration of the gillyweed's effect, Neville haltingly states, "I just . . . wanted . . . to help."[11] Neville has obvious familiarity with Harry—they've been classmates for three and a half years at this point, as well as fellow members of Gryffindor. However, it remains clear that Neville exists in Harry's periphery. It is also clear that Neville feels intimidated by Harry's reputation—which makes sense, given Neville's introverted disposition. Nevertheless, Neville acts as the surrogate Ron/Hermione in this scene. He is both the friend and confidant who willingly serves as Harry's second (replacing Ron), as well as the more knowledgeable witch/wizard from whom Harry usually gets aid (replacing Hermione). Harry himself verbally recognizes this fact when he states, "Well, it makes you a sight better than Ron or Hermione. Where are they?"[12]

Neville's provision of gillyweed continues to brighten his star for the viewer. His action gives him screen time and humor, as well as provides Harry someone to dialogue with in the absence of Ron and Hermione. The question, then, is not how this benefits Neville (as it clearly does), but why it was given to Neville in the film and not to Dobby? First, there is the practical explanation—it is logistically (and financially) easier to give lines and screen time to a human actor than to animate a CGI character. Second, Neville's love of herbology makes him a more natural choice to provide the gillyweed. Third, he probably ranks as the fourth most recognizable student (for viewers) at Hogwarts after Harry, Ron, and Hermione (with the possible exception of Draco Malfoy, the school's heel).

A fourth reasonable explanation comes from the timeline established with the publishing of the novels and the filming of the movies. The film version of *The Goblet of Fire* was released in 2005, two years after *The Order of the Phoenix* was published as a book. Screenwriter Steve Kloves (who wrote seven of the eight film scripts) and director Mike Newell almost certainly knew the events of book five before beginning to develop *The Goblet of Fire* for the big screen. As the prophesy foretelling Voldemort's eventual demise plays such a significant part of *The Order of the Phoenix*'s plot, the developers would have known that Neville's role in the series was about to become bigger. In light of this, it makes perfect sense to begin laying as much foundational material as possible to build Neville's on-screen character. This also directly coincides with Rowling's admissions of Neville's increasing importance, stating "I think he's already got a much bigger part.... Book five was a real turning point for Neville."[13] *The Order of the Phoenix*, both film and novel, bring Neville into the ranks of "significant characters." Amidst impending war preparations sparked by Voldemort's physical rebirth, the existence of the prophecy comes to Harry's attention. While finding and hearing the full prophecy becomes Harry's main quest, the rest of his time is spent establishing and training Dumbledore's Army: both of which heavily involve Neville. Furthermore, Neville's backstory is also established in *The Order of the Phoenix*. (It is important to note that few characters get as much backstory as Neville.)

While visiting Ron's father in the wizard hospital St. Mungo's, Harry, Ron, Hermione, and Ginny find themselves in the permanent-spell-damage ward of the hospital—essentially the wing of the hospital that houses patients with spell-induced dementia/Alzheimer's. It is here that they run into Neville and his grandmother, both of whom were visiting Neville's parents. Neville's grandmother reveals that she knows Harry and Hermione from Neville's descriptions and conversations about them, indicating their importance to him as friends. Additionally, she explains why Neville's parents are in the ward in the first place: they were "tortured into insanity by You-Know-Who's followers."[14] After the others express surprise and sadness, Harry reveals that he knew already by naming Bellatrix Lestrange as the person responsible. (Dumbledore had told him, swearing him to secrecy.)[15]

Neville's actions in this scene are caused by his introverted nature and his need to guard his privacy. As his impaired mother earnestly gives him a Droobles Blowing Gum wrapper as a gift, Neville slips it into his pocket, quietly defying his grandmother's advice to throw it away. The simple act shows a great deal about his love for his parents. He places importance on their role in his life even with their inability to raise him. Their legacy as "highly gifted Aurors" hangs over Neville's self-worth, especially as his grandmother laments that he lacks the skills necessary to become one. According to Neville, she is always "telling Professor Marchbanks I am not as good as my dad."[16] This admission, to Harry, Ron, and Hermione, is followed by an embarrassed Neville staring "fixedly at the floor."[17] His bumbling and shy nature is influenced, in part, by the thought of incapacitated parents who were once brilliant in their protection of their son. Neville's confidence level is connected to this parental absence in his life: they survived their brush with evil, but were left without their sanity. Neville, then, faced familial instability similar to Harry's. Neville performs a twofold action designed not to replace his parents, but to first avenge them by facing Bellatrix Lestrange and second, prove himself worthy of his parents' legacy. Both of these begin to come to pass in the end of *The Order of the Phoenix* and come to fulfillment by the end of *The Deathly Hallows*.

Neville undergoes a "strange and even slightly alarming change" after the news breaks that Lestrange and other evil witches and wizards have escaped the prison Azkaban.[18] All of Dumbledore's Army works harder after the prison break, but it is Neville who worked "harder than anyone else in the room," and improved "so fast it was quite unnerving."[19] It seems as though the motivation Neville needed to overcome his confidence issues came from the knowledge that he might get the chance to face Lestrange, which indeed happens during the climactic end of *The Order of the Phoenix*, occurring between members of Dumbledore's Army and Voldemort's Death Eaters for the possession of the prophecy. This is a pivotal battle for a number of reasons. First, Harry and his friends engage the dark forces head-on for the first time. Second, Harry's godfather Sirius dies in the battle. Third, it alerts the greater public to Voldemort's return. Fourth and finally, Neville stands next to Harry when Ron and Hermione have been taken out of commission.

In the resulting fight between the forces of good and evil, Hermione is hit by a curse that knocks her unconscious, Ron is hit with a laughing-gas curse leaving him nonsensical, Ginny breaks her ankle, and Luna stays to care for her. Only Harry and Neville remain capable of fighting.[20] There comes a point where Harry runs away from his friends, hoping to lead Voldemort's minions away, praying that "Neville would stay with Ron"—and it works when the forces of evil follow him.[21] The momentary respite is quickly lost, however, as Harry finds himself facing ten enemies at once. Neville once again throws himself in peril's way: "Neville was scrambling down the stone benches toward them."[22] He shouts from above, "He's dot alone! He's still god be!," (or "He's not alone! He's still got me!" had his nose not been bloodied).[23] What happens next is a series of events that place Harry and Neville firmly together as the heroic duo: if ever there were a moment when Neville's worth as a sidekick is felt, this is it.

Unfortunately and comically, the effect Neville has on the immediate situation is close to nothing: he only casts two and a half stupefy charms and is quickly seized from behind. Furthermore, once he is captive, the Death Eaters stop trying to persuade Harry and begin forcing him to watch Neville undergo torture. While he is being held, Neville's remarkable selflessness continues. Although it was foolhardy to reveal himself to a room full of older, more experienced enemies, he did it anyway. In this way, Neville is reminiscent of the American monomythic hero, as (previously) defined by Lawrence and Jewett: "a selfless superhero emerges to renounce temptations and carry out the redemptive task."[24] Neville's greatest heroic attributes are this selflessness and his ability to deny any temptations. Neville never gives in to any temptation offered by the enemy, nor does he engage in "sexually fulfilling activities,"[25] although that may be merely a matter of not following his narrative as closely as, say, Harry's infatuation with Cho Chang, or Ron's budding romance with Hermione. Lestrange, present in the room, wonders out loud "how long Longbottom lasts before he cracks like his parents. . . . Unless Potter wants to give us the prophecy."[26] Neville's response is consistent with his actions thus far: "DO NOT GIB ID DO DEM, HARRY!" as he kicks and writhes to free himself.[27] Regardless, Lestrange uses the torturing curse on Neville, sending him "twitching and screaming in agony" on the floor.[28] Before things get more out of hand, Harry holds out the prophecy, and the cavalry arrives.

As the battle begins around him in earnest, Harry's first act is to see to Neville, who is crawling along the floor. Neville confirms he's alright moments before Harry is grabbed by the neck and held aloft. As his windpipe is closed, Harry has mere moments to try and save himself. As Harry's situation seems grim, Neville *again* comes to the rescue by "[jabbing] Hermione's wand hard into the eyehole of the Death Eater's mask."[29] Neville's triumph does not last long, as another enemy appears and enchants Neville's legs into constantly and uncontrollably tap dancing. Neville's dancing legs ultimately destroy the prophecy: the glass ball eventually falls and is kicked by his flailing leg. Only Harry and Neville see the "recording," as it were, but they cannot hear the words spoken over the sounds of battle.[30] The prophecy, later revealed in full by Dumbledore, reveals Harry was not the only child who embodied the prophesied threat to Voldemort. The prophesy states: "The one with the power to vanquish the Dark Lord approaches. . . . Born to those who have thrice defied him, born as the seventh month dies . . . and the Dark Lord will mark him as his equal, but he will have power the Dark Lord knows not . . . and either must die at the hand of the other for neither can live while the other survives.[31] Harry's reaction to this information is to question whether the prophecy implies he is the one to vanquish Voldemort. Dumbledore informs him that two children were born at the end of July to parents who had three times escaped Voldemort's wrath: Harry and Neville. It is fitting, then, that Neville was by Harry's side when the prophecy's recording was lost. Additionally, the actions of Lestrange against Neville's parents now become clear: as Voldemort's most trusted lieutenant, she was sent to kill Neville while Voldemort went to kill Harry. In fact, the series mentions time and again that it was Harry's mother's counterspell of love that both saved Harry and defeated Voldemort. The famed lightning-bolt scar on Harry's forehead was a result of his mother's magic and Voldemort's demise. Any special powers Harry possesses come from two places: the connection he shares with Voldemort and the love he shares with others (an ongoing theme for Rowling). As previously stated, this knowledge of Neville's potential creates a situation of "what if," namely what if Voldemort had chosen to kill Neville instead—would his mother have saved *him* and created a lightning-shaped scar on Neville's forehead? Should the series include titles like *Neville Longbottom and the Sorcerer's Stone*? Speculating about the "what ifs" proves generally fruitless, as all retroactive speculation proves to be. This does not stop Neville's growing fan base from trying, however. As of September 2018, a Google search for "Neville Longbottom Alternate Theory" produces about 102,000 results. One top hit is a fan fiction about Neville-as-Harry, written by a Tumblr author called "ink-splotch." This particular fan fiction tries to re-envision the entire series, and has received considerable internet attention, being reposted by popular-culture sites like "PopSugar.com."

Dumbledore attempts to put these thoughts at rest by telling Harry that when he took it upon himself to kill the infant Harry, and not the infant Neville, Voldemort positioned Harry to fulfill the second part of the prophecy: "Voldemort himself would 'mark him as his equal'"[32] Be this as it may, Neville's involvement in the prophesy continues to make him an increasingly important member of the Harry Potter universe. In fact, the introduction of Neville's role in the prophesy creates a *new* Harry Potter mythos—beyond the imaginings of fan fiction—if you will. This falls directly in line with Doty's consideration of myths as a way to "model possibilities."[33] Suddenly, the perceived power Harry embodies grows to include Neville: he is a new wrinkle to a now familiar scenario, or, to put it another way, "the coded DNA of the human psyche calling us to refresh the dream."[34] Here, in *The Order of the Phoenix*, Rowling problematizes the uniqueness of Harry's quest. Where Harry was once the lauded, revered, and isolated young wizard who was responsible for Voldemort's first defeat, he now becomes only one potential fulfillment of that dream. Neville exists on a playing field parallel to Harry, brought into the light as a refreshment (and possible replacement) to the dream of vanquishing evil. At the same time, Rowling also undermines Harry's authority in this matter, at least from the perspective of him as the chosen hero.

The wizards who align themselves against Voldemort understand Harry's limitations. What keeps Harry in the fight, therefore, is his position as figurehead—placed there unwillingly as the object of Voldemort's wrath. The figurehead cannot be replaced without losing its symbolic effectiveness. However, it could be replaced if the new figurehead embodied similarly mythic possibilities, which Neville does. Knowing what "could have been" allows an astute reader (like the aforementioned fan-fiction writers) to re-create the previous four and a half books, placing Neville between the crosshairs: how would the books play out if shy, pudgy Neville had a lightning-shaped scar, and not the neglected, emotionally stunted Harry? Would Harry even have been brought up by his muggle Aunt and Uncle? (Probably, as Lestrange would have driven the Potters insane.) The worth of these musings comes from understanding Harry's precarious position as the prophetic hero as well as recognizing the potential of any of Neville's future actions.

Ultimately, these future actions see Neville rise to co-lead Dumbledore's Army in Harry's absence. This position brings him physical distress at the hands of the Voldemort-loyal teachers occupying the school, but does not dissuade him. In the film adaptation of this scenario, Luna Lovegood virtually becomes *his* sidekick. Recognizing that the actions of Dumbledore's Army during Neville's seventh year at Hogwarts occur while the narrative follows Harry, Hermione, and Ron, it is entirely conceivable that Rowling could fill a companion book telling of the trials Neville and the rest of the army experience in the meantime. What readers do get, aside from Neville's hurried recapitulation of his trials, are his actions during the Battle at Hogwarts: Voldemort's siege of the wizarding school. This is Neville's third significant battle. The first was at the Ministry of Magic in conflict over the prophecy, while the second took place in *The Half-Blood Prince* during the events culminating in Dumbledore's death.[35] (This second battle is short and mainly describes Harry chasing Snape. Neville and the others who are fighting are given only a few sentences.)

To understand Neville's importance in this third battle, a fair amount of description is needed to cover all of the pertinent actions Neville either takes or is involved in, beginning when Harry confides in him about the necessity of killing Nagini; Voldemort's huge snake is the final horcrux. As Harry heads to the forest to sacrifice himself, he takes the time to entrust this task to Neville: "The idea had come to him out of nowhere, born out of a desire to make absolutely sure.[36] Harry follows Dumbledore's example in bringing

Neville into the horcrux hunt. Harry calls it "crucial" to "make sure there were backups, others to carry on."[37] As he sets out to face his own death, he leaves behind Ron, Hermione, and Neville to finish the horcrux destruction: "now Neville would take Harry's place: There would still be three in the secret."[38] Neville responds without question, "Kill the snake? . . . All right, Harry."[39] It is important to note that Harry does not reveal the reason behind killing the snake, only that it needs to happen, especially if Ron and/or Hermione fail to do so. Neville's agreement, then, comes on blind faith in Harry.

After Harry's perceived death, Voldemort brings his inert body before the defenders of Hogwarts to gloat over his victory. As Voldemort begins lying about Harry, Neville charges toward Voldemort and breaks "free of the crowd" and is quickly disarmed.[40] Voldemort gives him the option to join the Death Eaters, but Neville, standing in sight of all of the defenders, shouts, "I'll join you when hell freezes over . . . Dumbledore's Army!"[41] In response, Voldemort summons the Sorting Hat from inside the school, places it upon Neville's head, and promptly sets it aflame. Neville breaks free at the same time Harry reveals himself to be alive, and the giant Grawp and some stampeding centaurs bulldoze into the crowd. Neville pulls the hat off, reaches inside, and pulls out Godric Gryffindor's sword: "With a single stroke Neville sliced off the great snake's head."[42] With the final horcrux destroyed, and Harry returned from the spiritual limbo he had been sent to, the battle turns in the heroes' favor and they defeat Voldemort once and for all.

There are (at least) two points of interest regarding Neville's actions before Voldemort. The first is the recognition that Voldemort calls him by name four times. Seldom in the series does Voldemort call a witch or wizard by name. (Although, to be fair, very seldom does Voldemort actually have dialogue.) He speaks of Dumbledore, Potter, Snape, and Lucius Malfoy by name—but never acknowledges others like Professor McGonagall, Hermione Grainger, any of the Weasleys, or the like. Granted, Voldemort only ever faces Dumbledore or Harry in dramatic fashion. In Neville's case, Voldemort repeatedly calls the young wizard by name. Perhaps this occurs simply because of Neville's physical presence, but there seems to be greater fictive resources in play.

Names and the power of affixing meaning to someone or something hold an important place in fantasy. One such example can be found in Madeleine L'Engle's *A Wind in the Door*, her second novel in a series of five YA fantasy novels. Trudelle Thomas defines L'Engle's use of naming as "a mode of knowing."[43] Thomas continues, explaining that in L'Engle's world, "Naming involves recognition; when a person Names another, she compassionately discovers their common ground (shared humanity or shared beingness). Naming fosters a deep understanding of another."[44] Thomas is careful to explain that while "Naming," in this sense, has less to do with actual names and more with "a way of knowing," to "Name another is to call him into being," which brings with it an indisputable act of power.[45] This act of power is present from the very beginning of the Harry Potter novels: Voldemort is known as "he who must not be named," and is often referred to as "You-Know-Who." By the end of the series, one's location can even be found out by speaking the name Voldemort. Consequently, by so pointedly naming Neville over and over, Voldemort exhibits a sense of shared beingness with Neville. Whether it comes from Voldemort's knowledge of who Neville could have been, or from a haughty sense of overconfidence, Voldemort is simultaneously affirming Neville's existence even as he attempts to undermine him.

The second point of interest is how Neville pulls Gryffindor's sword from the Sorting Hat. The hat was once a normal hat belonging to Gryffindor, but was animated by the four founders of Hogwarts to sort students into their houses. According to the hat itself, this occurred over a thousand years ago.[46] The hat also acts as a carrier for the sword of Gryffindor, regardless of the sword's location. Harry first pulls the sword from the hat in *The Chamber of Secrets*, when he killed Slytherin's basilisk.[47] The events within the Chamber of Secrets, then, involve *three* artifacts of Hogwarts' founders: the basilisk, the hat, and the sword.

During the Battle of Hogwarts, Neville pulls the sword from the hat even though the sword was not anywhere near Hogwarts, indicating both the connection between Gryffindor's artifacts and Neville's need for the sword (and/ or his worthiness, akin to drawing Excalibur from the stone). It is determined that Gryffindor's sword is effective in destroying horcruxes because of its use in killing the basilisk—an act infusing it with basilisk venom.[48] Considering how basilisk teeth destroyed Tom Riddle's diary and Helga Hufflepuff's cup, and how the sword subsequently destroyed the ring, locket, and Nagini—all five horcruxes destroyed by Harry and his allies were eradicated by Slytherin's basilisk. The final inanimate-object-horcrux, Ravenclaw's Diadem, is destroyed by a fiendfyre curse. (In the film version of *Deathly Hallows*, however, the Diadem is first stabbed by a basilisk fang and then thrown into the fire.)

Referring once again to the prophecy, it makes perfect sense that Neville plays such a significant role in defeating Voldemort, especially in regard to killing the snake. Nagini was Voldemort's most closely guarded horcrux as the snake never left his side. It is an interesting mix of wizards and witches that acts to destroy all seven of Voldemort's horcruxes: Dumbledore, Harry, Ron, Hermione, Vincent Crabbe, Neville, and Voldemort himself. It is not surprising that Dumbledore, Harry, Ron, and Hermione participate in destroying horcruxes. However, as the headmaster of Hogwarts and the most celebrated wizard alive, Dumbledore's role in the second defeat of Voldemort is surprisingly smaller than expected. Dumbledore's role, minus the destruction of Marvolo's Ring, is more about planning and intrigue than action. Harry destroys the diary and is involved in the removal of the horcrux inside himself, as well as the death of the physical body of Voldemort (not counted among the horcruxes, but technically a carrier of a part of his soul). Ron destroys the locket; Hermione gets rid of the cup. Crabbe is responsible for the fiendfyre curse that eliminates the diadem. Voldemort ends the horcrux inside Harry, as well as dying from his own rebounding killing curse. Neville, then, is in significant company as a destroyer of a horcrux. (The exception to the caliber of this company is Crabbe, who is unceremoniously denied his unintentional role in horcrux-destruction in the film.)

What ultimately sets Neville apart is the nature of this series of books. Given that Rowling wrote seven books, each chronicling a year of Harry's life, readers see all characters age and mature through the series's four thousand or so pages. Neville is just one of these characters given uncommon longevity. While fantasy series tend to have multiple books, few are popular enough to warrant more than three, four, or five, at most. Those that *do* stretch beyond a tetralogy are typically adult fare and extend far beyond "only" five books. The quintessential example of this is Robert Jordan's *Wheel of Time*, an adult series that stretched (beyond the author's own life) to fourteen volumes. A YA series with seven, then, is not the norm—although imitators abound since the publication of Rowling's series. In this regard, it would seem wrong of Rowling to neglect the maturation of early supporting characters—wouldn't Harry's friends also spend seven years maturing? However, some characters never develop beyond their initial characterization. Cho Chang is one who remains perpetually stagnant: she shows up as a love interest for Harry and spends the rest of the series in the periphery. Goyle, as another instance, began and ends his role in the series as a mindless lackey. Even juvenile antagonist Malfoy barely makes it out of adolescence in terms of his on-page growth. Malfoy reaches his textual peak as an unfortunate pawn in the game between Voldemort and Dumbledore. I am, perhaps, oversimplifying: from an extratextual standpoint, much has been written by Rowling to provide insight into and sympathy for characters like Malfoy. Regardless, it is clear that Goyle and Malfoy are villains and are not part of Harry's beloved cadre of friends and associates. To give them enough textual real estate to allow significant maturation would both detract from the heroes' stories as well as shift the focus away from the overall vision of good versus evil. Although in fairness to the series's complexity, it should be noted that Snape's narrative begins to delve into whether or not one's motivations makes someone "evil." It is also true that Dumbledore's own conflicted narrative begins to question this as well. However, the overarching vision of Voldemort being evil beyond redemption remains consistent (unlike Snape or Malfoy).

More significant shifts into moral/ethical grayness are evident in the grandiose visions of epics like George R. R. Martin's *A Song of Fire and Ice* (a.k.a. *A Game of Thrones*), where an ever-expanding collection of named characters get substantial backstory, development, an ambiguous allegiance to good or evil, and a chance to provide third-person narration. Nearly all characters in Martin's universe toe a gray line between good and evil, requiring the reader to reevaluate whether or not to feel sympathetic toward deceit, murder, rape, or incest. But Rowling's books are not Martin's: they do not tell the story of a cast of hundreds all bent on controlling a single continent. Instead they tell the story of how a boy (and his friends) grew up to finally vanquish a most feared dark wizard. It is within this story that Neville Longbottom, once a peripheral figure of comic relief, became one of the hero's most trusted sidekicks, and then (in that hero's absence) was elevated to take the role of secondary hero. Neville's growth, enabled and required by the sidekick separation from the hero, shows what is narratively and characteristically possible for a sidekick.

While Neville shows how a sidekick can grow into a hero when given enough time (a sort of literary Darwinism, perhaps), there is another significantly different possibility to a secondary hero's development. To illustrate this possibility, I show how Tenar from Ursula Le Guin's *Earthsea* series takes a path from separation to fulfillment and self-realization that is quite different from Neville's. Although Le Guin's series is fantasy, like *Harry Potter*, the similarities largely end there. *Earthsea* is a world of high fantasy, where the lifestyle and landscape adhere to the high-fantasy trope of mimicking medieval Europe, replete with swords, castles, superstition, fiefs and lords, and competing religions.[49] The inclusion of dragons, mages, wizards, witches, magic, dark sorcery, and some ever-present existential struggles with power, balance, and death place the six novels in Le Guin's series firmly into this subgenre. (It is important to note that the fifth published book, *Tales from Earthsea*, is a collection of short stories.) While *Harry Potter* also has dragons, wizards, and so on and so forth, it also intermingles with the real, contemporary world, which marks it as a decidedly different subgenre. Because of these differences, and perhaps in spite of them, Tenar exists as a much different example of a sidekick who leaves the fulfillment of a hero/sidekick relationship to develop further: Tenar's emergence from the sidekick role sparks a process that redefines how the *Earthsea* books are governed, read, and studied.

Placing Tenar into a position of sidekick is slightly difficult from a structural standpoint, considering that *The Tombs of Atuan* (the second book in the series) is Tenar's story in the same way *A Wizard of Earthsea* is Ged's. What is not difficult, however, is recognizing Ged as the undisputed hero of the first three novels. This is important because within each of these first three tales, Ged has a sidekick figure: book one, *A Wizard of Earthsea*, explored

Ged's early heroics alongside his foil-sidekick Vetch (recall the examination of Vetch from chapters 1 and 2). The third novel, *The Farthest Shore*, gives a much-older Ged a clearly defined younger sidekick in the youthful Prince Arren. Because Ged finds a new sidekick in each novel, *The Tombs of Atuan* reads as Tenar's sidekick origin story. This also gives her character a depth of backstory that is only ever paralleled by Ged's own coming of age tale in book one. While there are significant time lapses between each of the first three books, *Tehanu* (book four), begins as *The Farthest Shore* ends and then continues the narrative. In this way, *Tehanu* is the only direct sequel in the entire series up to this point. It is important to recognize that many years have passed between *The Tombs of Atuan* and the events that take place in *The Farthest Shore/Tehanu*: Ged is now the Archmage of all Earthsea and is much older. Tenar, once a young girl in *The Tombs of Atuan*, is a now a widow with two grown children. Before examining how this older Tenar becomes a secondary hero, I must first begin by exploring Tenar's relationship as Ged's sidekick when they first meet in *The Tombs of Atuan*.

Tenar's entire existence in *The Tombs of Atuan* is to function as the high priestess in a part of Earthsea geography far to the northeast of where Ged studied on the island of Roke. As a young child, Tenar was "eaten" by the evil "deities" the Nameless Ones in a ritual ceremony: setting her apart from all others as the One Priestess.[50] She alone is given access and essential dominion over the underground chambers that are the dwelling place of the Nameless Ones. It is clear from the beginning of the story that the Nameless Ones are a potent force of ancient evil. Ged later reveals their existence might best be described as elementals, earth-spirits of darkness.[51] Ged comes into the story as an interloper, captured inside the Nameless Ones' subterranean labyrinth when his quest for the lost half of the ring of Erreth-Akbe brings him to Tenar's domain. Tenar holds Ged hostage for a good portion of the novel. She does this against the wishes of her self-seeking overseer, Kossil, who would rather Ged be left to die.[52] Ged is the first man Tenar has ever laid eyes upon, in the technical sense, as all nonfemales living within the cloistered temple area are eunuchs. Tenar keeps Ged alive because of her fascination of him, although she is not entirely able to explain that fascination. Tenar has the upper hand in that she holds the key to Ged's captivity, but she is emotionally and socially underdeveloped compared to Ged (which makes sense considering her youthfulness and seclusion). Ged, as the hero on a quest, helps her realize how manipulated she has been, and she commits to leave her life behind.[53] Ged continues, offering her a choice: "Either you must leave me, lock the door, go up to your altars and give me to your Masters; then go to the Priestess Kossil and make your peace with her . . . or, you must unlock the door, and go out of it, with me."[54] The choice is something foreign and impossible for Tenar to even fathom. Her position as Priestess (a clearly brainwashed one at that) does not allow her to consider leaving; her soul has been "eaten" by those she serves. Ged recognizes the power of the Nameless Ones, but reveals that, while still "stronger than any man," they are far from the gods Tenar has believed them to be.[55] Furthermore, Ged offers her something she has never truly had before—open and honest trust:

> But I thought also of another thing between us. Call it trust. . . . That is one of its names. It is a very great thing. Though each of us alone is weak, having that we are strong, stronger than the Powers of the Dark. . . . I have trusted you from the first time I saw your face. . . . You have proved your trust in me. I have made no return. I will give you what I have to give. My true name is Ged.[56]

As previously mentioned, the power of names is paramount in Le Guin's series. To offer one's true name to another is to give them potential dominion over you—it is an act of the highest trust. In their article, "Le Guin's Earth-Sea: Voyages in Consciousness," Craig and Diana Barrow liken the mutual trust shared between Ged and Tenar as "a symbolic wedding," one occurring simultaneously with the restoration of the ring of Erreth-Akbe, "each bringing the other's half . . . as Ged reveals his true name."[57] Ged gave Tenar's true name to her only pages before, reminding the Priestess Arha (as she had known herself to be, meaning the "Eaten One") that her name was once Tenar.[58] The trust that Ged feels and offers in reciprocation invites Tenar to join her fate with his: trusting that he can help deliver them both out of the darkness and into freedom. When Tenar tells Ged, "I will come with you," she verbally acknowledges the partnership they have had since she shielded him from Kossil: they are partners in flight and in overcoming the evil that chases them.[59]

It can be argued that Ged and Tenar share the hero/sidekick roles as dual-protagonists, but this is largely based on a narrative point-of-view choice. Or the two might more accurately be described as hostage and captor-turned-admirer (a sort of reverse Stockholm syndrome). What cannot be ignored, however, is the chasm separating the two in terms of knowledge, confidence, and experience; in this case, clearly, Ged is the hero, Tenar the sidekick. Or perhaps not: maybe their roles are not so clearly defined. Holly Littlefield suggests that those who believe Tenar "must be rescued from her fate" take a "fairly simplistic interpretation" of the text.[60] Littlefield rightly points out: "When a fifteen-year-old girl single-handedly manages to outwit, entrap, and control the most powerful wizard in the land, it should be obvious that she is not a simpering, helpless female needing some knight in shining armor to rescue her. In fact, her strength is in many ways equal to or even greater than Ged's."[61] That fact Ged finds a powerful ally and counterpart in Tenar is indisputable, and Littlefield quotes Ged's confirmation of the power Tenar inherently possesses. However, even Littlefield must admit that Ged serves "as a catalyst" for Tenar's journey out of enslavement.[62] As this external catalyst, Ged remains the hero in their early partnership, a fact reinforced through how he saves her at the last moment. Tenar falters at the precipice of freedom, nearly succumbing to the power of the Nameless Ones once more, seeing Ged's face as "black and twisted like a demon's."[63] Ged says quietly, "by the bond you wear I bid you come, Tenar," and breaks the spell for good.[64]

The choice to cling to one another in a time of need also confirms Ged and Tenar as hero and sidekick. As *Tehanu* later shows, this connection deepens in the future. Tenar trades all she knows for freedom with Ged (a precious choice, regardless of how limited her experience has been). The parallels between *The Tombs of Atuan* and the ancient tale of Jason and the Argonauts cannot be ignored. (For the record, the other obvious parallel is with Theseus, Ariadne, and the labyrinth.[65]) Tenar (as the Medea figure) gives up all she knows to give the foreign hero an object of great power and then leave with him. While Tenar does not follow Medea's ultimately tragic path, Ged, like Jason, leaves her after they gain their freedom. Tenar confesses her sins to Ged, asking him to leave her behind on some forsaken island to live in exile.[66] Ged counteroffers to introduce her to the kingdom as the one by whom "an old evil was brought to nothing . . . the broken was made whole, and where there was hatred there will be peace."[67] After this, Ged would let her live with his old master Ogion on the island of Gont, where she might live and learn in peace. She asks Ged if he will come as well, to which he responds, "When I can I will come."[68] The book more or less ends there, and the reader does not see Tenar again until it is revealed in *Tehanu* that Goha, the widow who cares for the burned child Therru, is the grown-up Tenar.[69]

Tehanu does a great number of things in the world of Earthsea beyond simply continuing Tenar's story. Most significantly, it is a strong-feminist text, asking troubling questions about patriarchal power, female inequality, and justice for the marginalized. In doing so, it also begins theorizing about the true nature of magic within Earthsea: who has the right to perform magic, and what is the right way to do so? Peter Hollindale describes this fourth volume: "*Tehanu*, famously, is a feminist revisioning of Earthsea, in which Le Guin appeared to deconstruct her much-loved world."[70] Hollindale mirrors what Barrow and Barrow mentioned years before when stating that *Tehanu* "deconstructs the first three volumes of Earthsea, since Le Guin now must feel that she had overemphasized male power through romance and magic."[71] This is, indeed, exactly what Le Guin set out to do. In reference to her decisions in writing *Tehanu*, she wrote, "I couldn't continue my hero-tale until I had, as woman and artist, wrestled with the angels of the feminist consciousness. . . . Instead of the pseudo-genderless male viewpoint of the heroic tradition, the world is seen through a woman's eyes."[72]

In this viewpoint, the three main characters, Tenar, Therru, and Ged, all go on journeys of self-discovery. First, as an older woman, Tenar still holds prestige for her role in the events of *The Tombs of Atuan*, and still holds the potential to work magic; but she fights and resents the power that others have (or pretend to have) over her. Littlefield states that "as a middle-aged woman, [Tenar's] eyes have been opened, and she finds herself repeatedly questioning and condemning the laws, traditions, and policies that have caused women to be second-class citizens in Earthsea."[73] This new awareness and questioning eventually leads her to be instrumental in the changes that come in this book and the next, *The Other Wind*. Second, Therru has an aura of magic about her, and hints abound as to her eventual revelation as Tehanu, the child of dragons; but she lives in fear of the man who beat her, raped her, and threw her into a fire to die. Third, Ged comes back to Gont after he heals the rift between life and death and seats Arren on the throne of Earthsea; but he has been stripped of all magic in the process and must learn how to live life without it. The story is told almost exclusively from Tenar's point of view, akin to *The Tombs of Atuan*, making *Tehanu* the second volume of her story—just as *The Farthest Shore* was the second volume to Ged's story begun in *A Wizard of Earthsea*. *Tehanu* asks these kinds of questions, but not all of them find answers. Some answers come in the collection of short stories, *Tales from Earthsea*, while others finally come into focus in *The Other Wind*. Regardless, *Tehanu* marks a turning point in the series, and Tenar plays the pivotal role in that turning.

There are a number of ways to consider (or define) Tenar in this text. Among other things, she is a widow, a lover, a biological mother, an adoptive mother, an adoptive daughter, a healer, a guide, a confidant, a warrior, a dragonlord. Perhaps the most overarching and powerful way to look at Tenar is to look at the almost schizophrenic existence she has through her many names (remembering once again the importance fantasy attributes to names and the like): Arha, Tenar, and Goha. Each name means something else, and all three almost seem to have a different personality and purpose. Susan McLean suggests Le Guin based "Tenar" on the French *tenir*, or the Italian *tenere*, "both of which come from the Latin *tenere*, 'to have, to hold, to keep.'"[74] This meaning fits Tenar in both books, especially as she keeps Ged captive in *The Tombs of Atuan* and holds Therru as daughter in *Tehanu*. Goha, as defined in *Tehanu*, means "a white spider," which McLean considers an "appropriate symbol of women as artists and homemakers, people who make connections."[75] Goha, as a longtime resident of Gont, has made a home and a connection with the people there. Although Tenar is her dominant identity ("to have and to hold"), Goha and Arha seem to be talking and trying to exert themselves as the dominant identity. While stopping short of a more detailed or in-depth deconstruction study of Tenar's names, I cannot overlook the nature of naming, words, and magic in Earthsea: that all things are known by what they are and by what they are not.

The use-name of Goha brings with it all of the restrictions and subservience of a village widow. As Goha, Tenar plays the parts of subservient housewife and middle-aged farmer. She demurs to the whims of dignitaries and mages as befitting her identity as "a mere goodwife."[76] Arha comes back into her identity after Tenar is partially cursed by the book's other antagonist, the evil mage Aspen.[77] Although able to partially thwart Aspen's attempt to silence or cripple her (perhaps he meant to kill her, but the text is unclear as to the curse's nature), Tenar finds it hard to concentrate, speak, and think clearly for some time. She finds, however, that she is able to think in her native tongue. To do so, she relies on her identity as Arha: "Who she had been long ago, to come out of the darkness and think for her. To help her. As she had helped her last night, turning the wizard's curse back on him. Arha had not known a great deal of what Tenar and Goha knew, but she had known how to curse, and how to live in the dark, and how to be silent."[78] The entire text keeps Tenar bouncing back and forth between her identities. Arha helps her survive when she must face powers of darkness and fear. Goha allows her to interact with the people in the villages, but fails her when her son returns from life as a sailor/pirate and treats her like his maid/property.[79] Tenar, her true identity, interweaves with and utilizes her use-identities, allowing her to grapple with the way women have been excluded from the use of magic,[80] to take a stand against evil men intending to rape and kill her and Therru,[81] and to finally bind herself and Ged together as lovers.[82]

Tenar's ability to utilize different elements of her identity to deal with different scenarios mirrors reality, as it is well-documented that people utilize different personas and masks as needed to interact with others, all with different margins of success.[83] In this way too, *Tehanu* breaks with established Earthsea traditions. In *The Tombs of Atuan*, Ged told her "You must be Arha, or you must be Tenar. You cannot be both."[84] It would seem that contrary to this ultimatum, Tenar *can* be both—must be both and more than both—when she needs to be. In fact, when remembering how Arha is the child who "has no name" in her service to the Nameless Ones, Tenar has three names and yet no name all at once to serve her as she needs. Hollindale similarly sees Tenar as a conglomeration of personas and powers. He writes of Tenar's several roles: "She is confidante to Ogion dying. She is 'midwife' to Ged's anguished ordinariness; emasculated of his celibate wizardries, he is initiated by Tenar into male sexuality and love. She is Tenar of the Ring, the King's friend and mediator. . . . Above all, she is foster mother of the abused child Therru, who is dragonchild, least and greatest of Earthsea children."[85] Many of the roles Hollindale isolates are *Tenar's* roles, as Ogion, Ged, King Arren, and Therru all know her by her true name, although Therru perhaps knows her best as "mother," as the chapter told from her perspective reveals.[86] Hollindale also mentioned Tenar's interactions and humiliations at the hand of Aspen, most of which she endured as Goha, but ultimately it is as Tenar that she helped in his defeat.[87]

She is not alone in this, as we see Ged do something very similar. His use-name has long been "Sparrowhawk." After returning from his sojourn apart from the people of Gont, he shortens his use-name to "Hawk." This is not a major change, but "Hawk" implies, among other things, that this character is stronger, and perhaps not sparrow-sized or -powered any more. He is no longer linked to the identity of the Archmage he once was and can now no longer be. He also has a new version of himself to present to Tenar as her lover. In one very real and tangible sense, he has created a mature version of Sparrowhawk through which to experience the world anew. From Tenar's discussion with Aunty Moss it is revealed that male magic-users (sorcerers, mages, etc.) live lives of celibacy. Tenar is shocked at this thought, as she now must acknowledge the fact that Ged, quite possibly for the first time in his life, might have sexual urgings. Moss suggests that some believe there is a spell to cast away thoughts of sex, and describes them as spells of binding, so that no wizard might be tempted to use his power to fuel his lust.[88] The connection between male-magic users, celibacy, and the Roman Catholic church's institution of a celibate, male priesthood cannot be mistaken. If the men trained at Roke are the priests of the higher power of Earthsea, then the women who are barred from studying there are relegated to be "only" witches—lowly nuns, as it were (although none would care whether they stay celibate in *Earthsea*). However, as Hawk and Tenar come together as lovers, the notion of Ged's celibacy disappears, as does any residual obligation Tenar might have to a dead husband. Their union also fundamentally changes the dynamics of any future hero/sidekick relationship between them. This new reality must also accommodate the continued fostering of Therru, who considers Tenar her mother, and Ged her father.[89]

From the beginning of Ged's return to Tenar's life, their relationship is obviously not what it once was. For nearly the entire book, he needs Tenar more than she needs him. He needs her when he arrives sick and comatose. He needs her when he begins his long physical and mental recovery. He needs her when he must hide from the outside world. He needs her when they consummate their relationship. Ged is entirely in Tenar's debt because he does not know how to navigate a world without magic. Ged submits to Tenar's choices and guidance. The only exception comes when he protects Tenar by stabbing a would-be attacker through the abdomen with a pitchfork. Ged is the sidekick; Tenar is the hero. She is the self-sufficient power that cultivates future growth and influence (in both Ged and Therru). At times she does not even keep a sidekick, as Ged and Therru leave and come by her guidance and request. Tenar, when it is all said and done, is a new kind of sidekick. She did not stay mired in slow-moving development through story arc after story arc like Dick Grayson, languishing until the long-awaited day when the perennially youthful sidekick finally gets to . . . go to college (remembering, of course, that Dick does eventually come into his own as Nightwing, etc.). Nor did she continue on statically like Jeeves, Watson, or Bess Marvin/George Fayne: never changing or growing through countless volumes of adventures. While the changes undergone by Neville follow a path similar to Tenar's, his story as the "would-be Harry" merely hints at the radical redefinition Tenar brings to the understanding of her entire world.

The "secondary hero" is the form of "sidekick elevation" that occurs when sidekicks take part in narrative space ample enough for them to emerge in their own heroic roles. This is usually showcased in narratives that take place over multiple novels or through an extended publication history. The sidekick grows beyond the initially established hero/sidekick relationship, and moves into a space where such a relationship no longer fulfills the needs of the character. Neville Longbottom is given considerable literary territory in the *Harry Potter* series, bringing him from merely a laughable schoolmate of the hero to someone stalwart and confident standing on his own merits. Tenar similarly separates herself from the hero with whom she first appeared, but eventually pushes the understanding of how the very fabric of the *Earthsea* universe works.

NOTES

1. Roberta Seelinger Trites, "The *Harry Potter* Novels as a Test Case for Adolescent Literature," *Style* 35, no. 3 (2001): 481.
2. Ibid.
3. For just a few, see David Haber, "Neville Longbottom: The Other Chosen One." Beyond Hogwarts, last modified May 28, 2007, https://www.beyondhogwarts.com/harry-potter/articles/neville-longbottom-the-other-chosen-one.html; Krysti Yandoli, "Why Neville Longbottom Is the Best *Harry Potter* Character of All Time," Huffington Post, last modified December 6, 2017, https://www.huffingtonpost.com/2013/07/31/neville-longbottom_n_3682304.html; Elizabeth Entenman, "Ah, So This Is Why Snape Hated Neville Longbottom So Much," Hello Giggles, last modified August 22, 2016, https://hellogiggles.com/reviews-coverage/books/snape-neville-theory/.
4. Emily Asher-Perrin, "Neville Longbottom is the Most Important Person in *Harry Potter*—And Here's Why." Tor.com. Macmillan, last modified November 19, 2013. par. 1. https://www.tor.com/2013/11/19/neville-longbottom-is-the-most-important-person-in-harry-potter/.
5. Ibid., par. 6.
6. Ibid., par. 8.
7. J. K. Rowling, *Harry Potter and the Goblet of Fire* (New York: Scholastic, 2000), 491.
8. Ibid., 494.
9. *Harry Potter and the Goblet of Fire*, directed by Mike Newell (Burbank, CA: Warner Bros. Pictures, 2005), DVD.
10. Ibid.
11. Ibid.
12. Ibid.
13. J. K. Rowling, "Live Web Chat," *World Book Day Festival*, World Book Day, last modified March 4, 2004. http://www.accio-quote.org/articles/2004/0304-wbd.htm.

The Secondary Hero 89

14. J. K. Rowling, *Harry Potter and the Order of the Phoenix* (New York: Scholastic, 2003), 514.
15. Ibid., 515.
16. Ibid., 707.
17. Ibid.
18. Ibid., 553.
19. Ibid.
20. Ibid., 792.
21. Ibid., 799.
22. Ibid., 800.
23. Ibid.
24. John Shelton Lawrence and Robert Jewett, *The Myth of the American Superhero* (Grand Rapids: Eerdmans, 2002), 6.
25. William G Doty, *Mythography: The Study of Myths and Rituals*. 2nd ed. (Tuscaloosa: University of Alabama Press, 2000), 243.
26. Rowling, *Order of the Phoenix*, 800.
27. Ibid.
28. Ibid., 801.
29. Ibid., 802.
30. Ibid., 805.
31. Ibid., 841.
32. Ibid., 842.
33. Doty, *Mythography*, 94.
34. Ibid.
35. J. K. Rowling, *Harry Potter and the Half-Blood Prince* (New York: Scholastic, 2006), 599.
36. J. K. Rowling, *Harry Potter and the Deathly Hallows* (New York: Scholastic, 2007), 695.
37. Ibid., 696.
38. Ibid.
39. Ibid.
40. Ibid., 731.
41. Ibid.
42. Ibid., 733.
43. Trudelle H. Thomas, "Spiritual Practices Children Understand: An Analysis of Madeleine L' Engle' s Fantasy, *A Wind in the Door*," *International Journal of Children's Spirituality* 13, no. 2 (2008): 162.
44. Ibid.
45. Ibid., 163.
46. Rowling, *Goblet of Fire*, 176–77.
47. J. K. Rowling, *Harry Potter and the Chamber of Secrets* (New York: Scholastic, 1998), 319–20.
48. Rowling, *Deathly Hallows*, 304.
49. For more on high fantasy, see Brian Attebery, *The Fantasy Tradition in American Literature: From Irving to Le Guin* (Bloomington: Indiana University Press, 1980); Jared Lobdell, *Rise of Tolkienien Fantasy* (Chicago: Open Court, 2005); David Sandner, *Fantastic Literature: A Critical Reader* (Westport, CT: Praeger, 2004).
50. Ursula K. Le Guin, *The Tombs of Atuan* (New York: Atheneum, 1971), 7–10.
51. Ibid., 118.
52. Ibid., 76.
53. Ibid., 125.
54. Ibid., 126.
55. Ibid., 125.
56. Ibid., 127.
57. Craig Barrow, and Diana Barrow, "Le Guin's *Earthsea*: Voyages in Consciousness," *Extrapolation* 32, no.1 (1991): 35.

58. Le Guin, *Tombs of Atuan*, 105.
59. Ibid., 127.
60. Holly Littlefield, "Unlearning Patriarchy: Ursula Le Guin's Feminist Consciousness in *The Tombs of Atuan* and *Tehanu*," *Extrapolation* 36, no. 3 (1995): 248.
61. Ibid.
62. Ibid.
63. Le Guin, *Tombs of Atuan*, 136.
64. Ibid.
65. Barrow and Barrow, "Le Guin's *Earthsea*," 36.
66. Le Guin, *Tombs of Atuan*, 160.
67. Ibid., 161.
68. Ibid., 162.
69. Ursula K. Le Guin, *Tehanu* (New York: Atheneum, 1990), 17.
70. Peter Hollindale, "The Last Dragon of Earthsea," *Children's Literature in Education* 34, no. 3 (2003): 185.
71. Barrow and Barrow, "Le Guin's *Earthsea*," 42.
72. Ursula K. Le Guin, *Earthsea Revisioned* (Cambridge: Children's Lit. New England, 1993), 11–12.
73. Littlefield, "Unlearning Patriarchy," 251.
74. Susan McLean, "The Power of Women in Ursula K. Le Guin's *Tehanu*," *Extrapolation* 38, no. 2 (1997): 112.
75. Ibid., 113.
76. Le Guin, *Tehanu*, 92, 114.
77. Ibid., 122.
78. Ibid., 123.
79. Ibid., 205.
80. Ibid., 52.
81. Ibid., 169.
82. Ibid., 189.
83. Ronald Wardhaugh and Janet M. Fuller, *An Introduction to Sociolinguistics*, 7th ed. (West Sussex: Wiley-Blackwell, 2015), 256–57; see also Craig Calhoun et al., eds. *Contemporary Sociological Theory*, 3rd ed. (Wiley-Blackwell, 2012); Erving Goffman, *The Presentation of Self in Everyday Life* (New York: Doubleday, 1959); Wesley Longhofer and Daniel Winchester, *Social Theory Re-wired: New Connections to Classical and Contemporary Perspectives*, 2nd ed. (New York: Routledge, 2016).
84. Le Guin, *Tombs of Atuan*, 126.
85. Hollindale, "The Last Dragon," 186.
86. Le Guin, *Tehanu*, 219.
87. Hollindale, "The Last Dragon," 186.
88. Le Guin, *Tehanu*, 97–98.
89. Ibid., 219.

Chapter Four

The Sidekick Sequel

Reinventing Sidekicks through Parallel Novels

In the first two chapters, I established the prevalence of sidekicks in YA and other literatures, the critically and narratively important roles sidekicks take on in their relationships with their heroes, and ways sidekicks interact within specific surrogate-family relationships. The resultant "sidekick separation" often takes one of three avenues, the first of which was the focus of the previous chapter—the "secondary hero." This chapter will establish the second avenue, the "sidekick sequel," the way in which an author places the spotlight specifically on a preexisting sidekick. This is the next logical focal point, as I move outside and alongside the existing narrative tradition established for heroes and sidekicks.

This sidekick sequel is the literary reincarnation of preexisting sidekicks into protagonists of their own stories. This happens in a number of ways, most typically when a follow-up novel is told from the point of view of the sidekick. Remember that Twain took this very approach when he followed *The Adventures of Tom Sawyer* with *The Adventures of Huckleberry Finn*, taking a once-sidekick and turning him into the focus of his own novel—giving us an example of this tradition some 140 ago. Another notable (and more recent) repositioning is Beverly Cleary's *Ramona the Pest*, the second book in the much-loved *Ramona* series for elementary-school-aged children. The first in the series, *Beezus and Ramona*, was the story of nine-year-old Beatrice "Beezus" living with her younger sister Ramona. The little sister then becomes the focal point of the rest of the series. Beezus and Ramona, as characters, were *themselves* spin-offs from the *Henry Huggins* series. Or consider Judy Blume's character Sheila Tubman, who first appeared in *Tales of a Fourth Grade Nothing*, the first of the *Fudge* series following Peter

Hatcher and his little brother Farley "Fudge" Hatcher. Sheila headlines the sequel *Otherwise Known as Sheila the Great* (within which Peter and Fudge are only mentioned in passing), but the focus returns to Peter for the subsequent three books. This type of interconnectedness between stories occurs elsewhere in literature: take William Faulkner's use and reuse of Yoknapatawpha County or how Stephen King tied so many of his novels to the *Dark Tower* series. A less typical approach is to retell the original tale from the differing vantage point of another character, an approach commonly understood as a "parallel novel." Again, the parallel novel is not a new idea—some of the most famous include John Gardner's *Grendel*, Jean Rhys' *Wide Sargasso Sea*, Marion Zimmer Bradley's *The Mists of Avalon*, and Tom Stoppard's *Rosencrantz and Guildenstern Are Dead*. (Of course, the extent differs to which these texts interplay and interact with the original text.) The parallel novel has similarly proven attractive to contemporary authors. Recently, E. L. James, author of the controversial *Fifty Shades* series, published *Grey*, a retelling of book one from the perspective of Christian Grey. Another recent example is how Stephenie Meyer intended to publish *Midnight Sun*, a parallel novel to *Twilight*, but stopped short of a full publication when early chapters were hacked and released on the internet in 2008. Cinema has even given popular culture its fair share of parallelisms, as one needs to look no further than Robert Zemeckis's *Back to the Future* trilogy, as *Part II* interweaves new action and characters through scenes and scenarios from the first film. Disney also waded into these waters with its own version of *Rosencrantz and Guildenstern Are Dead*, aptly titled *The Lion King 1½*, where Timon and Pumbaa offer their perspectives on the events of the original *The Lion King*. To illustrate more fully the sidekick separation created by parallel novels, I offer two sidekick case-studies. The first is Shay from Scott Westerfeld's *Uglies* series and the two graphic novels *Shay's Story* and *Cutters*. Shay helps to establish a deeper look into how YA specifically utilizes a sidekick within a parallel novel. The second is Bean from Orson Scott Card's *Ender's Game* and *Ender's Shadow*, which offers a decidedly complex and in-depth consideration of sidekick elevation.

Scott Westerfeld's *Uglies* series (currently comprised of *Uglies*, *Pretties*, *Specials*, and *Extras*) is a relatively recent addition to the world of YA, as book one was published in 2005. (A new quartet set in the same world has been announced, the first of which, *Impostors*, was released in the fall of 2018). In the series, Westerfeld considers questions about identity and self-worth in an increasingly complex and technological society. In particular, the series overtly questions how adolescents derive self-worth in connection to their physical appearance. The world of *Uglies* is a science-fiction dystopia placed some three hundred years in our future (another example of YA's obsession with this subgenre). Physical appearance reigns supreme, beginning when children are moved out of their homes into the dormitories of

Uglyville. There, the children, now referred to as "uglies," impatiently await their sixteenth birthdays when they will undergo mandatory surgical enhancements to make them "pretties." Pretties are obsessed with being pretty, which, aside from a perfect physique and beautiful facial features, includes some combination of drinking, partying, eating, downing calorie-burning packets (to offset the eating), and hooking up with other newly attractive pretties. By and large, the populace does not give the surgery or these behaviors anything more than a cursory glance: it is entirely expected and normative. Joel Stein et al. provides some statements given by Westerfeld in reference to the series's prescience regarding today's society: "This is the first generation that thinks about plastic surgery as almost a given. . . . They're the first generation to grow up with the idea that plastic surgery is neither super-expensive nor a weird thing that only the maladjusted would do. The idea that the body is this thing you are given and you can't escape it—that no longer holds."[1] Westerfeld's contention that one can now escape the body he or she is given forms the foundation for *Uglies*, at least as far as the controlling government allows. An individual might have discretion regarding whether or not to undergo plastic surgery, but any subsequent choices (plastic surgery or otherwise) fall entirely under the discretion of a dystopian government: it is the major form of controlling the populace in this case.

When this dystopian element inevitably comes to light, it reveals that when uglies go under the knife, they unknowingly receive intentionally mind-numbing brain damage. While the damage is used as a form of conditioning, it is changeable and reversible for those who are an asset to those in control. This fictional premise is not new, as these things hardly ever are. Take, for just one example, "Harrison Bergeron," Kurt Vonnegut's short story about a government handicapping all individuals in an effort to achieve equality. Further parallels can be seen in the 1995 made-for-TV movie of the same title, starring Sean Astin and Christopher Plummer. In this version of the story, Harrison accepts an invitation to join the unaltered, unhindered ruling government. Eventually, after his lover Phillipa undergoes a forced lobotomy, he rebels in an effort to awaken the intelligence of the greater population, stating "You haven't made everybody equal, you've made 'em the same, and there's a big difference."[2]

In this now familiar dichotomy, where fictive dystopias necessitate either open revolution or flight to freedom, uglies in Westerfeld's series run away to begin their own way of life free from the cultural and physical restrictions of living a beautiful but shallow existence. These uglies are called Smokies, as their settlement is named "the Smoke." The conflict of the series comes from Smokies who return to the cities to entice others to leave the pretty life behind—something that main antagonist Dr. Cable tries to stop by any means possible. Tally Youngblood, the protagonist, is an interesting main character because of her reluctance to leave Uglyville—her entire focus and only desire is turning sixteen and going under the knife. Kimberly Downing Robinson remarks that Tally is "completely unaware that she is standing on the threshold of the archetypal 'hero(ine)'s journey.'"[3] Tally's unawareness of her potential as the hero enables the most important relationship in the *Uglies* novels: her friendship with Shay. Unlike Tally, Shay is acutely aware of what the approaching watershed means and takes the opportunity to run away. Before she does, she tries to open Tally's eyes to the possibilities beyond being pretty, and it is Shay's investment in her that ultimately convinces Tally to "leave home for 'a series of adventures beyond the ordinary, either to recover what has been lost or to discover some life giving elixir.'"[4] For Tally, it is a recovery of what has been lost: Shay.

Shay's role in the series is the on-again, off-again counterpart to Tally. Some reviewers refer to Shay and Tally as "frenemies," defining their relationship in the series as one of affection and conflict regarding their feelings for one another.[5] As it is Tally and Shay's relationship that drives the narrative, it is worthwhile to trace the major plot points of that relationship. Beginning in *Uglies*, Tally's desire to be a pretty allows her to be manipulated, time and again. Under coercion by Dr. Cable, Tally leaves to track down Shay and find the Smoke: Cable insists that Shay has been tricked into leaving, and as further incentive, withholds Tally's surgery until her return. Tally agrees that Shay must have been brainwashed in order to leave, a theory stemming mostly from their ongoing conversations about whether or not to travel away from the city. Tally's inability to convince Shay to stay in Uglyville also brings an element of guilt into the equation. When she finally makes it to the Smoke, it is her relationship with Shay that causes Tally to delay betraying the Smoke's location to Cable. Shay and Tally rely and confide in each other until the introduction of a love interest for Tally—which is when Shay gets tossed to the side, for the first but not last time. As Tally's de facto sidekick, Shay might best fall into the devil's advocate or foil roles. *Uglies* follows Tally from a limited omniscient third-person perspective, so the need for a narrative gateway does not necessarily apply. Instances of comic relief are few and far between in the entire series: a byproduct of its dystopian nature. The devil's advocate and foil roles are evident with the realization that Shay is everything Tally is not. Tally longs to be pretty; Shay desires to stay unaltered. Tally agrees to deliver the Smoke to Cable, while Shay bitterly resists any influence from the administration. Finally, Shay finds almost-boyfriends in David[6] and Zane,[7] only to lose them both to Tally, one after the other. In this way, then, Shay comes dangerously close to an embodiment of the antagonist-as-sidekick—a topic I have chosen to save for a later study.

Tally and Shay spend remarkably little time together, all things considered. Aside from the weeks they spend in the beginning of *Uglies* (covered in a few, cursory chapters), they are confined to a conversation here, a conversation there. Those opening weeks, however, firmly establish their interdependence for the rest of the series. Tally wants to embrace the pretty culture while Shay plans to run away. The bulk of the narrative covers Tally's relationship with David, especially after the Smoke is discovered and disbanded. While Tally and David are on the lam, however, their overarching concern is for David's parents, Shay, and the other Smokies that were captured. Shay is almost constantly on Tally's mind even though Tally is not always with her.

One of the reasons *Shay's Story* and *Cutters* are of increasing interest, then, is how they fill the gaps of Shay's narrative when she is separated from Tally. *Shay's Story* reframes the timeline of *Uglies*, giving life to Shay's background while bringing her story into dialogue with Tally's. An important difference to note here is that *Shay's Story* is a graphic novel, while the original series is not. The difference brings a consideration of a fixed, visual medium as well as the deepening understanding in the nature of Shay's character. The sequel to *Shay's Story*, titled *Cutters*, continues this new narrative by giving Shay's perspective during *Pretties*. (As of this writing, a third graphic novel to complement book three, *Specials*, has not been published. Considering how much time Shay and Tally spend together in *Specials*, it might not be necessary to reveal Shay's perspective.) In *Shay's Story*, we learn about Shay's early relationship with Zane, before either reached age sixteen. There was a kinship between the two of them long before either met Tally. Shay and Zane later pick up where they more or less left off, making Tally's interest, manipulation, and betrayal regarding Zane all the more potent. Zane was Shay's—and only Shay's—once upon a time. Of similar interest is Shay's time spent at the Smoke before Tally arrives: she saves a fellow runaway from drowning in a river, works hard to tame the land for use, and impresses the usually unflappable David. Although Shay's romance with David is somewhat ambiguous in *Uglies*, it finds foundation and intimacy in *Shay's Story*. David tells her his big, personal secret: he was born outside of the ugly/pretty civilization. David tells this to Shay right before he kisses her. (Not to call David a one-trick pony, but he follows a similar approach when he romances Tally.)

There are also significant fictive revisions being made here, and they significantly inform Shay's sidekick elevation. For instance, David's explanation for leaving Shay behind in Uglyville gets amended in *Shay's Story*. Originally, in *Uglies*, he tells Tally that Shay "chickened out," citing her desire to leave the city was because "her friends were." Furthermore, he states, "I almost told her to just forget about it, to stay in the city and become pretty."[8] *Shay's Story* reveals that David did, in fact, tell her to stay in Uglyville. David writes Shay a note, telling her "I know you're in love with me, and that's the wrong reason to leave home."[9] The eventual implications of this note are far-reaching. First, because the specifics of David's letter to

Shay are never shared with Tally, and Shay never offers to tell her this side of the story, the contradictory information is never overtly brought to bear. Had Shay informed her of David's duality, Tally might have approached the Smoke's greatest son with more reserve. (This is, of course, considering a narrative "what-if" scenario, which should only go so far in regard to this analysis: there is no greater consideration within the text itself, as was the case with Neville.) Second there is the question of David's character: he is, at least in this one instance, a liar. Considering the impact of David's relationship with Tally, a relationship where David is a pillar of virtue, any instance that might disrupt their union would seem potentially catastrophic. Unlike Tally, the reader now knows about this black mark on David's character, and it changes the reading of the entire series. Third, Tally and Shay might have bonded more completely if the whole truth had been told. More to the point, perhaps, as it is grounded in the text and not in a "what-if scenario," is Shay's decision to remain silent. Considering how integral romantic relationships are to this series, this silence gives Shay an element of power. Any number of times, Shay could have revealed her history with Tally in greater detail, but instead remained silent. Even from the beginning, then, Shay holds information in reserve that could, at the very least, act as a catalyst to disrupt the status quo. As a sidekick, this also serves to complicate the depth of Shay's relationship with Tally, as it complicates the level of trust shared between the two.

Fourth, and somewhat outside the scope of the text itself, is to question how much "right" an author has on revising works with or without an attempt to publish a new edition. One such revision that is largely accepted (and generally forgotten) is what Tolkien did in *The Hobbit*. In an effort to bring the actions of Bilbo Baggins into greater alignment with the vision of *The Lord of the Rings*, Tolkien produced the revised edition of *The Hobbit*, complete with an explanatory paragraph in the opening pages.[10] These revisions included various alterations of passages dealing with the Ring, such as the famous "Riddles in the Dark" chapter. If there was ever an outcry regarding the changing nature of *The Hobbit*'s text, I am unaware of its existence today. However, there are other situations where a change is met with significant audience opposition. Perhaps the most notable is George Lucas's decision to make Greedo shoot first in the Cantina scene with Han Solo in the 1997 special edition of *Star Wars: A New Hope*. Unlike with Tolkien's changes, Lucas's changes are largely reviled and still incite contention.

However unpopular revisionist actions can be, considering them brings me back to the central question of this chapter: to what extent does a parallel novel (turning a sidekick into a protagonist) impact the way we read the original, central story? Or, perhaps more succinctly, how does this parallel novel impact the way we characterize sidekicks? Shay's decision to remain silent about David is an apparent impact, especially if remembered throughout the entirety of their narrative in *Cutters*. One interesting historical by-product is the effect had on scholarship that may have come between publications, understanding that scholarship helps a reader interpret the text at hand. Take, for instance, what happens when considering the narrative structure of these sets of Westerfeld's stories. Because of how completely *Uglies*'s narrative structure follows Tally, much of Shay's actions, beliefs, and thoughts are left to the imagination during the principle novels. This partly creates narrative tension as it leaves an element of the unknown to both Tally and the reader (as all good first-person or limited-omniscient narratives do). The resolution of this tension comes with revelation; Dr. Cable reveals her hidden manipulations of Tally and/or Shay, or David's mother shows Tally the cure to the brain lesions, and so on and so forth.

The absence of Shay's part of the narrative will lead some readers and critics to do one of two things: take Tally's assumptions and conclusions at face value, or read between the lines in an effort to understand Shay's motivations. One such critic, YA author Robin Wasserman, takes the latter approach. Wasserman offers a close reading of the series in an effort to show how overlooked and undervalued Shay is in an initial read-through. Wasserman argues that Shay is "not a sidekick, she is a hero. A hero with the misfortune to be trapped in someone else's story."[11] Throughout her analysis, written before *Shay's Story* was published, Wasserman creates a compelling case: throughout the first three books, Shay shows initiative, loyalty, and insight. Tally, on the other hand, makes terrible decisions, gets forgiven for them time and again, and betrays her friends and values for the sake of her physical attraction to David and Zane. Wasserman puts it this way: "Shay blazes a trail for Tally, right up the side of a mountain. Shay extends a hand to Tally, and helps her to the summit. Shay and Tally admire the view . . . then Tally pushes Shay over the cliff. Lather, rinse, and repeat."[12] Throughout her analysis, Wasserman makes it clear that Tally owes a considerable amount to Shay, but Tally nonetheless repeatedly betrays her in one way or another. Tally's heroics, therefore, are based on stealing ideas and recognition from Shay. This potentially places Shay into a number of character roles. Maybe she *is* the hero, as Wasserman points out that "the very thing Tally *pretends* to do—while in reality being blackmailed by Dr. Cable—Shay actually *does*."[13] Or perhaps she is the older, wiser figure offering guidance to the hero: "Again and again, Shay figures things out and then explains them to her best friend . . . Shay is just smarter."[14]

Another YA author, Diana Peterfreund, offers a similarly themed evaluation of Shay's relationship with Tally. In response to fans' advocating for being on either "Team David" or "Team Zane" (a play on fans' affiliation with either Team Jacob or Team Edward in the love-triangle debate from *Twilight*), Peterfreund suggests a third option for Tally's romantic affections: "Team Shay." As Wasserman has to fill in the blanks with Shay's motivations, so too does Peterfreund offer an interpretation of the series's events through her own specific lens. Although she recognizes that any suggestion or innuendo regarding a romance between Tally and Shay would largely be ignored or refuted, Peterfreund nevertheless presents what-might-be, at least if we considered the possibility of attraction between the two amidst the plethora of suggestive dialogue and scenarios. She begins by rightly establishing that Shay "cares very deeply about what Tally thinks of her."[15] Referencing the times when Tally tried to create computer-generated versions of what Shay's face would look like postoperation, Peterfreund asserts that it is "desperately important" for Shay that Tally "like her for who she is."[16] She takes the notion further, marking how Tally is *"fantasizing about Shay's* [potential new face]," and asks the reader to consider what Shay's reaction might be if she knew that "Tally is thinking about her so much?"[17] Admitting that her thesis is largely grounded in intellectual fancy, Peterfreund maintains an exaggerated tone when discussing the romantic implications of Tally and Shay's friendship. However, exaggeration aside, Peterfreund draws from a considerable amount of textual evidence supporting her position. In fact, if it were not for Shay's admission that she was upset over Tally's "stealing" of David, Peterfreund would not need to admit intellectual indulgence. This instance may very well be the only supporting evidence for Shay's heterosexuality found in the first three books. While looking at the changing nature of the relationship, Peterfreund considers Shay's motivations at the end of *Pretties* when she helps Dr. Cable turn Tally into a Special. As a new Special herself, she has been given the opportunity to bring Tally into the fold of a newly established (and somewhat above the law) group of Specials: the Cutters.[18] In this case, romantic notions notwithstanding, Peterfreund makes a compelling argument:

> Now, however, Shay knows exactly what she is doing. She tried being friends with Tally. It didn't work. This time, she wants more. She wants to possess Tally and subjugate her completely. If status is what Tally wants, if what will make Tally love Shay is status, then Shay will shove status down her throat. She will be better than David, the leader of the Smoke; better than Zane, the founder of some silly, pretty clique. Not only will Shay be a Special, but she'll also be in charge of an elite team of Specials. And on the off chance that Tally still doesn't fall into line after being dazzled by what Shay has become, well, she'll force it on her.[19]

The context of Tally's change into a Special and the rest of the narrative in *Pretties* support Peterfreund's suggestions. A friendship with Tally as equals has not benefited Shay; it has instead caused the destruction of the Smoke, the forceful operation turning Shay into a pretty, and the disruption of the ignorant bliss that accompanies that change. Tally has twice left Shay's friendship behind in order to spend time with the leader of their social spheres. She alienates Shay and opens up deep emotional distress leading to self-harm. As Shay brings Tally into the world of Specials, all of this changes: Shay is the one in charge. They no longer share equal status. If Tally were to spend extra time with the leader of her social group, it would be with Shay. This is, ultimately, Shay's sidekick elevation: she is the new leader, while Tally is undeniably the follower.

Some of what Peterfreund and Wasserman postulate regarding Shay's behind-the-scenes actions is later disproven in *Shay's Story* and *Cutters*. However, these two critics have essentially tried to do what Westerfeld does in his parallel graphic novels: create a backstory to fill in the narrative gaps. Moreover, they have entered into a conversation of intellectual inquiry in the face of ambiguous scenarios within the text. Westerfeld's choice to publish the parallel graphic novels allows him to revisit the series, bring Shay into focus as a counterprotagonist, and retroactively remove the ambiguity allowing Wasserman and Peterfreund to offer varied readings of his text. The attention given to Shay in these new novels, however, suffers from its inability to escape from Tally's story line and break new ground. Therefore, the way we track her sidekick elevation is subsequently affected. Everything that happens in *Shay's Story* must coincide with what happens in *Uglies*. The only new substantive information or drama provided by *Shay's Story* is the specific nature of Shay's romance/nonromance with David. Three years before having had the opportunity to read *Shay's Story*, Wasserman went to great lengths in her suppositions to consider David's treatment of Shay and their relationship. Wasserman recognizes David's tendency toward duplicity and self-delusion when it comes to Tally and Shay. Furthermore, Wasserman points out that although David is "so disgusted with Shay" and her decision to not leave Uglyville the first time, he "somehow fails to notice that . . . *Tally* chickened out on her first chance."[20] Continuing on, Wasserman asks what David's motivations might have been in involving himself with Shay romantically "*in the first place?*" if he felt so strongly that Shay was "a pathetic follower" and a "coward."[21] While some of those postulates are again, disproven, when read in light of *Shay's Story*, considering they were made on soon-to-be-outdated information, Wasserman can hardly be held accountable. So too are Peterfeund's suggestions disproven when reading *Cutters*, but only in part: although Shay is forced to change into a Special, her misinterpretation of Tally's motivations remains, as well as her desire to bring her back into good graces. The way *Shay's Story* (and *Cutters* for that matter) is hindered in its ability to strike out on its own will strike a chord with popular culture enthusiasts, as George Lucas's second *Star Wars* trilogy infamously suffered from the same restrictiveness. (Furthermore, don't all prequels suffer from this same fundamental problem?) When viewers (or readers) know the inevitable outcome, what power does the conflict have?

Westerfeld's graphic novels lack this power. However, *Ender's Shadow*, my second example of this kind of parallel novel, does not.

Although completing Ender's principal story over twenty years ago, Orson Scott Card continues to publish new additions to the science fiction novels comprising what is known as the "Enderverse." He began with *Ender's Game* in 1985 and wrote a parallel novel to that original story in 1999 titled *Ender's Shadow*. *Ender's Game* and *Ender's Shadow* fit perfectly into the debate on defining YA, as the subjects of these books are children, but what happens to them is a far cry from what constitutes normal childhood development. Andrew "Ender" Wiggin begins the story told in these two books at age six. The students he works and trains with are treated like soldiers, complete with officers, uniforms, and battle simulators. Ender even encounters physical threats, resulting in his killing two older bullies in self-defense. He is ultimately the commander who successfully leads an interplanetary strike force against untold billions (if not trillions) of alien creatures, destroying their homeworld and eradicating their species—all before he turns twelve. Using children as weapons of mass destruction brings on-going ethical questions into play, and the debate surrounding *Ender's Game* continues even while its leadership and tactical qualities have helped it become required reading for members of the United States Marine Corps.[22] Card himself has gone on record regarding this debate, stating, "I have never written a single piece of YA fiction . . . my work has never been marketed that way until Tor put a YA cover and a new ISBN on Ender's Game . . . long after it had become popular with young readers."[23] The novel has been noted to complicate the very definition of YA as it is "providing and almost immediately beginning to dismantle a framework that ostensibly distinguishes children and adults . . . [offering] greater insights into the instability of these distinctions and implicitly highlight[ing] the overlapping spaces between them."[24] The duality between the portrayal of children and adults through *Ender's Game* and *Ender's Shadow* finds its beginning, at least in part, in the advanced mental capacities of the novels' protagonists.

In the original and first novel, *Ender's Game*, Ender leads a group of children/students in a series of war games intended to prepare them to be the next generation of military leaders in a forthcoming war against an alien species named the Formics. His sidekick, Bean, is included in this group. To be fair, Bean is Ender's sidekick in that he is the only character who even remotely fulfills this role. Ender's teachers intentionally isolate him in hopes that his leadership abilities will grow out of necessity. Bean, as one under Ender's command, is capable of achieving a lasting relationship based on physical proximity alone—but not one seemingly based on equality, as could have been the case with Ender's peers Alai and Petra. Ender fosters Bean's education as well as confides in him. Apart from Ender taking confidence in Bean, there is little in *Ender's Game* to suggest a more evenly distributed, reciprocal relationship between the two boys. (In *Ender's Game*, much of Ender's relational development involves how he interacts with his sister Valentine.) The change in relationship comes with *Ender's Shadow*. Like *Shay's Story* and what it does to *Uglies*, *Ender's Shadow* retells the plot of *Ender's Game* from Bean's perspective. This provides an intriguing complication to Bean's relationship with Ender: even as he is the protagonist from the book's point of view, he is very clearly Ender's sidekick. (Card wrote both novels in a third-person, limited-omniscient point of view, but chooses to focus the narratives on Ender and Bean, respectively.)

To say that Bean becomes a hero merely by "getting his own book" is far too simplistic. As has often been the case, having one's own book does not make one a hero (or a sidekick, for that matter). What makes Bean's narrative in *Ender's Shadow* unique from the standpoint of hero/sidekick pairings (and uniquely different from Tally and Shay) is the level to which the partnership is changed after the publication of the parallel novel. Christine Doyle notes that the second novel "does alter, or at least disturb, many readers' views of Ender."[25] Doyle attributes this to the book's effectiveness and "power," even supplying anecdotal testimony from young adults who had "a preference for Bean and *Shadow* because of a dislike for what they perceive[d] as Ender's 'weakness' in both books."[26] Doyle presents this dislike as an opportunity for further study, and while I do not look into why readers might view Ender's occasional indecisiveness or empathy as weakness, I am very much concerned with the shift regarding a reader's view of Ender. To that end, Bean could have easily languished in sidekick purgatory throughout the duration of *Ender's Shadow*. Instead, Card uses the opportunity to create a cyclical relationship between Ender and Bean, allowing both to occupy the position of hero in their actions. Bean firmly chooses to position himself in the sidekick role, a decision he makes logically, understanding where his weaknesses lie in light of Ender's strengths. However, this decision is made with the full knowledge that he *could* surpass Ender as the hero if he so desired. Again, as a way of contrast, Shay never had the opportunity to choose her role as sidekick (although that gets somewhat complicated in *Specials*). Like the other graduates of Battle School, Bean applauds the choice of Ender as his commander. Until this decision (and to a certain extent even afterward), Bean is regarded as humanity's backup plan; if Ender fails in any way, Bean would be called upon to take over. In fact, it is made clear that those in charge argued whether to keep Ender as the chosen savior of humanity instead of Bean. Faced with the decision to embark on his own, Bean chooses to remain.

Looking first at what *Ender's Game* has to offer in terms of Bean's role as sidekick, Bean proves himself a highly competent individual—even at his young age. He apparently first meets Ender when he is assigned to Ender's first command in Battle School: Dragon Army. As seen from Ender's perspective, the reader finds that Ender unwillingly (and almost uncontrollably) chooses to isolate Bean from the rest of the army. Ender realizes his actions, but continues to set Bean apart in an unconscious attempt to raise him above the rest of the "soldiers," albeit at the expense of the others despising Bean. Ender knows they may easily resent the younger, smaller recruit, asking himself, "Why am I doing this? . . . making one boy the target of all the others?"[27] During the first practice session of Dragon Army, which is also their first encounter, Ender calls upon Bean four times to give intelligent answers to his questions—bringing attention to Bean while setting him apart from the other soldiers. At the end of the session, Bean asks Ender for a platoon command, stating: "I can be the best man you've got, but do not play games with me."[28] Ender responds to Bean's request for responsibility with, "I made sure they *all* noticed you today. They'll be watching every move you make. All you have to do to earn their respect now is be perfect."[29] In this way, Ender has set up a scenario for Bean that mirrored his own rise to command—excellence by means of isolation. All the while, Ender thinks, "Why had he done to Bean what had been done to Ender by commanders that he despised?"[30] After some introspection, Ender answers his own question: "I am hurting you to make you a better soldier in every way. . . . That's why they brought you to me, Bean. So you could be just like me."[31] Although he recognizes the commander/soldier dynamic he shares with Bean, Ender almost defiantly ends his inner soliloquy with, "But I'll be watching you, more compassionately than you know, and when the time is right you'll find that I am your friend, and you are the soldier you want to be"[32] In their article on the link between Card's novels and the genre of the school story, Christine Doyle and Susan Louise Stewart also comment on Card's pattern of isolating the students with more potential. While their ultimate intention is to investigate how Card shifts a school story into the postmodern, they offer many helpful insights into the complementary nature the books have. In their example on isolation, they write that although the strategy "of isolating Ender, then Bean" is "torture for both," the boys eventually recognize that the absence of such isolation would necessitate them to integrate themselves into "the rest of the gang," a move leading toward mediocrity and anonymity.[33] What are needed, therefore, are not integration and duplication, but isolation and invention: "the battle ahead requires them to be extraordinary."[34] Ender marks Bean as someone to join him in extraordinary achievement as early as their initial interaction.

    The next significant back and forth between Ender and Bean comes after Ender's army wins its second battle in one day—a battle that was nevertheless stacked against them. That night, Ender sends Bean a private message, "See me at once."[35] Bean goes down the corridor to Ender's personal room. Inside, they converse about the nature of the Battle School and about why students like themselves were brought up and advanced at such an early age.[36] Ender asks Bean, point blank, why they made him a soldier so young. Bean answers, "Because they need us, that's why. Because they need somebody to beat the buggers. That's the only thing they care about."[37] Ender answers, "It's important that you know that, Bean."[38] As they continue talking, Bean realizes that whether or not he meant to, Ender confided in him—to share some of the struggle that he faces as the chosen hero of the impending war. As Ender is speaking, "Bean looked at him and realized that the impossible was happening. Far from baiting him, Ender Wiggin was actually confiding in him. Not much. But a little. Ender was human and Bean had been allowed to see."[39] Ender lowered his defenses in front of one of his soldiers for the first time since coming to the battle school. There had been instances where Ender shared friendship and camaraderie, certainly, but never a moment of unveiled vulnerability. Ender has invited Bean into a new level of relationship, a place where no one else had ever (nor would ever) be invited while the world looked to Ender to lead the next war.

Sara K. Day offers an interesting view regarding Ender's choice of Bean as his "right-hand man."[40] Day points out that not only does Bean think "like a solider, devising strategies and intuiting the opponents' weaknesses" which Ender certainly finds useful, but Bean also exhibits additional traits Ender finds perhaps even more admirable: "Ender ultimately seems to align the qualities he notes in Bean—including, notable, *goodness*—as traits associated with adulthood."[41] The overarching purpose of Day's article is to explore how the relationship between childhood and adulthood is problematized in Card's novels: "Card examines, blurs, and even eliminates the lines that are frequently drawn between ideas of children and beliefs about adults."[42] Day suggests that one of these lines is truth-telling; while the adults always tell half-truths or ambiguities, and the children tend to despise these behaviors, the children themselves also lie, "often just as easily as adults do, and especially Ender himself."[43] Recognizing Bean's "*goodness*" as a more admirable exemplification of adulthood (more admirable than lying, in this case) brings Bean into a position of value and emulation. He is one who can "simultaneously embody childhood and adulthood": he is, "like Ender, . . . a personification of border areas . . . able to be understood both as a young child and already an adult."[44] Ender sees Bean as one who can positively counteract his own areas of inadequacy. Part of this is his goodness, and another part is his intellect and cleverness.

While Bean's attributes and goodness (though undoubtedly complicated by *Ender's Shadow*), might be two reasons Ender chooses Bean, other rationales have been offered. For instance, Tim Blackmore suggests that Card meant the text as a "replacement for the military paradigm" through the fictional focus on "the warrior who lives inside it."[45] As part of this goal, Blackmore states that "Bean is the catalyst for Ender's ambivalence about his life as a warrior."[46] Blackmore bases this claim on the way Ender treated

Bean in their first encounter, creating the same isolation he himself experienced. Eventually, Ender admits that he "had never, except perhaps with Bean, used his power to hurt someone."[47] This admission, according to Blackmore, marks a "massive upheaval in Ender's paradigm."[48] Perhaps it was an unconscious decision for Ender to isolate Bean in the manner in which he did, but it was definitely a deliberate action to bring Bean into the fold as a sidekick. Recognizing Bean's impact in Ender's paradigm shift from a warrior to a peacemaker certainly explains Card's reasoning in making Bean a sidekick. (It also certainly explains Card's subsequent reasoning in making Bean the focus of a parallel novel.)

Whatever the rationale, whether harboring qualities of goodness or utilizing actions as a catalyst, once Bean has been brought into Ender's confidence, Ender gives him the assignment to think outside of the box, to "be clever," and "think of solutions to problems we haven't seen yet" and gives him a list of people from which to handpick a special squad for training.[49] As their conversation has lasted past the lights-out deadline, Ender allows Bean to stay the night in his cabin—another trusting act in the new relationship. The importance of this scene becomes even more apparent when this same passage takes place in *Ender's Shadow*. This dual telling of the scene from both novels' perspectives makes it one of the more pivotal scenes regarding Ender and Bean's relationship. It is also significant because even in *Ender's Game*, it is told from Bean's point of view (at least, from a third-person point of view following Bean). Bean is successful in his assignment, as he is in all things presented to him. Dragon Army becomes the only undefeated army in the history of the battle school, and Ender is graduated early to be sent, unprecedentedly, straight to command school. Bean is with him when he gets the order to leave the battle school, but the two of them do not see one another for some time; it is not until Ender begins controlling actual space battles that they reunite. Bean's involvement in that part of the narrative is relatively inconsequential, at least, that is, until reading about his experiences in *Ender's Shadow*.

When Card writes *Ender's Shadow*, everything Bean attempts takes on deeper significance, and Card paves the way for an even stronger argument for how Bean-as-sidekick evolves into something more. Bean's newly supplied backstory establishes that he was a stolen embryo with altered genetics, giving him incredible intelligence at an impossibly young age.[50] This accounts for his outstanding performance during Battle School, and this enhanced intelligence also gives Bean insight into the goings-on of the Battle School, as well as an understanding of global politics and interplanetary tactics. What Bean lacks, however, are the interpersonal skills of the other students. Bean notices, time and again, that Ender has the ability to demand the best from his soldiers while still remaining a figure of respect and compassion. Bean concludes that it is innate in Ender, and it is something he could never hope to learn or reason into. The recognition of these innate talents helps Bean bring himself closer to Ender.

The reader also learns in *Ender's Shadow* that Bean's relationship to Ender began long before he ever served in Ender's army. Upon arriving at Battle School, Bean finds himself constantly being compared to Ender. At first, he is unsure whether or not the comparison is a hindrance or an advantage. His mind is finally made up when he must make a decision about his future. During an exploration of the air intake system, Bean discovers his genetically enhanced nature by eavesdropping on a conversation between his teacher, Dimak, and the commander of Battle School, Colonel Graff. Graff questions Bean's legal status as a human, suggesting Bean's mysterious genetics make him as much of a threat as an asset. When he returns to his bunk that night, Bean comes up with a plan to assuage any fears Graff might have over his status as a human: "His perfect camouflage . . . quelling their fears and bringing him both safety and advancement. He had to become Ender Wiggin."[51] To develop his interpersonal skills in light of Ender's example, Bean engages in a number of social experiments. The most important thing he does during his quest to become Ender, however, is to handpick the roster making up Dragon Army. Dimak invites Bean into his office and confronts him about his hacking of the teachers' computer system. Instead of a reprimand, however, Dimak puts Bean's intellect to the test: build a hypothetical army out of unseasoned students and/or those assigned for transfer.[52] Bean tests Dimak by asking whether or not he can put himself into the commander's position and guesses from Dimak's reaction that the hypothetical army is a real one, and is intended for Ender. Dimak admits nothing, but it is obvious that Bean has indeed guessed the assignment's true intention; he compiles the list and submits it.

Of those included in Ender's misfit army, two students are of note. The first is Bean himself. While it might have seemed extremely unlikely for Bean not to add himself to Ender's army, he does have that option. However, since this assignment comes after his decision to hide behind Ender, to "become" him, sidling up to the older soldier makes perfect sense. The other notable inclusion is Nikolai, Bean's only friend. In the same way that Ender only chooses to confide in Bean, Bean only chooses to confide in Nikolai. (This exclusivity makes sense, considering Bean's initial lessons in trust were broken by his first real adult guardian, Sister Carlotta).[53] Nikolai is described throughout the book as merely an average student among the very gifted attendees of Battle School. Elsewhere he might have stood out, but in a school of geniuses, he struggles with the schoolwork in the classroom and the tactics in the battle room. Bean vacillates on the issue of adding him, judging Nikolai's abilities to be behind the others chosen, but knows what the opportunity would mean. In the end, he adds him simply because, as he says to himself, "I want him."[54] Nikolai more or less fits into a sidekick role for

Bean, fulfilling the space of friend and confidant, as a sense of reliance gradually occurs between them: sometimes even a sidekick needs a sidekick.

To solidify their connection further, it is revealed to the reader that Nikolai is the child from whom Bean was cloned: they are brothers, genetic twins aside from Bean's alteration. After this fact comes to light (to the reader, not to Bean or Nikolai), Nikolai has a conversation with Anderson (another Battle School teacher) in which Nikolai describes his relationship with Bean: "sometimes he's the little brother and I am looking out for him, and sometimes he's the big brother and he's looking out for me."[55] Anderson then suggests that Nikolai and Bean are friends, but Nikolai corrects him with, "I told you. I am his brother. Once you get a brother, you do not give him up easy."[56] In many ways, this interchange is a moment of sentimentality for Card. A few scant paragraphs after unveiling Bean's true genetic identity, one which the reader would already have connected to Nikolai, Card gives Nikolai an opportunity to take ownership of Bean as an older brother without an awareness of their biological connection. With the exception of the family reunion at the end of the novel, Nikolai has no role to play in the greater battle against the Formics: his narrative ends when Bean gets sent to Command School.

Until Bean walks into Dragon Army's barracks, the only meaningful relationship he has is with Nikolai. Once he enters the barracks, however, he meets Ender for the first time. From the privileged narrative standpoint of *Ender's Shadow*'s narration, it is Bean who has always had the advantage over Ender: he is smarter, more wary of the leadership, has done more investigating regarding the nature of Battle School, and has already guessed the true intentions of the next Formic altercation/war—although he has allowed himself to be misled regarding this fact.[57] Bean also knows he has handpicked Ender's entire army for him—stacking the deck in Ender's own favor as much as possible. Bean has done all of this is in spite of the fact that Ender remains a mystery to him in person, in ability, and in myth. Although Bean constructs the army to give *himself* as much opportunity as possible under Ender's leadership, Bean's actions are also based in the faith he has in the Ender mythos—he has staked his own chances on what he has heard about the incredible Ender Wiggin. Throughout *Ender's Shadow*, there is an unmistakable aura of hero worship around Ender. Adding even more to this aura/mythos is the *literary* mythos surrounding Ender as a character, stemming from his role and writings as the Speaker for the Dead (the subject of other *Ender's Game* sequels). If the reader has already read *Ender's Game*, he or she already knows the outcome of all the major plots regarding Ender. The tension over whether or not Ender will survive the mental strain of his "training" is gone, as is the shock of the revelation that Ender has fought and won an actual war instead of a simulation. What the reader of *Ender's Shadow* gets instead are the aloof musings Bean gives regarding his guesses as to

Ender's mental processes. These musings, what Bean refers to as "his private theology," are what create the intrigue of *Ender's Shadow*: because the plot is (probably) already known by the reader, the real drama lies in how Bean's psychological and philosophical study of Ender in turn drives the development of their partnership.[58]

The drama of Bean's study comes to the forefront again when examining Bean's perspective of his first conversation with Ender: the one in which he asks for a toon command. Afterward, Bean reflects on the conversation, the dialogue of which is repeated almost verbatim from *Ender's Game*: "Today he found out that all this time Wiggin didn't even know Bean existed. Everybody compared Bean to Wiggin—but apparently Wiggin hadn't heard or didn't care."[59] Up until this point, Bean has operated under the reputation his intelligence has built for him, as the most intellectually revered student in the entire school. Suddenly, Bean's carefully (and intentionally) created protection means nothing. This reversal actually supports Bean's private theology: the object of his study and devotion (for it can be considered as such) would cease to exist if Ender acted in any manner that might undermine that created image. Although Bean admits surprise and disappointment in Ender's actions ("Unlike you, Wiggin, I *do* give the other guy a chance . . . you screwed up with me today"),[60] Doyle and Stewart liken Ender's behavior toward Bean (and eventually that of Bean toward his own troops) as a natural by-product of his new role as a teacher. They consider this as part of Ender's coming to "understand and accept some of the principles that guide these former 'enemies' they have now joined. Adopting some aspects of the 'status quo' becomes essential in order to accomplish their larger purpose."[61] Ender's larger purpose is to take his army and help it reach its potential. It is logical, then, that he employs tactics he has undergone himself. Their first face-to-face meeting actually upholds the expectations Bean held about Ender, whether Ender (or Bean) knows of them or not. Bean expected to find a colleague who could finally engage him on his level of higher function. Instead, he found someone who demanded excellence without discrimination; a teacher who would never give away dominance or leadership for anything other than successfully achieving a purpose. Bean does not find the possibility for equal partnership: the best he can hope for is to become his new teacher's most trusted subordinate—his sidekick.

Bean finally achieves this trusted position with Ender when he is called into his room to receive the "think outside the box" assignment. Looking at this moment from the extended version found in *Ender's Shadow*, three newly unique pieces of the story come to light. The first is the revelatory moment where Ender lets his guard down. In the retelling, after "Ender was letting Bean see that he was human," the narration adds, "Bringing him into the inner circle. Making [Bean] . . . what? A counselor? A confidant?"[62] Both titles hold differing connotations. To call Bean a "counselor" would put him in a position of power or authority over Ender, if only momentarily. To properly counsel Ender, Bean would need the authority to potentially instruct him in an advised course of action. At the very least, it makes them peers—allowing for a back and forth exchange of ideas and information. A "confidant," on the other hand, might hold any level of power within the relationship, depending on the sensitivity of the information at hand. If Bean has, in fact, been made Ender's confidant, he has been granted a level of intimacy beyond the other soldiers; his commander trusts him enough to keep their conversations secret.

The second unique piece established in this retelling is Bean's choice to keep himself in the sidekick role. Up until now, even with Bean's mythification of Ender, there has been tension regarding whether or not Bean would surpass him. Because of his increased intelligence, Bean knows about his high regard in the eyes of the Battle School faculty: some consider him the second-best hope after Ender, others consider him the best before Ender. Here, however, in Ender's room, Bean admits his inadequacies in leadership. He thinks:

> I'm glad enough that the burden is on Ender, . . . because I have more confidence that Ender can bring it off than that I could. Whatever it is that makes men love the commander who decides when they will die, Ender has that, and if I have it no one has yet seen evidence of it. Besides, even without genetic alteration, Ender has abilities that the tests didn't measure for, that run deeper than mere intellect.[63]

Bean not only contemplates his shortcomings as a leader, but also postulates regarding Ender's unmeasurable qualities: that which "makes men love the commander who decides when they will die." Doyle and Stewart similarly weigh in on Ender's ability as a commander, citing his "deep empathy" as the driving force behind why "his troops follow him."[64] If it is, indeed, Ender's empathy that makes him a great commander, then their pairing makes perfect sense: Bean is the analytical genius, while Ender is the emotional maven. Doyle and Stewart also recognize how this empathy requires everyone to keep Ender in the dark regarding the actual war: the fact that "he understands the foe" also means he "could never go into battle willing to win at all costs."[65] In this way too, Bean's advanced intellect allows him to recognize where Ender's skill surpasses his own. It proves a significant enough difference that Bean chooses to follow Ender. Before entering into his cabin that night, Bean had been using Ender as the means to several ends: survival from the persecution he faces from the faculty as a genetically modified human, and searching for someone among his classmates who might recognize his own abilities for leadership.

The third change to the retelling of this scene in *Ender's Shadow* is Bean's continued reflection upon his new assignment (or assignments, as the narrative suggests). While he contemplates potential advantages of the use of stupid tactics in the battle room, Bean also realizes he now has a role in the tactics outside of the battle room: he must help protect Ender from the threat of physical enemies. Bean sees that he "can help" Ender where it truly counts: in the battle against the Formics. He determines to forsake "geometry and astronomy and all the other nonsense" in order to find time to research how animals "wage war"—especially "hive insects," as they are Earth's closest living parallel to the Formics. This is a result of Bean's more intellectual perspective on the matter at hand, as well as Ender's insistence that Bean know the true reasons behind Battle School. The other real (and in many ways, more immediate) threat to Ender is the hatred Bonzo (one of the aforementioned bullies) has for him. Bean, having experienced this kind of animosity when "growing up" on the streets of Rotterdam, knows firsthand the danger Ender faces. He determines to "watch [Ender's] back" as best as he is able.[66]

This passage is even more unique, from a narrative standpoint, as it is the only "shared" scene in both books that does not include a version from Ender's point of view. This moment is the lone instance of Bean's point of view in *Game*, and that view expands in *Shadow*. In judging Bean's status as a hero, then, we have a one-sided view of the exchange, as all others have Ender's thoughts from *Game* and Bean's from *Shadow*. An interesting element of Doyle and Stewart's study included side-by-side excerpts from the two novels, placing Ender on the left and Bean on the right. They contend that such a practice allows the reader to "see how Ender and Bean complete each other."[67] While they do not specify how exactly Ender and Bean complete one another, Doyle and Stewart do recognize that "both construct similar facades in order to establish their authority, but when they separate, those facades collapse and each boy is left trembling, further isolated, angry, and disillusioned."[68] It is clear that the similarities stemming from the two characters' viewpoints do bring the two of them into closer connection.

In light of such similarity, an intriguing plot point is the reader's inability to judge Bean's guesses about Ender's motivations in this meeting. Card, to the point of annoyance, constantly "allows" Bean to mentally work his way through all possible outcomes to a given scenario, weighing what other factors could be at play, and how other people might react—all in an effort to show Bean's heightened mental prowess. The problem with this cognitive approach, especially in the moment where Ender confides in Bean, is Bean's inability to judge emotional or irrational decisions (with the exception of thinly veiled anger, like in the case of Bonzo's anger toward Ender). This one interchange between Bean and Ender—again, completely from Bean's point of view in both novels—hides all chance of looking into Ender's compassionate thought processes. Perhaps, though, this hiding of Ender's thoughts is not problematic; it instead preserves the sanctity of Ender's innermost perceptions regarding Bean. Hiding part of Ender's consciousness from the reader promotes a mystery similar to the personal religion Bean bases around the legend of Ender.

In light of the lack of revelation regarding Ender, the scene where he leaves Battle School for Command School is the first of the two most pivotal in terms of Bean's sidekick relationship with Ender and thus for the elevation of such a relationship. Right before Ender leaves for Command School, he leads his army in their final battle. This fight, as told in *Ender's Game*, pits Dragon army against Griffin and Tiger armies: the first battle against two armies at once. Ender goes into this battle in an emotional daze. Earlier that day he had fought his way out of an ambush by Bonzo, in which Ender unknowingly killed the hateful older student.[69] Going into the army battle, Ender thinks, "I am sick of the game. No game is worth Bonzo's blood pinking the water on the bathroom floor. Ice me, send me home, I do not want to play anymore."[70] From this emotional perspective, Ender tosses out all of the rules (after a suggestion from Bean), uses the forsaken strategy of a battle formation, and breaches the enemy gate before immobilizing all of their forces.[71] The narration tells the reader nothing regarding how this plan comes together, other than, "Ender grinned. 'OK. Why not. Let's see how they react to a formation.' Bean was appalled. 'A formation! We've never done a formation in the whole time we've been an army!'"[72] All moments that follow, including the victory, seemingly belong solely to Ender and his brilliance. After reading the same battle from *Ender's Shadow*, however, there are some significant changes to this scene. First of all, the level of Ender's melancholy is deepened to the point where he would be "allowing himself to be part of a screen of frozen soldiers, pushed through the battle by someone else, [it] was as close to sleeping through it as he could get."[73] The screen is a part of the formation Ender chose to employ, but there again is another change: "As it turned out, Ender's plan was to use another of Bean's stupid ideas . . . a screen formation of frozen soldiers."[74] In giving Bean the credit for the strategy, Card also omits Bean's incredulous reaction to the suggestion to use a formation. Finally, after Ender decides to ride along as part of the screen, he "left everything up to Bean to organize. 'It's your show,' he said." One soldier calls Ender's actions as "trust, Bean old boy," but Bean inwardly thinks: "That's despair."[75] Bean promptly carries out his plan, including personally assuring the victory in the end.[76] In this final battle, therefore, Bean is not only the sidekick to the hero, he *is* the hero outright: Ender has quit mentally, physically, and emotionally. This variant perspective is entirely found in *Ender's Shadow*; if the parallel novel didn't exist, the brilliance and credit would remain with Ender.

In the immediate aftermath of the battle, Dragon Army's toon leaders and their seconds are all promoted. Bean finds himself as the new leader of Rabbit army. The Dragon Army barracks are in disarray in light of eighteen of the army's leaders transferred to command other armies. While this continues, one of the toon leaders, Fly Molo, comes to Bean (with the other toon leaders in tow) and states, "Bean, somebody's got to tell Ender. . . . We thought . . . since you're his friend. . . ."[77] Even though this stuns Bean, he reasons, correctly, that only he "had been taken inside Ender's confidence," and that in the eyes of his fellow soldiers, he was "the closest thing to a friend they had seen Ender have since he got command of Dragon."[78] Bean acknowledges this fact and goes to see Ender, when Ender is receiving his orders to go to Command School. One new point (exclusive to *Shadow*) comes to light in this moment. As Ender leaves his room, he pauses: "He turned to Bean, took his hand. To Bean, it was like the touch of the finger of God. It sent light all through him. Maybe I am his friend. Maybe he feels toward me some small part of the . . . feeling I have for him."[79] Remembering Bean's private theology, his ongoing study of the Ender mythos, equating Ender's touch to "the finger of God" falls right in line. The moment of intimate physical connection, something that had never before been mentioned or alluded to in either novel, acts as a passing of the torch, or the laying on of one's mantle. The parallels between this moment and Elijah's passing of his mantle to Elisha moments before being brought into heaven are numerous.[80] Bean ends the scene in private reflection, concluding: "Ender gave [his life] meaning."[81]

Although Bean spends time at Battle School without Ender, as well as passing time traveling to meet up with him (and others) at Command School, the final essential moment between the hero and the sidekick comes in the final battle Ender fights. Card designs this ultimate battle, the attack on the Formic home world, to mirror Ender's last battle in Battle School. Ender is similarly broken when he comes to this point: exhaustion and frayed nerves have led him to despair once again. He sees the imbalance of power, his own "eighty fighters, against at least five thousand, perhaps ten thousand enemy ships."[82] His mind tempts him to quit, "I do not care anymore" and "You can keep your game. If you will not even give me a chance, why should I play?"[83] (Remember that at this point, Ender does not realize he faces real enemy forces: he still believes it is a simulation.) What brings him into action is hearing Bean's voice: "Remember, the enemy's gate is *down*."[84] Ender decides to mimic his actions in Battle School. He groups his forces and sends them on a suicide mission toward the planet—where the pilots use a molecular weapon to destroy all matter on the planet as well as all of the surrounding ships in a chain-reaction.[85]

Bean's involvement in this scene, as shown in *Ender's Shadow*, is significantly more than what it first appeared. In the chapters leading up to the final battle, Bean's role in the battles grows in both reach and authority. Graff tells him that "it's all the more important that you watch everything. Be there for him . . . you're his backup."[86] The other children in Ender's command were "finally becoming aware that Bean was following the whole battle, not just his part of it," causing them to pass along to Bean their approval.[87] When the final battle begins, Ender hesitates, and those in control offer Bean the command: "A light blinked on . . . all he had to do was press a button, and control of the battle would be his. They were offering it to him, because they thought that Ender had frozen up."[88] Bean waits, however, and wisely so. Although he understands the implications of the real battle before them, he has no plan, no course of action, and does not see how they could successfully get the molecular weapon in range of the planet.[89] Bean offers his advice about the enemy gate as an ironic joke meant to reflect the impossibility of the situation ahead. Ender takes it and runs with it, however, to the stunning success of the entire war. Yet Bean still has one more moment of impact. As the ships fly toward the planet, all but two are destroyed. Bean quietly, and on his own volition, tells one of these last ships to set off the molecular weapon within his own ship, beginning the chain-reaction before the ship was destroyed. Without this decision, the suicide run would have likely failed.[90]

Yet, Bean refuses to acknowledge his role in the decision-making, telling Graff after the fact, "I only knew that I had no plan at all. . . . Maybe it made him think of a plan. But it was him. It was Ender. You put your money on the right kid."[91] Graff responds with "I think perhaps you pulled each other across the finish line."[92] Graff's words undoubtedly summarize the purpose behind *Ender's Shadow*: layering a counternarrative within the original novel that creates complications and alterations as it retells a familiar story. Bean has become unique in this sense, as he was not only Ender's sidekick, but in refusing to take over the hero's role, he consciously sacrifices his own chance at glory. Bean becomes the sacrificial hero by *not* becoming the hero. Card has used the parallel novel to refine a new avenue for the sidekick. This is not the only new avenue Card develops with *Ender's Shadow*; Doyle and Stewart spend considerable time arguing their assertion that Card took the school story, a "highly traditional form," and deviated from the traditional "structural conventions in significant ways."[93] Some of these ways include a "highly unusual narrative approach," "utilizing multiple voices within the novels in innovative ways," and that "the teachers are seen as complex characters."[94]

In addition to these innovations on the school story, Card also shows innovation when it comes to treating sidekicks within a closed literary universe. The in-depth exploration of Bean in a parallel novel not only augments the experience of reading the original story, but changes the very nature of that story and of his and Ender's characters. Westerfeld did something similar with Shay and Tally in the *Uglies* series, but stopped short of where Card took the idea. Westerfeld gave Shay two graphic novels; Card has published four sequels to *Ender's Shadow*, with a fourth sequel forthcoming. (This does not count Marvel Comics' ongoing series of comics based on Ender and

Bean's time at Battle School, begun in 2008.) Both Card and Westerfeld, writing within the past sixteen years, have tangibly demonstrated how a well-executed parallel novel can help a sidekick become more than what was once originally intended in terms of characterization: The resulting counternarrative or paranarrative can deepen the initial story line by building intricacies within characters who were not previously at the forefront of the narrative.

NOTES

1. Joel Stein et al., "Nip. Tuck. Or Else." *Time*, vol. 185, no. 24 (June 29, 2015): 46.
2. *Harrison Bergeron*, directed by Bruce Pittman, aired August 13, 1995, on Showtime, https://www.youtube.com/watch?v=XBcpuBRUdNs.
3. Kimberly Downing Robinson. "*Uglies*," *Interdisciplinary Humanities* 27, no. 2 (2010): 151.
4. Ibid.
5. Scott Westerfeld, Devin Grayson, and Steven Cummings, *Uglies: Shay's Story* (New York: Ballantine, 2012); Diana Peterfreund, "Team Shay," in *Mind-Rain: Your Favorite Authors on Scott Westerfeld's Uglies Series*, ed. Scott Westerfeld (Dallas: BenBella, 2009), 42.
6. Scott Westerfeld, *Uglies* (New York: Simon Pulse, 2011), 228–29, 287.
7. Scott Westerfeld, *Pretties* (New York: Simon Pulse, 2011), 23.
8. Westerfeld, *Uglies*, 237.
9. Westerfeld, Grayson, and Cummings, *Uglies: Shay's Story*, 9.
10. J. R. R. Tolkien, *The Hobbit* (New York: Ballantine, 1974), 9.
11. Robin Wasserman, "Best Friends for Never," in *Mind-Rain: Your Favorite Authors on Scott Westerfeld's Uglies Series*, ed. Scott Westerfeld (Dallas: BenBella, 2009), 20.
12. Ibid., 21.
13. Ibid., 24.
14. Ibid., 22.
15. Peterfreund, "Team Shay," 43.
16. Ibid.
17. Ibid., 44.
18. Westerfeld, *Pretties*, 346; Scott Westerfeld, *Specials* (New York: Simon Pulse, 2011), 3–5.
19. Peterfreund, "Team Shay," 48.
20. Wasserman, "Best Friends," 31.
21. Ibid.
22. "Revision of the Commandant's Professional Reading List." Marines: The Official Website of the United States Marine Corps., last modified May 17, 2017. https://www.marines.mil/News/Messages/Messages-Display/Article/1184470/revision-of-the-commandants-professional-reading-list/.
23. Orson Scott Card, "Looking Back." YALSA, 2008. http://www.ala.org/yalsa/booklists/awards/bookawards/margaretaedwards/maeprevious/anniversary.
24. Sara K. Day, "Liars and Cheats: Crossing the Lines of Childhood, Adulthood, and Morality in *Ender's Game*," *English Studies in Canada* 38, no. 3–4 (2012): 212.
25. Christine Doyle, "Orson Scott Card's Ender and Bean: The Exceptional Child as Hero," *Children's Literature in Education* 35, no. 4 (2004): 317.
26. Ibid.
27. Orson Scott Card, *Ender's Game* (New York: Starscape, 2002), 161.
28. Ibid., 165.
29. Ibid., 166.
30. Ibid., 167.
31. Ibid., 168.
32. Ibid.

33. Christine Doyle and Susan Louise Stewart, "*Ender's Game* and *Ender's Shadow*: Orson Scott Card's Postmodern School Stories," *The Lion and the Unicorn* 28, no. 2 (2004): 191.
34. Ibid.
35. Card, *Ender's Game*, 195.
36. Ibid., 196.
37. Ibid., 196–97.
38. Ibid., 197.
39. Ibid.
40. Day, "Liars and Cheats," 217.
41. Ibid.
42. Ibid., 224.
43. Ibid., 220.
44. Ibid., 217.
45. Tim Blackmore, "Ender's Beginning: Battling the Military in Orson Scott Card's *Ender's Game*," *Extrapolation* 32, no. 2 (1991): 125.
46. Ibid., 137.
47. Card, *Ender's Game*, 245.
48. Blackmore, "Ender's Beginning," 138.
49. Card, *Ender's Game*, 198.
50. Orson Scott Card, *Ender's Shadow* (New York: Tor, 2000), 173.
51. Ibid., 186.
52. Ibid., 217–19.
53. Ibid., 79.
54. Ibid., 224.
55. Ibid., 262.
56. Ibid.
57. Ibid., 154–55.
58. Ibid., 244.
59. Ibid., 244–45.
60. Ibid., 244.
61. Doyle and Stewart, "*Ender's Game* and *Ender's Shadow*," 193.
62. Card, *Ender's Shadow*, 297.
63. Ibid., 300–1.
64. Doyle and Stewart, "*Ender's Game* and *Ender's Shadow*," 192.
65. Ibid.
66. Card, *Ender's Shadow*, 301.
67. Doyle and Stewart, "*Ender's Game* and *Ender's Shadow*," 196.
68. Ibid.
69. Card, *Ender's Game*, 211–12.
70. Ibid., 215.
71. Ibid., 216–18.
72. Ibid., 216.
73. Card, *Ender's Shadow*, 342.
74. Ibid.
75. Ibid., 343.
76. Ibid., 344.
77. Ibid., 349.
78. Ibid.
79. Ibid., 291.
80. 2 Kings 2:9–14.
81. Ibid., 292.
82. Card, *Ender's Game*, 292.
83. Ibid., 293.
84. Ibid.
85. Ibid., 295.
86. Card, *Ender's Shadow*, 440–41.

87. Ibid., 442.
88. Ibid., 447.
89. Ibid., 449.
90. Ibid., 454.
91. Ibid., 457.
92. Ibid.
93. Doyle and Stewart, "*Ender's Game* and *Ender's Shadow*," 186.
94. Ibid., 186, 192.

Chapter Five

The Self-Aware Sidekick

Studying Sidekicks in First-Person Sidekick Superhero Stories

The third and final form of sidekick separation is perhaps the most structurally revealing of the three forms in regard to the sidekick's elevation. The kind of novel studied here is a very specific genre, one that has become increasingly popular for today's YA authors, as it moves the primary narrative point of view to that of the sidekick, beginning a new and unique story for the sidekick outside of the tradition established in chapters 3 and 4. I call the main characters in these books "self-aware sidekicks," but only in two specific ways. The first is the narrative choice: these are stories of a young adult protagonist who is a sidekick to a caped-superhero, told from a first-person point of view. Hence, he or she is acutely "aware" of being a sidekick to a superhero. The second is the author's awareness of, and often less-than-subtle homage to, the caped-superhero tradition, especially Batman and Robin. These kinds of "self-aware sidekick" novels come at a time where other "self-aware" or "heroes in the real world" characters are receiving their time in the popular culture spotlight. For instance, the aforementioned *Teen Titans Go! To the Movies* (2018) is a comedic turn on comic book sidekicks, so much so that the entire plot of the film hinges on Robin's desire for his own cinematic movie—all to prove he is more than a sidekick. Brian Tallerico calls the film a "clever, funny examination of its very existence."[1] Tallerico continues, likening the film's antics/jokes to those in other films, like *Deadpool* (2016) and *The LEGO Batman Movie* (2017), which "serve as meta commentaries on the superhero genre of films that so dominate the marketplace."[2] For instance, during one of the film's sequences, the Titans travel through time to stop the origin stories of heroes like Superman, Wonder

Woman, Aquaman, and Batman, looking at the covers of classic comic books to double-check their success; they know they have succeeded when the hero disappears from the cover. Along these lines of self-awareness, Deadpool has had two movies released in the past two years (*Deadpool 2* was released in 2018, a mere two years after the first film). A character who has consistently broken the literary "fourth wall" and spoken directly to the audience, Deadpool has also referred to the speech balloons and narrative boxes on the physical pages of his comic books, and cut through pages of a comic book to speak to himself in the past. This practice of playing with convention by allowing characters to break the fourth wall shows up now and again in superhero comics, with a few notable standouts including Animal Man, She-Hulk, and Grant Morrison's *The Multiversity: Ultra Comics*. Other long-standing characters that are self-aware (or hyper-aware) of their existence as comic book characters include Mr. Mxyzptlk and Bat-Mite, two mischievous imps from the fifth dimension, obsessed with interfering with Superman and Batman, respectively.

The "self-aware sidekick" novels, however, stop just short of breaking the fourth wall, and never address the reader. They fall more in line with the "hero in the real world" scenario, seen in comics and/or films like *Kick-Ass* (2010), *Kick-Ass 2* (2013), Christopher Nolan's Batman trilogy (*Batman Begins* [2005], *The Dark Knight* [2008], and *The Dark Knight Rises* [2012]), *The Green Hornet* (2011), and *The Punisher* (2004). These films exist under a premise where ordinary people, without superpowers, take it upon themselves to put on a mask and seek justice against evil. *The Dark Knight* even doubles down on this premise, as the opening sequence involves Batman-copycats trying to stop nefarious activity. Although the "self-aware sidekicks" studied in this chapter do have superpowers, elements of the worlds in which they exist are meant to mimic the "real world" as much as possible. Furthermore, the "self-aware sidekick" novels recognize and play within the same superhero conventions that more metacognizant creations like *Deadpool* or *Teen Titans Go! To the Movies* break or disregard. The "self-aware sidekick" texts present a paradox: these sidekicks are the focus of their own novels while nevertheless functioning as heroes' seconds. While this closely resembles Conan Doyle's use of Watson as the narrator of the bulk of the Sherlock Holmes stories, there are three important differences. One, Watson is never truly the focus of the tale—Holmes is; two, Watson is a grown man, not a young adult; three, Holmes is a detective, not a superpowered, caped crime fighter (although similarities do exist). The self-aware sidekick novels studied in this chapter are Jack Ferraiolo's *Sidekick*s and John David Anderson's *Sidekicked*. Two of Anderson's other novels, *Standard Hero Behavior* and *Minion*, would fit in nicely as similarly themed texts and could easily offer continued insight into this world from more angles. *Standard Hero*

Behavior is a high-fantasy sidekick novel, and *Minion* is a villain's sidekick's tale taking place in the same literary universe as *Sidekicked*.

Both of these texts, in one form or another, deal very directly with the sidekick separation established in chapter 2. As was the case with texts studied in chapters 3 and 4, each brings a new kind of wrinkle into this scenario. Ferraiolo's work portrays the coming-of-age of a young man who must balance the responsibilities of school, social life, and fighting crime with his father-figure hero. Anderson's narrative follows a similar vein, but creates an absentee father situation. Both texts are notably and significantly different in their characterization of sidekicks than all previously studied examples.

In particular, this type of novel makes the sidekick question his or her role through the entire text. The readers see an intimate look at the characters' thoughts, which are often fixated on becoming heroes. The narrative drive of the self-aware sidekick novel is to constantly make sidekicks think beyond the confines of "sidekickery." There is no casual acceptance of their lots as sidekicks; there is no Watsonesque mentality of contentedness in remaining a sidekick forever. The larger point of these novels is to challenge the status quo, to question why sidekicks are kept at the side. In doing this, the entire narrative position of the sidekick is redefined: in fact, it could be said that they are not sidekicks at all at this point, as they are undoubtedly the protagonists, even while not the "hero." In the case of Anderson's novel, Andrew Bean is a sidekick in name only—his superhero refuses to mentor him. In Ferraiolo's novel, Scott Hutchinson is not a true sidekick either: he unknowingly acts as a popularity gimmick and financial draw for an aging hero losing his grip on what is right and wrong. As these sidekicks aren't sidekicks, and aren't necessarily even treated as sidekicks, but are without a doubt the main focus of each respective text, the question becomes, "What are they?"

The answer is simple: they're something new.

Within the context of YA themes, this new question of identity is further complicated. Central questions like "Who am I?" and "Who will I become?" are deepened when the apprenticeship itself is in question. If becoming a hero someday is suddenly not guaranteed, then what will become of a sidekick? I begin with Ferraiolo to set the stage for this illustration, as the world of *Sidekicks* is the most stereotypically superhero of the two texts. However, it is Anderson's text that brings what I consider the most interesting twists on the dynamic.

Ferraiolo's *Sidekicks* places the adolescent Scott Hutchinson, a.k.a. Bright Boy, alongside Trent Clancy, a.k.a. Phantom Justice, the hero of New York City. As a YA text, it makes perfect sense that Scott struggles to balance being a crime fighter by night and a student by day. The first chapter firmly places this text into YA territory: after saving an attractive woman as she fell off of a building, Bright Boy experiences an erection (something difficult to hide in his Robinesque shorts). A helicopter news crew films the action, and later replays the footage repeatedly on public television. If the experience and the repeated news coverage weren't enough, Scott finds his sidekick identity lampooned throughout his school the next day. Socially, Scott barely fits in, having no friends and no social group to associate with. The life of a sidekick has consumed his attention. The fulfillment he found in being Bright Boy allowed him to readily accept his social marginalization when not in costume. Subsequent to his unfortunate news coverage, he finds himself alienated from the only part of his persona in which he found solace—sparking the identity crisis that drives the novel. Scott's identity crisis is more than just the major plot conflict, it is also the device through which the novel works to redefine the sidekick role, and this crisis and redefinition can be seen through a number of different combinations of elements within the text. There are three that showcase his struggles best. The first is the nature of his relationship with his superhero, Phantom Justice. The second is how a newfound romance challenges his constrictions as a sidekick. The third is how his old relationship with Phantom Justice and his new relationship with his newfound romance conflict to further challenge his superhero convictions.

To understand how Phantom Justice and Bright Boy interact, it is important to establish the parameters of their fictional world: here, heroes and villains are cataloged by the nature of their power(s). The three categories constituting one as "super" are plus strength, plus speed/reflexes, and plus intelligence.[3] Both Bright Boy and Phantom Justice belong to the biological category of "plus strength/plus speed" or "plus/plus," which is a somewhat common combination. Plus intelligence often appears as a super's only gifted trait, and the likelihood of a triple plus (plus strength, plus speed/reflexes, plus intelligence) is very low. In this world of pluses, Trent's Phantom Justice embodies the Batman figure as much as Scott's Bright Boy embodies the Robin figure: he is a mysterious and rich crime fighter who adopted an orphaned young boy. Their physically imposing butler/trainer/housekeeper Louis Sullivan is a modified placeholder for Alfred. All of this is obviously intentional, as any twist placed upon the superhero genre entails beginning with the familiar.[4] In fact, the situation in which Scott finds himself (adolescence impeding his ability to wear a costume designed for a child) further mirrors the frustrations felt by Dick Grayson in comics chronicling Robin's decision to become Nightwing.[5] Scott faces increasing hostility from Trent in regard to his request to wear a more appropriate costume,[6] which eventually comes to a head almost violently.[7] The hostility Trent directs toward Scott grows throughout, leading to the book's major twist, as well as the major change to Scott's definition of sidekick: the revelation that Trent has long been orchestrating his hero-villain face-offs as a source of financial and popular success. This news comes in the form of a chapter from Trent's third-person perspective. This chapter tells of Trent's long-term financial agreement with his archnemesis Dr. Chaotic: they stage epic battles for payment by companies who conspicuously place products to be shown during the television coverage.[8]

Additionally, it is later revealed that Trent has been killing other pluses when it was either opportunistic or necessary to keep his position as the sole hero of the city.[9] Once the reader knows of Trent's murderous actions, everything understandably changes. His heroics, at least of late, are nothing of the sort. Scott, then, no longer has a true hero to be sidekick to. In addition, the details surrounding the death of Scott's parents become suspect, leading one to speculate whether or not Trent arranged for their death. Scott's adoption and training was a calculated step taken by Trent to increase his popularity: a move that would garner more cash flow from a younger demographic. As Scott begins to challenge Bright Boy's costume, he is more of a liability than an asset in the eyes of his mentor and guardian. In fact, this liability issue has probably been brewing for some time. Trent states to Dr. Chaotic that he would love to "leave Bright Boy bleeding in an alley somewhere," using the death of his sidekick to "boost the ol' numbers."[10] Ferraiolo has obvious knowledge of comic book history, here employing the sidekick as a "draw for younger readers" scheme.[11] The killing of a sidekick to boost popularity/readership alludes to the Batman story-arc *A Death in the Family*, in which the fate of Jason Todd, Dick Grayson's successor to Robin, was left in the hands of readers. The readers were asked to participate in a phone-in campaign to vote whether or not Jason Todd were to live or die: the final vote resulted in his death.[12]

Scott eventually finds himself cast aside by Trent—who believes he killed Scott with a modified overdose of adrenaline.[13] (Scott is saved by a group of supers operating as an underground resistance against Trent's growing megalomania.) Scott is now a sidekick without a hero, although it is likely his work and world as a sidekick were always shams. He was never truly a sidekick because the battles he and Trent fought were mostly all staged. Now, almost unavoidably, Scott assumes the responsibility of hero: he is asked to be the sole "good guy" challenging Trent without knowing all of the details, players, or even the final outcome. What makes Scott's situation even more unique is that the first villain he faces as a hero is his former mentor, the one who taught him how to be heroic. Such irony is typical of the new form of sidekick that Ferraiolo has crafted. Although Scott's heroics as Bright Boy have been fabricated as part of an ongoing financial scheme, he has still been brought up believing the mantras regarding protecting the innocent, bringing evildoers to justice, and so forth. Without bringing him into the fold, Trent needed to maintain the integrity of an honest-to-goodness sidekick. In this manner, Trent trains the hero who ultimately helps foil his plans. Scott has been a "nonsidekick" to a villain for years.

The revealing skintight costume that brings Scott into growing conflict with Trent brings us to the second way Ferraiolo redefines his sidekick: a newfound romance that challenges Scott's contentedness as a sidekick. At its core, *Sidekicks* is a love story between Scott and Allison Mendes. The prospect of such a love seems impossible for two reasons: (1) it begins when Scott is at his lowest emotional level seen in the story, and (2) Allison is the secret identity for Dr. Chaotic's sidekick, Monkeywrench. (Allison's sidekick moniker, Monkeywrench, is likely a not-so-subtle reference to Miller's *The Dark Knight Returns*, where Batman calls Dick his "monkeywrench."[14]) Scott and Allison have unknowingly been sworn enemies for years. Scott's emotional low begins with the news coverage of his erection. It mortifies him, and as his schoolmates actively make fun of Bright Boy, his entire outlook on his life seems dire:

> Basically, I have no life (social or otherwise) as Scott, and now my hero identity is not comfortable anymore either. I mean, becoming Bright Boy has always been my escape. Have a bad day as Scott? No problem! Just slap on the uni, go out, bust some skulls, and become a hero to millions. But now, that's completely changed. My stupid costume has made me [a] joke. And I feel stuck.[15]

Feeling stuck is new territory for Scott, as he has always had the outlet of experiencing fame and adoration as the successful Bright Boy. Scott can no longer find solace by being Bright Boy, and the sexual nature of his humiliation makes it even more personally distressing.

Recognizing the connection between an inability to act and Scott's desire to disappear into the character of Bright Boy brings to mind one of the more interesting tropes of YA texts (or any other text for that matter): the concept of hiding behind a mask, of maintaining a dual identity. In both YA and in real life, the "masks" worn by young adults are often personas adapted and applied in different situations. This falls directly in line with what Penelope Brown and Stephen Levinson refer to as "face": the sociolinguistic notion commonly used in terms of "saving face" and/or "losing face." (It should be noted that Brown and Levinson base their notion of face on Erving Goffman's 1967 study, *Interaction Ritual: Essays on Face to Face Behavior*.) Face, or the "public self-image that every member wants to claim for himself [or herself]," comes in two aspects: positive or negative.[16] Positive face is "the positive consistent self-image . . . claimed by interactants," which "crucially" includes the desire for such a self-image to be perceived positively by other members of society.[17] In this case, then, Scott feels the need to save his positive face, as his outward social identity is being ridiculed instead of "appreciated and approved of."[18]

Because Scott cannot admit to being Bright Boy, and his peers have made that once positive identity undesirable, his other option is to act upon "negative face," which is a "freedom of action and freedom from imposition," again, understanding that this is based upon communicative interaction.[19] Ronald Wardhaugh and Janet Fuller interpret negative face as the "desire to be unimpeded by others' actions."[20] The difficulty in creating an outward self-identity free from imposition rests in each other's cooperation in maintaining that face. Unfortunately for Scott, his peer group would likely not allow him the use of either positive or negative face, as they ridicule his desire to be Bright Boy as well as harass any attempt to save his negative face by acting outside of their influence (an action gladly taken up by the school's bully, Jake). Furthermore, considering that positive and negative face occur within the framework of Brown and Levinson's Politeness Theory, true use of positive and/or negative face would require actual communication between Scott and his peers.[21] However, from his standpoint as both outside observer and direct recipient of their scorn, he nonetheless feels unable to act, and any true communication is impossible.

Finding himself with no foreseeable course of action is a natural step within the maturation process. It is not until Dr. Chaotic and Monkeywrench return that Scott has a force acting upon him sufficient enough to "unstick" him, as it were. A number of years have passed since the last confrontation with Dr. Chaotic, and were it not for Trent's sagging popularity, they may never have faced off again. Monkeywrench, always assumed by Scott to be a boy, now has a new costume that hides both face and any features that might now reveal her as a female. A few altercations occur in which Dr. Chaotic reveals his renewed antagonism toward Phantom Justice. More importantly, Monkeywrench heckles Bright Boy about his publicized erection. Things change during another run-in, when Bright Boy and Phantom Justice confront Dr. Chaotic and Monkeywrench inside a warehouse complex. Scott's focus is entirely on Monkeywrench:

> The only things that exist in the world right now are Monkeywrench and my hatred for him ... and he hasn't even noticed yet. He's watching the exchange between Chaotic and Phantom, because that's what we sidekicks usually do; we stand around and wait for the main event to start, and then we fight. I mean, that's why we're called sidekicks; if we were supposed to start the fighting, we'd probably be called *frontkicks* or something.[22]

Ferraiolo succinctly sums up the role typically played by comic book sidekicks: wait while the heroes talk to the villains, wait until the heroes or villains begin to fight, and so on. Regardless of what is expected of him as a sidekick (and Ferraiolo's moment of metacognition), Scott loses his cool and rushes into a fight with Monkeywrench before his awaited cue. During the fight, they topple onto an adjacent building, crash through the roof, and land inside. The impact causes Monkeywrench's mask to come off. Scott, recognizing her, asks in disbelief, "Allison?"[23] Realizing her identity has been compromised, she frantically attacks him until she succeeds in taking his mask off as well.

As they face each other, in costume but maskless for the first time, they reach an impasse: Allison recognizes it as "mutually assured destruction."[24] If either were to say something about the other's secret, then the other would reveal all the other's secrets. Although this is a moment of sudden and unforeseen intimacy (for it is indeed an intimate moment, somewhat akin to Adam and Eve in the Garden of Eden, "naked, and they felt no shame"[25]), the full impact is somewhat lost—Allison barely knows him, and she thinks his name is Steve. Regardless of this mistake, Scott leaves the fight with a new wrinkle in his life: he has an unparalleled intimacy with a girl he considers to be one of the more attractive (and unattainable) in his grade.

The actual beginning of their romantic relationship ends up being easier on Scott's part than he had imagined. After a day of ignoring him (and causing him some understandable confusion), Allison pulls Scott into a janitor's closet to talk him down from attempting something drastic to get her attention.[26] During their conversation, Allison reveals that Dr. Chaotic is her father, as well as explaining her reluctance to consider her and her father's actions as "villainous." Because they are still in school, Allison escorts Scott to their next class and promptly obtains an excuse for the two of them to leave for independent study.[27] Finally alone, Scott and Allison talk about their respective lives as sidekicks, whether or not Allison considers her father a villain or merely a man guided by misunderstood principles, and how they should both adopt new costumes. Scott desires a costume that does not create moments of indecency, and Allison wants a costume that does not conceal her femininity. After the two of them dress in new, edgier, and more comfortable outfits, they spar over a few buildings until they end up kissing on top of a truck. The "fight" and kissing are recorded and posted on the internet.[28] Bright Boy and Monkeywrench are the talk of his school the next day.[29]

In the span of one day, everything in Scott's life changes: his archenemy is a girl who goes to his school, she takes an active interest in him, he finds a new costume that does not make him self-conscious, and he kisses said girl. As he walks through the halls of his school, listening to everyone talk about how exciting it is that Bright Boy and Monkeywrench are a couple, he thinks, "for the first time in years, I feel good about both of my selves. I feel like I have a secret worth having again, and oddly enough, it makes it easier to keep."[30] Bright Boy's newfound popularity falls directly in line with what Ingrid Schoon writes regarding positive youth development. Within a greater context of chances and opportunities influencing youth development, Schoon recognizes the "long-standing question" inherent when studying "the individual and the context in which s/he is embedded."[31] Schoon goes on to recapitulate previous arguments: "On the one hand, it is argued that social context and conditions shape individual attributes and characteristics. . . . Alternatively it has been argued that individuals enter environments selectively by choice or through constraints imposed by their psychological characteristics."[32] Scott's school is his social context, one he must enter without choice, and—until this moment—has had psychological constraints imposed upon him by the ridicule of the student body. Furthermore, the social context introduced by Allison shapes his "individual attributes and characteristics" more than any other up to this point. A third social context for Scott regards Trent, and the physical distance apart from Trent in which the other two happen. Additionally, the new costume was obtained with the knowledge that Trent would not approve. Furthermore, Scott's new relationship with Allison is also something entirely taboo under Trent's rule. Scott asserts his own opinions and desires for the first time when they would evoke real-world consequences. Allison's presence in Scott's life allows him to act in direct conflict with what Trent would condone. In this way, Scott begins to shed his sidekick subservience. Furthermore, and more to the point in this case, Scott begins to move out of the oppression and control of an untrustworthy and psychologically abusive guardian (although Scott does not know that yet).

As Scott begins to move away from that oppression toward making his own decisions regarding right and wrong, it seems that he might be the only character in the book who holds a consistent conviction for seeking justice. This conviction is the aforementioned third element in Ferraiolo's sidekick redefinition. Trent's search for justice is obviously fake, or at best, long-ago corrupted. Dr. Chaotic's apparent motivation is a warped sense of justice; according to Allison, Dr. Chaotic believes he works to right certain injustices ignored by the confines of the law.[33] His underlying motivation also includes the financial arrangement with Trent. Allison begins to show signs of true conviction, which complicates the matter of exactly who ends up playing hero/sidekick at the end of the novel. While Scott holds the only overt conviction for seeking justice, there are those, like Allison, who either develop a sense for justice or reveal hidden motivations to uphold righteousness. These others include Louis, and Jake (the aforementioned bully at Scott's school). For most of the text, Jake is known only as a bully "as dumb as a bag of hammers" who picks on Scott on a regular basis.[34] However, after Trent shoots Scott with the dart of adrenaline, it is Jake who saves him. Jake is a plus intelligence who has long been employed in keeping Scott safe by encouraging the separation between Scott and his persona as Bright Boy.[35] Louis is another secret plus intelligence, although it is unclear whether or not he is a plus speed/plus strength as well.

While Louis and Jake have worked for the greater good all along, Scott is the only one who acts without knowing about the intrigue or deception going on. As such, his is an apparently purer form of "right"; for Scott, there are no gray areas and no compromises. This issue of determining right from wrong is hugely important in the world of heroes and sidekicks. In *Sidekicks*, this kind of morality falls directly in line with Trent's actions and Scott's reactions. Paul Bloomberg offers two basic understandings of morality. The first deals with "how one ought to behave toward others."[36] As Bloomberg continues to define this type of interpersonal consideration, he places it alongside justice, that which is "understood loosely to encompass all fair dealings between people."[37] Morality and justice, according to Bloomberg, are "often seen to have the same scope," bringing the understanding of one into alignment with an understanding of the other.[38] While the essays in *Morality and Self-Interest* become increasingly nuanced in regard to justice and whether or not one has sufficient reason to be socially just,[39] recognizing the fundamental connection between morality, justice, and how heroes/sidekicks must therefore act gives perfect context to the evaluation of Scott's actions in the latter half of *Sidekicks*.

What makes Scott's situation even more unique, and therefore worth more weight in the redefinition of sidekick, is the source of his commitment to justice: it was taught to him by the corrupted Trent. This is, again, the great irony in the text. The opportunistic and two-faced Trent instilled Scott's unwavering belief in fighting for good. As a six-year-old adoptee, it makes perfect sense that Scott would believe the dogma of his mentor/father figure—even if his father figure didn't believe it himself. Scott's childlike belief lets him act without hesitation when it comes to the final confrontation with Trent. In fact, Scott acts on those ideals in an act of faith when he confronts Trent at the end of the novel. His concern is for Allison's well-being (she was taken after Scott was given the adrenaline). In his search for her, Scott follows the direction of Jake, who speaks to him telepathically. Scott does not know about the various parts of the plan to defeat and discredit Trent: an Allison body-double has been given to Trent without his knowledge and there is a hidden camera broadcasting Trent's actions and confession. Additionally, and still unbeknownst to Scott, Louis and Allison are alive and well, and have been working with Jake (and others) to stop Trent for some time. Blind faith, then, is the closest approximation for what Scott exhibits as the lone heroic "tool" of the coalition working to stop Trent.

But could that lone hero have been someone else? Although *Sidekicks* is told from Scott's point of view, there arises another consideration: if Dr. Chaotic was working for the side of justice all along, that would mean Allison is another superhero sidekick. While Scott's unique situation calls without question for a redefinition of sidekick, Allison's actions complicate things even further, as she essentially helps deputize Scott to defeat Trent. Could a case be made for making Allison the hero of Scott's sidekick-as-hero novel? In many ways, yes. Allison provides a test case as equally intriguing as Scott. As a multifaceted character partially obscured through the nature of the first-person narration, Allison's actions and motivations are in question until the very end of the text. In terms of conflict, she shares, albeit partially, in Scott's major conflict: her parent. Scott's final conflict with his surrogate father is no accident (remembering from chapter 2 the importance of parental relationships in YA texts). In the same fashion, Allison has issues with her own father. According to Allison, Dr. Chaotic (real name Dr. Edward Simmons) is actually a passably good father. Regardless that he had an underage child take part in the elaborate fakery of Trent's good versus evil battles (somewhat akin to Batman's enlisting Carrie Kelly in *The Dark Knight Returns*), Allison notes that even when he had been sent to prison, her father always kept their lines of communication open: "My dad never stopped talking to me. . . . Even when he went away, we still talked."[40] Allison tells this to Scott only after Dr. Chaotic found out that about the changed costumes and public kissing: Dr. Chaotic has stopped talking to her.[41]

After all is said and done, it becomes clear that Allison was at least somewhat in the know when it came to Dr. Chaotic's plan(s) for defeating Trent: she allowed her father to create the body double used to trick Trent into thinking she was dead, she laid low and pretended to be dead while her father went to help Scott, and she waited in their old lab to help Scott finish Trent in front of the camera. Whether or not she knew that her father would sacrifice himself is unclear, although it is clear that he understood what was needed to save his daughter. Dr. Chaotic's sacrifice and Scott's willingness to confront Trent in an attempt to save Allison align with what Sonya Sachdeva et al. suggest: namely that "the choice that conflicts with selfishness can often be seen as morally right."[42] Although perceived as a villain, Dr. Chaotic exhibits morally justifiable behavior. Scott's morality is also intact. Although, to be thorough, Bloomberg would likely discount Dr. Chaotic and Scott's actions as moral or just because they lack the impartiality necessary, as "agents must not see their own interests, of the interest of their families, communities, etc., as having any special standing whatsoever in the decision procedure that determines what ought to be done."[43] This disqualifies any motivation regarding Allison, as Scott and Dr. Chaotic are obviously partial. However, because stopping Trent counts toward the greater good and safety of the citizens of New York, the claim for Scott's well-adjusted morality stands.

Even more to the point than the complicated parental relationship is Allison's hero/sidekick dynamic with Scott. During one of their dates, they hear a cry for help. Scott takes the lead, but Allison physically diffuses the situation. Afterward, she tells Scott of her remorse for not having helped more people in her past. Their work together is mutually deferential and comes with an ease of two who have been connected for years. Considering their similarities in age and experience, the question whether or not one plays the hero while the other plays the sidekick is convoluted. The book ends with

Allison and Scott heading out to answer a cry for help, free of their obligations to sidekick for Dr. Chaotic or Trent. Allison jokes about changing her name to "the Viper," while Scott could be "the Viper's assistant."[44] While this is said in jest, a final revelation that Allison also possesses plus intelligence puts her into the more intellectually advantageous position to assume the lead. Considering she was responsible for nearly all of their romantic decisions (skipping class, new costumes, when and how to kiss) also suggests her comfort in making command choices. Complicating this dynamic even further is the involvement of Jake and Louis, who have already shown their abilities in strategy and plan execution—which Scott has followed in lieu of making his own plans. Scott ends the novel by reaffirming his resolve to follow plans set out by Jake, Louis, and even Allison. While Scott's credibility does not hinge on his need to be the one making the decisions, he remains the "hero" of his self-told novel without becoming a "full-fledged hero" or ever embodying a typical sidekick position.

John David Anderson's *Sidekicked* also deals heavily with the desire to become a sidekick, but takes that premise in a completely different direction than Ferraiolo and *Sidekicks*. Anderson's text is based on a premise very similar to Ferraiolo's, and it could have been analyzed instead of Ferraiolo in the beginning of this chapter, as both establish a sidekick/protagonist in a world of superheroes. There are, however, at least two significant differences between the two texts. The first is that teenaged *Sidekicked* protagonist, Andrew Bean, does not get the girl in the end despite a good deal of romantic tension between him and Jenna, another sidekick. The second is Andrew's superhero/father figure is not a hypervigilant do-gooder (or even a villain masquerading as a do-gooder)—he is, in fact, a drunken recluse. Considering the weight these facts have on the redefinition of Andrew as a sidekick, *Sidekicked* provides the most insightful material in deciding just how far YA has taken sidekicks from their original inception.

Sidekicked takes place in a fictional city called Justica, where superheroes are born with their powers (attributed to unexplained genetic differences). Thirteen-year-old Andrew calls himself the Sensationalist because his senses are heightened far beyond those of a normal human. One important element that sets *Sidekicked* apart from other metanovels is Andrew's involvement with a secret sidekick training program code-named Highview Environmental Revitalization Organization (or H.E.R.O.), which allows Andrew and five other specially gifted middle school students to hone their abilities and train with their assigned superheroes.[45] Andrew and his fellow sidekicks-in-training treat H.E.R.O. like an elective extracurricular activity, which is, in fact, its cover at Highview Middle School. The concept of a sidekick training program is not unique to *Sidekicked*, as it has been used in a number of novels, comics, and films over the years. Notable examples include virtually any incarnation of Marvel's X-Men (particularly when focusing on Xavier's

"School for Gifted Youngsters"), Disney Channel's *Sky High* (2005), Revolution Studio's *Zoom* (2006), and DC's "Teen Titans." What makes H.E.R.O., and more specifically Andrew, unique is his status as a sidekick without a hero. The hero assigned to mentor him is the Titan, described during his heyday as "Nearly indestructible. Fists of iron. Nerves of steel. Heart of Gold."[46] The current-day Titan, however, tells Andrew "You do not want to be my sidekick . . . I am sorry. I just can't right now," essentially leaving him in sidekick limbo.[47] Andrew's hero will not mentor him, and as he's been told to be patient, he will not likely be assigned a new hero any time soon.[48]

Andrew's situation problematizes the status quo as he is a character who, according to the "Superhero Sidekick Code of Conduct," must act with conviction to honor his sworn allegiance to the Titan, but that same conviction forces him to respect the Titan's request that he keep his distance.[49] This Code of Conduct establishes a common morality for all the students in H.E.R.O., as well as the heroes they are attached to. The four rules of the code include a sidekick's commitments to: "always use his powers in the service of justice and honor" (helping those in need); never "compromise his super's secrets or his own"; protect innocent bystanders and "never take a life" as long as there is another option; accompany, protect, walk with, and trust in his super "above all else."[50] As a consequence of the Titan's desire to be left alone, Andrew essentially must function on his own. (Anderson himself acknowledges this fact, calling Andrew a "sort of a sidekick" because "to be a sidekick you have to have someone to stand beside and . . . you know . . . kick with."[51]) Furthermore, this absence of a superhero guiding force is the basis of nearly every form of conflict in the book. The Titan was once the most celebrated and powerful superhero the city (and probably the world) had known. Now, however, he has dropped off the grid and has become a drunken recluse. Every major plot thread leads toward forcing the Titan to reappear and assert himself once more. His absence also sets up a scenario where Andrew questions his self-worth regarding this father figure's absence in his life. (It should be emphasized that Andrew's home life is very stable. His mother and father live together with no sign of marital discord, and their concern for him is illustrated repeatedly. Nevertheless, Andrew keeps his identity as the Sensationalist a secret from them. Considering the nature of the text, his parents function in a very limited capacity beyond allowing Andrew to attend H.E.R.O.)

The absentee father figure makes Andrew eventually take a stand on his own—he chooses to stand and fight regardless of, or in place of, the reclusive Titan. Andrew has three conversations with the Titan over the course of the book; four if you count one given in flashback. The most important is the third; Andrew is summoned to learn the truth about the Titan's reclusiveness. Andrew hears the story of the Titan's decision from another reclusive and semiretired hero, Jim Rediford; the Titan is wracked with guilt over the death of a villain at his hands. Andrew enters the other room to speak with the Titan:

> I know what happened. It's the same with me sometimes. I see things. And hear things. From miles away. I know they're coming, and it pisses me off because I know I can't do anything about them. You can't save everybody, as much as you'd like to. It's just not possible. I know that. But that does not mean you stop trying. The city is in danger. You're in danger. The Code says I am supposed to stand beside you. To follow you. But I can't stand by you if you will not get up.[52]

This speech is interspersed with a good deal of description and introspection on Andrew's part, who all the while tries to spark some reaction from the hero who should have been mentoring him all along. Nothing happens: "The Titan does not move."[53]

An interesting insight into both Andrew and the Titan at this point comes from Bree Picower. While Picower explains the tools of inaction as they apply to social justice educators and the common disconnect between teaching social justice and acting upon those teachings, the tools of inaction can help explain why the Titan does not respond to Andrew. This, in turn, gives insight into Andrew's renewed commitment to action. Two tools of inaction mentioned by Picower are at play here. The first is the "tool of postponement," which suggests that the person in question would need "[his or her] temporary circumstances changed" so that he or she "would be better able to take action."[54] Another way to explain this tool of inaction is to state, "I'll do something when it affects me."[55] For the Titan, the circumstances that would need changing are his guilt/depression, his misunderstanding of what happened in the past (as he was not entirely culpable), and his physical deterioration due to inaction and alcohol consumption. He also does not act until he can no longer avoid it: he only does something when it affects him. Andrew does not have this choice. He finds himself neck-deep in the whole scheme from the beginning. The second tool working here is a tool of dismissal, the tool of "I can't make a difference."[56] This tool, according to Picower, comes from a sense of "powerlessness," allowing the Titan to "dismiss participating in something that [he] thought was hopeless."[57] The hopelessness for the Titan is not so much that justice will not be achieved, but that it would be hopeless *for him* to try to help achieve it. Because the city's current hero, the Fox, seems to have all things under control, any act on the part of the Titan would feel "as pointless as spitting in the wind."[58] Andrew, on the other hand, feels powerless every day of his life. However, he does not let this lead him into inaction, but the opposite.

The speech Andrew gives marks a turning point. In more than one way, this acts as Andrew's last effort as a sidekick. Up until this point, Andrew has tirelessly held faith in the Titan. While the public questioned his whereabouts, and other supers begrudgingly accepted the Titan's slide into obscurity, Andrew never lost faith that his mentor might snap out of it and becomes the behemoth of justice he once was . . . until now. After giving his speech, and seeing the Titan's nonreaction to it, Andrew wants to "scream at him," to "kick him off the bed," to "force him . . . to apologize."[59] He does not, citing the reason that "I just can't make myself believe anymore."[60] The Titan's choice to sit and not react to Andrew's speech is the final rejection. From this moment on, Andrew is on his own. The climax of the novel comes shortly thereafter, as does the plot twist revealing Jenna's involvement in the villain's actions. (Jenna's assigned hero is the Fox, who turns out to be the vengeful returned daughter of a former nemesis of the Titan.) Before finding this out, Andrew embarks on his own attempt to save those in harm's way—aided in part by his desire to find and save Jenna. Anderson layers rejection upon rejection onto Andrew: the Titan's repeated rejections; the pseudo-rejection of Jenna (although it seems as though she would have chosen Andrew had she not ended up in prison); the difficulty in having a largely intellectually useful power instead of something physically intimidating. These rejections are what stand between Andrew and whether or not he is a traditionally defined sidekick.

The basis of Andrew's impassioned speech to the Titan no doubt finds its germination in a conversation he has with Jenna. This conversation is arguably the most important piece of the novel. It also becomes intriguing from a romantic point of view as it ends with Jenna's kissing Andrew. Andrew's relationship with Jenna further aligns the text with a YA audience: he finds himself in a love triangle. Andrew works to determine whether or not Jenna prefers him or newcomer Gavin. Gavin, a sidekick with powers almost entirely different from Andrew's (his skin can become almost impenetrable, making him something akin to X-Men's Colossus, or even the Hulk), almost instantly complicates the long-held affection Andrew has had for Jenna. The love triangle continues to marginalize Andrew, already something of the outsider in H.E.R.O. due to the nature of his powers; instead of Jenna's agility and strength or Mike's power to shoot electricity from his hands, Andrew can sense "Sodium chloride . . . one crystal dissolved in about two ounces of water."[61] The triangle plays out over the course of the novel, including Jenna's inviting both Gavin and Andrew on a date (at the same time), kissing both of them (at different times), and admitting her confusion over whom she likes.

Jenna's liberties with Andrew's feelings regarding a potential romance have a significant impact on Andrew's embodiment as a sidekick, as they fundamentally change how he sees himself. Andrew begins the novel as a never-been-kissed seventh grader harboring romantic feelings for his closest female friend. As the novel progresses, Andrew must grapple with Jenna's interest in him, including her kissing him,[62] which is entirely new territory. In terms of his development as a young man, this is part and parcel of the maturation process—or at least is not uncommon. The effect it has on his shifting personal awareness is significant, however, but not in the same sense as Scott's relationship with Allison in *Sidekicks*. For Andrew, the new connection with Jenna is always complicated, fragmented, and confusing. What it does grant him, aside from classic middle school angst, is an opportunity to face evildoers in the heat of battle. During the date to which Jenna invites both Andrew and Gavin (a fund-raising event including all of the city's wealthy patrons), the villains of the book attack and force the three sidekicks to engage. Andrew protects the city's mayor as he tries to get him out of the building—an act that proves his worth, but one given to him by Jenna. Andrew's powers keep him alive, but do not help in thwarting the enemy. Jenna's invitation brings Andrew into an unforeseen and unsanctioned moment of heroism, but keeps him within the realm of sidekickery: Jenna and Gavin call the shots until the Fox arrives. Furthermore, Andrew goes unrecognized as a superpowered entity by the police officers who show up. After successfully getting the mayor out of harm's way, Andrew tries to reenter the fray. However, as he's not wearing a mask, he is "just Andrew," and is evacuated along with everyone else.[63] When the mayor gives a statement on the news that night, Andrew waits for him to "say something, to call us out."[64] All the mayor says, however, is a thank you to the Fox and "all the other nameless heroes who helped to stop this vicious attack."[65] Andrew feels this is enough, because "even being a nameless hero is still better than being no hero at all."[66] While being a nameless hero allows Andrew to feel some long-overdue pride in his abilities, making him feel like he "finally [has] a secret that's worth keeping," his actions were not necessarily those of a *super*hero.[67] In this way then, as a sidekick facing evil without a hero, mask, costume, or utility belt to aid him, Andrew broadens the scope of who might qualify as a sidekick or in what circumstances a sidekick might emerge. To further strip him of any kind of sidekick moniker, H.E.R.O. is suspended after the attack.[68] Andrew is now not even a sidekick-in-training to an absent hero: he is only a gifted ordinary citizen.

Understanding the implications of Andrew's identity as an ordinary citizen leads back to the aforementioned, all-important conversation he has with Jenna. This conversation also reveals how Jenna impacts the sidekick status quo. As they sit outside of the school, Jenna turns to Andrew and asks, "Do you think I am good? A good person, I mean?"[69] What follows is perhaps the longest conversational back-and-forth in the book. Jenna presses Andrew's answers, making him question exactly what he believes "being good" really means. Even his general answer does not satisfy her: "You do the right thing most of the time, and you make some mistakes, but you learn from them, and you try to help other people or at least stay out of their way, and you do not kill anybody and you're, you know, basically good."⁷⁰ Andrew's answer fairly represents what "doing-one's-best" might look like for a sidekick-in-training. Jenna, however, finally cuts to the chase: "Sometimes I do not think there really is a good and bad. . . . At least, not the way we are always taught. Sometimes I think there are just choices and consequences."⁷¹ She follows this with the increasingly complex yet familiar moral dilemma whether the ends justify the means. The answer Andrew finally comes up with is rooted in increasing confusion as he attempts to "figure out why she is asking me all of this." He tells her, "I do not *know*, Jenna. It's neither [good nor bad] . . . you did what you thought was right."⁷² For Andrew, this makes the most sense in a convoluted situation. In light of what Andrew inherently knows as a conscientious human being, as well as a sidekick trying to live up to the Superhero Sidekick Code of Conduct, doing what seems right at the time is enough. Jenna, unbeknownst to Andrew (or readers for that matter), grapples to reconcile the disparate elements of the Fox's plan: would Jenna ultimately do good by aiding the Fox to secretly kill the Titan, making the Fox the greatest hero the city has ever known? This would allow the two of them, theoretically, to do unquestionable good in the future. Jenna and Andrew's conversation carries the heaviest implications of the novel: so much so that Anderson suggests that teachers ask guided questions concerning "the difference between good and evil, right and wrong."⁷³

Furthermore, the back-and-forth between Andrew and Jenna mirrors David Schmidtz's explanation of typical arguments involving morality. Schmidtz states, "Even so, when people argue about whether something like affirmative action is right, they have a shared understanding that it *matters* whether affirmative action is right."⁷⁴ While it does not matter exactly what two or more people might be arguing, the point Schmidtz makes is that they have a vested interest and deeply seated belief that the argument matters. Part of Schmidtz's writing is intended to offer a counterargument to previously published writings on morality, namely whether or not acting on moral grounds requires a "special kind of reason."⁷⁵ Schmidtz's answer suggests that morality does *not* need to prove any kind of special reason before one takes action. Even without proof of these special reasons, Schmidtz states that "we have [a] basis for saying we *ought* to conform to commonsense morality," which coincides directly with his choice of title: "Because It's Right."⁷⁶ In the case of *Sidekicked*, Jenna obviously cares about the outcome of their conversation—she is the discussion's instigator, and she has the most to lose depending on the outcome. Andrew cares about the topic as well, even though his morality is not in question.

Andrew has easy answers, in part because he does not actively serve as a sidekick. Jenna, however, has come to believe that "there's an awful lot of gray in the world."⁷⁷ Because the Fox is a villain-turned-hero intent on retribution, Jenna is more of a tool to be used than a sidekick to be trusted.

Unlike Trent hiding the truth from Scott in *Sidekicks*, the Fox has chosen to bring Jenna into her plans: to help her manipulate the public's view of who is heroic and who is not. When the final confrontation occurs, however, Jenna chooses Andrew over the Fox—largely in part because of their friendship and the previous conversation on morality. When thinking of Jenna in terms of the whole narrative, she does not quite fit the typical sidekick mold either. In fact, if judging Jenna by the book's internal Superhero Sidekick Code of Conduct, she fails all four at some point or another, and fails several of them a number of times. Jenna could similarly be considered a criminal accomplice, a double-agent, or a "confused, powerful, and impressionable" thirteen-year-old.[78]

Jenna's scenario creates a sidekick-definition problem as complicated as the one presented by Andrew. This plays into another reoccurring theme Anderson uses throughout the novel: that it's not about Andrew. While this might make the paradoxical metanovel even more of a paradox, the phrase "it's not about you" is spoken to Andrew no fewer than four times (or five, if you count Andrew's personal question, "Is it me?" when the Titan refuses to mentor him; the Titan squeezes his shoulder in comfort, suggesting that no, it is not he.[79]). The first two "it's not about you" are spoken by Mr. Masters, the teacher in charge of H.E.R.O. He says it to Andrew as a way to explain the Titan's apparent disinterest in mentoring him.[80] Jenna says the third to Andrew during their conversation about good and evil.[81] Finally, one of the villain's henchmen, the Jack of Clubs, says the fourth right before he attempts to kill Andrew. After the Jack of Clubs says "I am sorry, kid, really. This is not about you," Andrew thinks, "Why does everybody keep *saying* that?"[82] The moment of cognition pays off beyond the obvious comedic effect. Andrew recognizes there are forces acting that he cannot see; part of the mystery of the novel comes from his unveiling who is behind the criminal activity. The connection Andrew has with the Titan, weak though it may be, is what continually brings Andrew into harm's way: the Fox wants to flush the Titan out of hiding. On the surface, it is all about the Titan. From this standpoint, Andrew is nothing more than a bystander in his own novel. In fact, although he is present at the final showdown, it is Jenna who defeats the Fox and saves Andrew and the Titan. Jenna points out that when it comes to their education as sidekicks, they are at the guidance of a single individual. She states, "Just like Mr. Masters was using you . . . shaping us all into what *he* thought the world needed in order to save it. That's the way it works, Drew."[83] Furthermore, even the title, *Sidekicked*, suggests the past-tense action of kicking someone aside—which is what seems to be happening to Andrew over the course of his own tale.

Although Andrew is something of a bystander in the wrong place at the wrong time throughout his own story, the way his story resolves offers something beyond what Ferraiolo's text offers: Andrew gladly embraces a future as a nonsidekick (at least for the time being). The Titan sees Andrew at the bowling alley again, this time to tell him he is officially retiring. He offers Andrew the chance to be his sidekick for one night, to "probably find some robbers to rough up, rescue some old ladies. Maybe try to dig up some drug dealers or something."[84] Andrew lets him off of the hook, citing that he "Didn't bring my mask."[85] As Andrew watched the Titan walk away, he muses about how he might be "paired up with" a new hero someday, but "for now, I really do not care . . . my friends are waiting for me inside. And I am feeling normal for a change."[86] In many ways, this is what Andrew has asked for all throughout the book. Jenna asks him if he wants to be normal, and he responds with "[e]very day."[87] When Andrew visits Jenna in prison, she asks him again if he has "ever wanted to be normal," to which he gives "pretty much the same answer. 'Yeah. Sometimes. Maybe.'"[88] Although he ends the tale as a sidekick-in-training without a hero, his world is complete, and he is content. By definition, to be a sidekick is to have someone to follow and learn from. Andrew, by the end of the novel, is not a sidekick, and that's okay.

These self-aware sidekick novels, *Sidekicks* and *Sidekicked*, share something rather important: the sidekicks have an ultimately untrustworthy hero. Looking back once more at Watson and Holmes, it is striking that Watson, as sidekick, also told and narrated their adventures. Watson never doubted Holmes, and never needed to (although this sometimes gets complicated), and therefore never needed to assume the role of master detective in his stead. Watson writes the Sherlock Holmes stories (or Conan Doyle writes them from Watson's point of view, whichever one prefers), but never shows signs of ambition beyond his role. Scott and Andrew, however, change that established role by actively desiring the hero role as they narrate their own novels. They do so by engaging with and adapting YA conventions. By the end of *Sidekicks*, Scott does not need to be the hero deciding what to do or whom to save. Scott remains the hero of his self-told novel without becoming a "full-fledged hero" or ever achieving a typical sidekick position. Andrew is something different altogether: the younger of the two characters studied, his sidekick separation at the end of his novel is the most complete. Instead of going forth with the intention to become a hero, Andrew achieves a state of personal contentedness beyond (or in spite of) his sidekick identity.

NOTES

1. Brian Tallerico, review of *Teen Titans Go! To the Movies*, directed by Aaron Horvath and Peter Rida Michail, RogerEbert.com, July 23, 2018, https://www.rogerebert.com/reviews/teen-titans-go-to-the-movies-2018.
2. Ibid.
3. Jack Ferraiolo. *Sidekicks* (New York: Abrams, 2011), 31.

4. For more on the idea of changing "superhero iconography," see Alex S. Romagnoli and Gian S. Pagnucci, *Enter the Superheroes: American Values, Culture, and the Canon of Superhero Literature* (Lanham: Scarecrow, 2013), 81–87.

5. Romagnoli and Pagnucci, *Enter the Superheroes*, 46–47; Kristen Geaman, ed. *Dick Grayson, Boy Wonder: Scholars and Creators on 75 Years of Robin, Nightwing and Batman* (Jefferson: McFarland, 2015), 118.

6. Ferraiolo, *Sidekicks*, 47.
7. Ibid., 174.
8. Ibid., 115–17.
9. Ibid., 212, 252–53.
10. Ibid., 117, 116.

11. Bradford W. Wright, *Comic Book Nation: The Transformation of Youth Culture in America* (Baltimore: Johns Hopkins University Press, 2001), 17; Romagnoli and Pagnucci, *Enter the Superheroes*, 172.

12. Romagnoli and Pagnucci, *Enter the Superheroes*, 47–48; Jim Starlin and Marv Wolfman, *Batman: A Death in the Family* (1988; New York: DC Comics, 2011), 107–8.

13. Ferraiolo, *Sidekicks*, 237.
14. Frank Miller, *The Dark Knight Returns* (New York: DC Comics, 2002), 82.
15. Ferraiolo, *Sidekicks*, 68.

16. Penelope Brown and Stephen C. Levinson, *Politeness: Some Universals in Language Usage* (Cambridge: Cambridge University Press, 1987), 61.

17. Ibid.
18. Ibid.
19. Ibid.

20. Ronald Wardhaugh and Janet M. Fuller, *An Introduction to Sociolinguistics*, 7th ed. (West Sussex: Wiley-Blackwell, 2015), 257.

21. Ibid., 256.
22. Ferraiolo, *Sidekicks*, 76.
23. Ibid., 80.
24. Ibid., 83.
25. Gen. 2:25.
26. Ferraiolo, *Sidekicks*, 104.
27. Ibid., 110.
28. Ibid., 158–59.
29. Ibid., 157.
30. Ibid., 163.

31. Ingrid Schoon, "Life Chances and Opportunities in Times of Social Change: Evidence from Two British Birth Cohorts," in *Approaches to Positive Youth Development*, ed. Rainer K. Silbereisen and Richard M. Lerner (London: SAGE, 2007), 163.

32. Ibid.
33. Ferraiolo, *Sidekicks*, 134.
34. Ibid., 34.
35. Ibid., 242–46.

36. Paul Bloomberg, ed. *Morality and Self-Interest* (New York: Oxford University Press, 2008), 3.

37. Ibid.
38. Ibid.
39. Ibid., 15–30.
40. Ferraiolo, *Sidekicks*, 181.
41. Ibid.

42. Sonya Sachdeva et al., "The Role of Self-Sacrifice in Moral Dilemmas," *Plos ONE* 10, no. 6 (2015): 2.

43. Bloomberg, *Morality and Self-Interest*, 3.
44. Ferraiolo, *Sidekicks*, 309.
45. John David Anderson, *Sidekicked* (New York: HarperCollins, 2013), 30.
46. Ibid., 68.

47. Ibid., 78.
48. Ibid., 52.
49. Ibid., 41.
50. Ibid.
51. John David Anderson, *Sidekicked: Teacher's Guide* (johndavidanderson.org, 2013), 1.
52. Anderson, *Sidekicked*, 292–93.
53. Ibid., 293.
54. Bree Picower, "Tools of Inaction: The Impasse between Teaching Social Issues and Creating Social Change," *Teachers and Teaching: Theory and Practice* 21, no. 7 (2015): 914.
55. Ibid., 915.
56. Ibid., 918.
57. Ibid.
58. Ibid.
59. Anderson, *Sidekicked*, 293–94.
60. Ibid., 294.
61. Ibid., 139.
62. Ibid., 180.
63. Ibid., 243.
64. Ibid., 251.
65. Ibid.
66. Ibid.
67. Ibid., 254.
68. Ibid., 258.
69. Ibid., 171.
70. Ibid., 173.
71. Ibid., 175.
72. Ibid., 179.
73. Anderson, "*Sidekicked*: Teacher's Guide," 3.
74. David Schmidtz, "Because It's Right," in *Morality and Self-Interest*, ed. Philip Bloomberg (New York: Oxford University Press, 2008), 81–82.
75. Ibid., 81.
76. Ibid., 82, 79.
77. Anderson, *Sidekicked*, 368.
78. Ibid., 369.
79. Ibid., 78.
80. Ibid., 51.
81. Ibid., 174.
82. Ibid., 197.
83. Ibid., 369.
84. Ibid., 372.
85. Ibid., 373.
86. Ibid.
87. Ibid., 180.
88. Ibid., 369.

Conclusion

Studying sidekicks fills a significant hole within the discipline of literary studies, as very few (if any) studies have devoted full attention to this type of character to this extent. Most studies that do mention sidekicks use them in a cursory or passing consideration. Here, however, in dedicating my entire focus on the sidekicks and how they interact with, work with, react against, and ultimately separate away from their heroes, I have attempted to rectify this oversight. It has also been stimulating and gratifying to find such ongoing development for sidekicks within YA. In fact, I would go as far as to suggest that YA's treatment of the sidekick has been indispensable to the evolution of this character (and will no doubt continue in this regard).

While the four well-established sidekick roles have long been utilized in detective novels, comic books, and/or fantasy texts, YA has recently shown at least three ways a sidekick can evolve beyond these "original" or classic characterizations of a hero's sidekick. The processes through which sidekick elevation can occur offer a complex look into the ways the boundaries of sidekick use have been changed. Three such processes have been outlined here. The "secondary hero" has the broadest overall appeal and possibility, as it taps into an author's freedom for further character development over sequential stories. That decision still needs to be intentional and dynamic, however, as many sidekicks never evolve beyond their initially established roles. Narrowing the focus comes to the "sidekick sequel," a specific version of the parallel novel. It is arguable that the sidekick-focused parallel novel offers the greatest level of complexity when it comes to elevating a sidekick. This complexity comes from the inherent narrative challenges and opportunities that accompany retelling a previously established narrative. If the intention also includes maintaining fidelity to the original novel, threading or interweaving new and challenging developments to characters/sidekicks or events presents a literary quagmire through which to successfully navigate. The third avenue for evolution, the "self-aware sidekick novel," wipes the literary slate clean (or offers a new slate entirely) and allows for unrestricted sidekick development. This avenue also taps into the history of comic book superheroes, as the sidekicks in question are keenly aware of the traditions they embody from the beginning of their narratives. In this way—and I believe this to be an important distinction—the self-aware sidekicks build upon their foundational forebears and forge new literary ground for the sidekick character.

Furthermore, aligning with the idea of building upon a foundation and forging new ground, part of the expressed purpose for this study has been to establish such a foundation for studying sidekicks. Future scholars (including myself) can (and should) build upon this foundation by deriving continually deeper insights regarding sidekicks within scholars' respective fields of specialization. The foundation established here is only a work in part: as is the case with ever-developing fields of literary study, much work remains to be done. I previously alluded to a number of theoretical lenses and/or considerations that I intentionally did not use or pursue, mostly in the interest of keeping this study tightly focused. Some of these considerations inevitably and unavoidably made their way into the analysis regardless, and they have made the greater study stronger. However, there remains a rich array of possible explorations to consider; when I began my study of sidekicks, I only partially understood how fruitful this avenue of literary study could be.

One question that remains regards how to consider the many sidekicks that "fall away" into an antagonist role, or vice versa when an antagonist becomes a sidekick. For instance, *The Lord of the Rings* brings Gollum into the Frodo/Sam dynamic, and gives Frodo an untrustworthy, antagonistic second sidekick—made all the more concrete after Frodo sends Sam away. On a lesser scale, Harry Potter's relationship with Ron often strains to the point of argument and resentment. *Harry Potter and The Deathly Hallows* even finds Ron angrily leaving Harry's side for a considerable amount of time. The antagonistic sidekick would be an intriguing topic for a YA study or even a fan fiction study, as the "frenemy" appears in these kinds of literature, especially when involving conflict between friends and relatives. In and of itself, fan fiction exists as a macrocosm of study opportunity: how does the fan fiction community use sidekicks? Or, in what ways can studying the fan fiction community reveal the influence it has on its inspirational text(s), and vice versa? As authors can (and often do) interact with their fan bases/readers during the writing process, the potential influence fans and fandom have on subsequent books (and characters) cannot be overlooked.

Another consideration that arose, but was too unwieldy to include is the pantheons of sidekicks in a given fictive "universe." For example, the cinematic *Star Wars* universe presents a great number of hero/sidekick pairings:

Han Solo and Chewbacca, C-3PO and R2-D2 (who are themselves, at any given time, sidekicks to several major characters), and even the ewoks from *Return of the Jedi*. The characters who can use the force even have built-in apprentice/master relationships: jedi/padawan, sith/apprentice. Some of the more recent incarnations of *Star Wars* films, television, comics, novels, and video games following the original trilogy's cinematic release are arguably geared toward a younger audience. For instance, the television show *Star Wars: The Clone Wars* would be particularly conducive to this kind of study: it is a YA, computer-animated series that develops the relationship between Jedi Knight Anakin Skywalker and his Padawan Ahsoka Tano over the course of seven seasons (as of 2018).

One of the richest untapped veins of sidekick research is the animal sidekick. Again, to keep even this short consideration manageable, I will limit the possibilities here to YA texts. Children's books like Beverly Cleary's *Henry and Ribsy* heavily rely upon the boy-and-his-dog story line. On the opposite end of the spectrum are personified animals, particularly those found in virtually every animated Disney feature (Sven, Flounder, Abu, Meeko, Pascal, etc.). When it comes to fantasy and mystery, the animal sidekick becomes something else again in worlds less constricted by "natural" laws of nature and physics. Returning to the example of Jennifer Strange in *The Last Dragonslayer*, the Quarkbeast is a better sidekick to Jennifer than Tiger in many ways—he accompanies her on more errands, he has a preexisting relationship with her at the book's outset, and he is an intimidating physical presence. In a general sense, animal sidekicks range from less intelligent and nonverbal to highly intelligent.

Along the lines of highly intelligent animal sidekicks, but in a move that takes the complexity of the animal sidekick to even greater depths, Philip Pullman's fantasy trilogy *His Dark Materials* has a unique vision of the animal sidekick. Pullman pairs female hero Lyra with her animal sidekick Pantalaimon (a male). Pantalaimon is highly intelligent and acts as Lyra's conscience in many regards: he is Jiminy Cricket to Lyra's Pinocchio. Pantalaimon is only one example of Pullman's *dæmons*; all of Pullman's human characters have an opposite-sex animal counterpart. They are essentially an external, tangible manifestation of a character's soul. The textual, extratextual, and philosophical implications abound.

A third example of the variation of the animal sidekick can be found with Gurgi's devotion to his hero Taran in Lloyd Alexander's high fantasy pentalogy, *The Chronicles of Prydain*. Alexander describes Gurgi as something between an animal and a man—someone who does not quite fit with either world, and who has consequently been shunned by both. I look to Gurgi, therefore, as one who exists as both a human companion and an animal sidekick. I suggest that one of the more emotionally fulfilling elements of

Alexander's series is watching the devotion grow between Gurgi and Taran, who are ultimately destined to be separated.

Similar to Gurgi and Taran in *Prydain* is Grover in *Percy Jackson and the Olympians*. As a satyr, Grover is Percy's part-animal sidekick. Characters like Gurgi and Grover bring to mind questions asking what it means to be human. As Gurgi has been shunned by both "natural" humans and beasts, he is therefore something entirely unique even as he performs as though he were a human (and yes, "performs" brings with it any number of increasingly complex avenues of investigative potential). Furthermore, as a satyr in the Percy Jackson universe, Grover has a physical connection to the earth: opening the door for an ecocritical and/or other ecological reading.

In a move that could be used to study animal sidekicks, antagonistic sidekicks, or entire pantheons of sidekicks, a much more detailed and complete study of gross constituent units of sidekicks could prove enlightening. This kind of study would necessarily delve much more deeply into the theories behind structuralism. Naturally, as is the case with many structuralist studies, the logical reaction would be to take the opportunity to then challenge or deconstruct the initial study. Such an ongoing semiotic conversation regarding sidekicks would undoubtedly be useful.

Bibliography

"The 100 Best Young Adult Books of All Time." *Time*. Accessed December 18, 2018. http://time.com/100-best-young-adult-books/.
Alexander, Lloyd. *The Castle of Lyre*. New York: Random, 1990.
Anderson, John David. *Sidekicked*. New York: HarperCollins, 2013.
———. *Sidekicked: Teacher's Guide*. johndavidanderson.org. 2013.
Aristotle. *The Rhetoric and the Poetics of Aristotle*. Translated by W. Rhys Roberts and Ingram Bywater. New York: McGraw, 1984.
Asher-Perrin, Emily. "Neville Longbottom Is the Most Important Person in *Harry Potter*—And Here's Why." Tor.com. Macmillan. Last modified November 19, 2013. https://www.tor.com/2013/11/19/neville-longbottom-is-the-most-important-person-in-harry-potter/.
Attebery, Brian. *The Fantasy Tradition in American Literature: From Irving to Le Guin*. Bloomington: Indiana University Press, 1980.
Baker, Deirdre F. "Reader at Large: Musings on Diverse Worlds." *Horn Book Magazine* 83, no. 1 (2007): 41–47.
Barrow, Craig, and Diana Barrow. "Le Guin's *Earthsea*: Voyages in Consciousness." *Extrapolation* 32, no.1 (1991): 20–44.
"Batman: The Legacy Continues." *Batman: The Animated Series. Vol 1*. Burbank, CA: Warner Home Video, 2004. DVD.
Bell, J. L. "Success in Stasis: Dick Grayson's Thirty Years as a Boy Wonder." In *Dick Grayson, Boy Wonder: Scholars and Creators on 75 Years of Robin, Nightwing and Batman*, edited by Kristen Geaman, 8–27. Jefferson: McFarland, 2015.
Blackmore, Tim. "Ender's Beginning: Battling the Military in Orson Scott Card's *Ender's Game*." *Extrapolation* 32, no. 2 (1991): 124–42.
Bloomberg, Paul, ed. *Morality and Self-Interest*. New York: Oxford University Press, 2008.
Brown, Penelope, and Stephen C. Levinson. *Politeness: Some Universals in Language Usage*. Cambridge: Cambridge University Press, 1987.
Buchanan, Ron. "'Side by Side': The Role of the Sidekick." *Studies in Popular Culture* 26, no. 1 (2003): 15–26.
Calhoun, Craig, Joseph Gerteis, James Moody, Steven Pfaff, and Indermohan Virk, eds. *Contemporary Sociological Theory*. 3rd ed. Wiley-Blackwell, 2012.
Campbell, Joseph. *The Hero with a Thousand Faces*. New Jersey: Princeton University Press, 1972.
Card, Orson Scott. *Ender's Game*. New York: Starscape, 2002.
———. *Ender's Shadow*. New York: Tor, 2000.
———. "Looking Back." YALSA. Accessed December 28, 2018. http://www.ala.org/yalsa/booklistsawards/bookawards/margaretaedwards/maeprevious/anniversary.

Cart, Michael. *Young Adult Literature: From Romance to Realism*. Chicago: ALA, 2010.
Carter, Betty. "Adult Books for Young Adults." *The English Journal* 86, no. 3 (1997): 63–67.
Cervantes, Miguel de. *Don Quixote*. Edited by Diana de Armas Wilson. Translated by Burton Raffel. New York: Norton, 1999.
Chatman, Seymour. *Story and Discourse: Narrative Structure in Fiction and Film*. Ithaca, NY: Cornell University Press, 1989.
Collings, Michael R. "The Epic of *Dune*: Epic Traditions in Modern Science Fiction." In *Aspects of Fantasy: Selected Essays from the Second International Conference on the Fantastic in the Arts*, edited by William Coyle. 131–39. Westport: Greenwood, 1981.
Collins, Suzanne. *The Hunger Games*. New York: Scholastic, 2008.
Coogan, Peter. *Superhero: The Secret Origin of a Genre*. Austin: MonkeyBrain, 2006.
Corliss, Richard. "Can Pixar Still Go Up?" *Time*. Last modified June 24, 2013. http://content.time.com/time/magazine/article/0,9171,2145505,00.html.
Culler, Johnathon. *Structuralist Poetics: Structuralism, Linguistics and the Study of Literature*. London: Routledge, 1975.
Day, Sara K. "Liars and Cheats: Crossing the Lines of Childhood, Adulthood, and Morality in *Ender's Game*." *English Studies in Canada* 38, no. 3–4 (2012): 207–25.
Dirda, Michael. "Holmes and Away." *New Statesman*. November 7, 2011: 42–43.
Doty, William G. *Mythography: The Study of Myths and Rituals*, 2nd ed. Tuscaloosa: University of Alabama Press, 2000.
Doyle, Arthur Conan. *A Study in Scarlet*. Edited by Owen Dudley Edwards. Oxford: Oxford University Press, 1999.
Doyle, Christine. "Orson Scott Card's Ender and Bean: The Exceptional Child as Hero." *Children's Literature in Education* 35, no. 4 (2004): 301–18.
Doyle, Christine, and Susan Louise Stewart. "*Ender's Game* and *Ender's Shadow*: Orson Scott Card's Postmodern School Stories." *The Lion and the Unicorn* 28, no. 2 (2004): 186–202.
Dyer, Carolyn Stewart, and Nancy Tillman Romalov, eds. *Rediscovering Nancy Drew*. Iowa City: University of Iowa Press, 1995.
Edlund, Ben. *The Tick: Omnibus: Sunday through Wednesday*. Quincy: New England Comics, 1995.
Edwards, Owen. "Introduction" to *A Study in Scarlet*, by Arthur Conan Doyle. Edited by Owen Edwards, ix–xxxviii. Oxford: Oxford University Press, 1999.
Entenman, Elizabeth. "Ah, So This Is Why Snape Hated Neville Longbottom So Much." Hello Giggles. Last modified August 22, 2016. https://hellogiggles.com/reviews-coverage/books/snape-neville-theory/.
Ferraiolo, Jack. *Sidekicks*. New York: Abrams, 2011.
Fford, Jasper. *The Last Dragonslayer*. New York: Houghton, 2012.
Foote, Stephanie. "Bookish Women: Reading Girls' Fiction: A Response to Julia Mickenberg." *American Literary History* 19, no. 2 (2007): 521–26.
Francus, Marilyn. "Virtuous Foundlings and Excessive Bastards." *The Eighteenth Century* 49, no. 1 (2008): 87–94.
Frye, Northrop. *Anatomy of Criticism: Four Essays*. Princeton: Princeton University Press, 1957.
Garbowski, Christopher. "The Comedy of Enchantment in *The Lord of the Rings*." *Christianity and Literature* 60, no. 2 (2011): 273–86.
Geaman, Kristen, ed. *Dick Grayson, Boy Wonder: Scholars and Creators on 75 Years of Robin, Nightwing and Batman*. Jefferson: McFarland, 2015.
Goffman, Erving. *The Presentation of Self in Everyday Life*. New York: Doubleday, 1959.
Greenblatt, Stephen, ed. *The Norton Shakespeare*, 2nd ed. New York: Norton, 2008.
Haber, David. "Neville Longbottom: The Other Chosen One." Beyond Hogwarts. Last modified May 28, 2007. https://www.beyondhogwarts.com/harry-potter/articles/neville-longbottom-the-other-chosen-one.html.
Harrison Bergeron. Directed by Bruce Pittman. Aired August 13, 1995, on Showtime. https://www.youtube.com/watch?v=XBcpuBRUdNs.
Harry Potter and the Goblet of Fire. Directed by Mike Newell. Burbank, CA: Warner Bros. Pictures, 2005. DVD.

Herbert, Frank. *Dune*. New York: Penguin, 1990.
Hogan, Walter. *Humor in Young Adult Literature: A Time to Laugh*. Lanham: Scarecrow, 2005.
Hollindale, Peter. "The Last Dragon of Earthsea." *Children's Literature in Education* 34, no. 3 (2003): 183–93.
Hoppenstand, Gary, ed. *The Dime Novel Detective*. Bowling Green: Bowling Green University Press, 1982.
The Incredibles. Bird, Brad, dir. 2004; Walt Disney Home Entertainment, 2005. DVD.
Inness, Sherrie A. "Is Nancy Drew Queer? Popular Reading Strategies for the Lesbian Reader." *Women's Studies* 26, no. 3–4 (1997): 343–72.
Jung, C. G. *The Archetypes and the Collective Unconscious*. Translated by R. F. C. Hull. New Jersey: Princeton University Press, 1981.
Jurgens, Dan, Jenny Ordway, Louise Simonson, and Roger Stern. *The Death of Superman*. New York: DC Comics, 1993.
Keene, Carolyn. *Nancy Drew Mystery Series: The Secret of Shadow Ranch*. New York: Grosset, 2002.
Lawrence, John Shelton, and Robert Jewett. *The Myth of the American Superhero*. Grand Rapids: Eerdmans, 2002.
Lee, Harper. *To Kill a Mockingbird*. New York: Warner, 1982.
Le Guin, Ursula K. *Earthsea Revisioned*. Cambridge: Children's Lit. New England, 1993.
———. *Tehanu*. New York: Atheneum, 1990.
———. *The Tombs of Atuan*. New York: Atheneum, 1971.
———. *A Wizard of Earthsea*. New York: Houghton, 1968.
Levi-Strauss, Claude. *Structural Anthropology*. Translated by Claire Jacobson and Brooke G. Schoepf. New York: Basic, 1963.
Littlefield, Holly. "Unlearning Patriarchy: Ursula Le Guin's Feminist Consciousness in *The Tombs of Atuan* and *Tehanu*." *Extrapolation* 36, no. 3 (1995): 244–58.
Lobdell, Jared. *Rise of Tolkienien Fantasy*. Chicago: Open Court, 2005.
Longhofer, Wesley, and Daniel Winchester. *Social Theory Re-wired: New Connections to Classical and Contemporary Perspectives*, 2nd ed. New York: Routledge, 2016.
Lynch, Paul. "Not Trying to Talk Alike and Succeeding: The Authoritative Word and Internally-Persuasive Word in *Tom Sawyer* and *Huckleberry Finn*." *Studies in the Novel* 38, no. 2 (2006): 172–86.
Lyon Clark, Beverly, ed. *The Adventures of Tom Sawyer: A Norton Critical Edition*. By Mark Twain. New York: Norton, 2007.
"Marvel Movies: Marvel Cinematic Universe (MCU)." Marvel. Accessed December 28, 2018. https://www.marvel.com.
McLauchlin, Jim. "Batman's 10 Greatest Robins." Newsarama. Last modified March 23, 2018. https://www.newsarama.com/15683-ranking-the-robins-from-10-to-1-yes-there-are-10.html.
McLean, Susan. "The Power of Women in Ursula K. Le Guin's *Tehanu*." *Extrapolation* 38, no. 2 (1997): 110–18.
Miller, Frank. *The Dark Knight Returns*. New York: DC Comics, 2002.
Morrison, Grant, Andy Kubert, and Jesse Delperdang. *Batman and Son*. New York: DC Comics, 2007.
Mortimer, John. "Introduction" to *The Best of Wodehouse: An Anthology*, by P. G. Wodehouse, ix-xvi. New York: Random, 2007.
Nadeau, Frances A. "The Mother/Daughter Relationship in Young Adult Fiction." *The ALAN Review* 22, no. 2 (1995): 14–17.
Nikolajeva, Maria. *The Rhetoric of Character in Children's Literature*. Lanham: Scarecrow, 2002.
Nilsen, Alleen Pace, and Kenneth L. Donelson. *Literature for Today's Young Adults*. 8th ed. Boston: Pearson, 2009.
Pagnoni Berns, Fernando Gabriel, and César Alfonso Marino, "Outlining the Future Robin: The Seventies in the *Batman Family*." In *Dick Grayson, Boy Wonder: Scholars and Creators on 75 Years of Robin, Nightwing and Batman*, edited by Kristen Geaman, 28–39. Jefferson: McFarland, 2015.

Palumbo, Donald. "The Monomyth as Fractal Pattern in Frank Herbert's *Dune* Novels." *Science-Fiction Studies* 25, no. 3 (1998): 433–58.
Panek, LeRoy Lad. *The Origins of the American Detective Story*. Jefferson, NC: McFarland, 2006.
Paretsky, Sara. "Introduction" to *The Secret of the Old Clock*, by Carolyn Keene, n. pag. Bedford: Applewood, 1991.
Peterfreund, Diana. "Team Shay." In *Mind-Rain: Your Favorite Authors on Scott Westerfeld's Uglies Series*, edited by Scott Westerfeld, 41–53. Dallas: BenBella, 2009.
Picower, Bree. "Tools of Inaction: The Impasse between Teaching Social Issues and Creating Social Change." *Teachers and Teaching: Theory and Practice* 21, no. 7 (2015): 908–22.
Pierce, Tamora. *Alanna: The First Adventure*. New York: Simon, 2005.
———. *In the Hand of the Goddess*. New York: Simon, 2005.
Pittman, L. Monique. "Dressing the Girl/Playing the Boy: *Twelfth Night* Learns Soccer on the Set of *She Is The Man*." *Literature Film Quarterly* 36, no. 2 (2008): 122–36.
Plato. *Phaedrus*. Translated by W. C. Helmbold and W. G. Rabinowitz. New Jersey: Prentice, 1956.
Prieto-Pablos, Juan A. "The Ambivalent Hero of Contemporary Fantasy and Science Fiction." *Extrapolation* 32, no. 1 (1991): 65–80.
Puente, Maria. "Always Someone Right by Superheroes' Side." *USA Today*. Last modified January 13, 2011: 2D. Academic Search Complete.
Rehak, Melanie. *Girl Sleuth: Nancy Drew and the Women Who Created Her*. Orlando: Harcourt, 2005.
"Revision of the Commandant's Professional Reading List." US Marine Corps. Last modified May 17, 2017. https://www.marines.mil/News/Messages/Messages-Display/Article/1184470/revision-of-the-commandants-professional-reading-list/.
Reynolds, Richard. *Super Heroes: A Modern Mythology*. Jackson: University Press of Mississippi, 1994.
Riordan, Rick. *Percy Jackson and the Olympians: The Lightning Thief*. New York: Hyperion, 2005.
———. *Percy Jackson and the Olympians: The Sea of Monsters*. New York: Hyperion, 2006.
Robertson, Robin. "Seven Paths of the Hero in *Lord of the Rings*: The Path of Love." *Psychological Perspectives* 52, no. 2 (2009): 225–42.
"Robin Rising." *Batman: The Animated Series. Vol 1.* Burbank, CA: Warner Home Video, 2004. DVD.
Robinson, Kimberly Downing. "*Uglies*." *Interdisciplinary Humanities* 27, no. 2 (2010): 151–54.
Romagnoli, Alex S., and Gian S. Pagnucci. *Enter the Superheroes: American Values, Culture, and the Canon of Superhero Literature*. Lanham: Scarecrow, 2013.
Rowling, J. K. *Harry Potter and the Chamber of Secrets*. New York: Scholastic, 1998.
———. *Harry Potter and the Deathly Hallows*. New York: Scholastic, 2007.
———. *Harry Potter and the Goblet of Fire*. New York: Scholastic, 2000.
———. *Harry Potter and the Half-Blood Prince*. New York: Scholastic, 2006.
———. *Harry Potter and the Order of the Phoenix*. New York: Scholastic, 2003.
———. "Live Web Chat." World Book Day. Last modified March 4, 2004. http://www.accio-quote.org/articles/2004/0304-wbd.htm.
Sachdeva, Sonya, Rumen Iliev, Hamed Ekhtiari, and Morteza Dehghani. "The Role of Self-Sacrifice in Moral Dilemmas." *Plos ONE* 10, no. 6 (2015): 1–12.
Sandner, David. *Fantastic Literature: A Critical Reader*. Westport, CT: Praeger, 2004.
Schatz, Thomas. *Hollywood Genres: Formulas, Filmmaking, and the Studio System*. New York: McGraw, 1981.
Schmidtz, David. "Because It's Right." In *Morality and Self-Interest*, edited by Philip Bloomberg, 79–101. New York: Oxford University Press, 2008.
Schoon, Ingrid. "Life Chances and Opportunities in Times of Social Change: Evidence from Two British Birth Cohorts." In *Approaches to Positive Youth Development*, edited by Rainer K. Silbereisen and Richard M. Lerner, 157–71. London: SAGE, 2007.

Shackleford, Dean. "The Female Voice in *To Kill a Mockingbird*: Narrative Strategies in Film and Novel." *Mississippi Quarterly* 50, no. 1 (1996): n. pag. Academic Search Complete.
Smith, Sidonie, and Julia Watson. *Reading Autobiography: A Guide for Interpreting Life Narratives*, 2nd ed. Minneapolis: University of Minnesota Press, 2010.
Spinrad, Norman. *Science Fiction in the Real World*. Carbondale: Southern Illinois University Press, 1990.
Starlin, Jim, and Marv Wolfman. *Batman: A Death in the Family*. New York: DC Comics, 2011.
Stein, Joel, Katy Steinmetz, and Steven Borowiec. "Nip. Tuck. Or Else." *Time* 185, no. 24 (2015): 40–48.
Tallerico, Brian. Review of *Teen Titans Go! To the Movies*, directed by Aaron Horvath and Peter Rida Michail. RogerEbert.com, July 23, 2018, https://www.rogerebert.com/reviews/teen-titans-go-to-the-movies-2018.
Thomas, Trudelle H. "Spiritual Practices Children Understand: An Analysis of Madeleine L' Engle' s Fantasy, *A Wind in the Door*." *International Journal of Children's Spirituality* 13, no. 2 (2008): 157–69.
"The Tick vs. the Idea Men." YouTube. Accessed August 23, 2017. https://www.youtube.com/watch?v=EJ9ErONcHe8.
Tipton, Nathan G. "Gender Trouble: Frank Miller's Revision of Robin in the *Batman: Dark Knight* Series." *The Journal of Popular Culture* 41, no. 2 (2008): 321–36.
Tolkien, J. R. R. *The Hobbit*. New York: Ballantine, 1974.
———. *The Return of the King*. New York: Ballantine, 1974.
———. *The Two Towers*. New York: Ballantine, 1974.
Toner, Christopher. "Catastrophe and Eucatastrophe: Russell and Tolkien on the True Form of Fiction." *New Blackfriars* 89, no. 1019 (2008): 77–87.
Trites, Roberta Seelinger. *Disturbing the Universe: Power and Repression in Adolescent Literature*. Iowa City: University of Iowa Press, 2000.
———. "The *Harry Potter* Novels as a Test Case for Adolescent Literature." *Style* 35, no. 3 (2001): 472–85.
Twain, Mark. *The Adventures of Tom Sawyer*. 1876. Edited by Lee Clark Mitchell. Oxford: Oxford University Press, 1998.
Waid, Mark, and Alex Ross. *Kingdom Come*. New York: DC Comics, 2008.
Walker, Jeanne Murray. "Rites of Passage Today: The Cultural Significance of *A Wizard of Earthsea*." *Mosaic* 13, no. 3–4 (1980): 179–91. JSTOR.
Wardhaugh, Ronald, and Janet M. Fuller. *An Introduction to Sociolinguistics*, 7th ed. West Sussex: Wiley-Blackwell, 2015.
Ware, Michele S. "'True Legitimacy': The Myth of the Foundling in *Bleak House*." *Studies in the Novel* 22, no. 1 (1990): 1–9.
Wasserman, Robin. "Best Friends for Never." In *Mind-Rain: Your Favorite Authors on Scott Westerfeld's Uglies Series*, edited by Scott Westerfeld, 19–39. Dallas: BenBella, 2009.
Watson, George. "The Birth of Jeeves." *Virginia Quarterly Review* 73, no. 4 (1997): 641–52. Academic Search Complete.
Werlin, Nancy. "Get Rid of the Parents?" *Booklist* (July 1995): 1934–35.
Westerfeld, Scott. *Pretties*. New York: Simon Pulse, 2011.
———. *Specials*. New York: Simon Pulse, 2011.
———. *Uglies*. New York: Simon Pulse, 2011.
Westerfeld, Scott, Devin Grayson, and Steven Cummings. *Uglies: Shay's Story*. New York: Ballantine, 2012.
Wodehouse, P. G. *The Best of Wodehouse: An Anthology*. New York: Random, 2007.
Woloch, Alex. *One vs. the Many: Minor Characters and the Space of the Protagonist in the Novel*. Princeton: Princeton University Press, 2003.
Wood, Daniel Davis. "Character Synthesis in *The Adventures of Huckleberry Finn*." *The Explicator* 70, no. 2 (2012): 83–86.
Wright, Bradford W. *Comic Book Nation: The Transformation of Youth Culture in America*. Baltimore: Johns Hopkins University Press, 2001.

Yandoli, Krysti. "Why Neville Longbottom Is the Best *Harry Potter* Character of All Time." Huffington Post. Accessed December 6, 2017. https://www.huffingtonpost.com/2013/07/31/neville-longbottom_n_3682304.html.

Zuckerman, Phil. "Publishing the Applewood Reprints." In *Rediscovering Nancy Drew*, edited by Carolyn Stewart Dyer and Nancy Tillman Romalov, 41–46. Iowa City: University of Iowa Press, 1995.

Index

The Adventures of Detective Barney, 44
The Adventures of Huckleberry Finn, 25, 91
The Adventures of Tom Sawyer, 11, 24–25, 26, 91; Huckleberry Finn, 24–26; Tom Sawyer, 24–26
Alexander, Lloyd, 56, 61, 63, 141
Alger, Horatio, 44
Anderson, John David. See Sidekicked
archetypal studies, 1, 5, 6, 7, 19
Aristotle, 2
Asher-Perrin, Emily, 71
Avengers: Infinity War, 2

Back to the Future, 92
Baker, Deirdre F., 59
Barrow, Craig, 34, 83, 84
Barrow, Diana, 34, 83, 84
Batman: The Animated Series, 45–46
Batman Begins, 118
Batman/Bruce Wayne, 42, 43–49, 121
Batman Family comic, 45
Beezus and Ramona, 91
Bell, J. L., 44, 45
The Big Bang Theory, 17
Bildungsroman, 11, 21, 70
Blackmore, Tim, 103
Bloomberg, Paul, 126, 127
Blume, Judy, 16, 91
Bradley, Marion Zimmer, 92
Brown, Penelope, 122–123

Buchanan, Ron, 11, 16, 32

Campbell, Joseph, 5, 72; heroic cycle, 6; monomyth, 5, 7, 63, 75
Campbell, Patty, 11
Captain America: The Winter Soldier, 2
Card, Orson Scott, 12, 92, 100, 104, 109, 112. See also Ender's Game series
Cart, Michael, 10, 29
Carter, Betty, 10, 32
Castle, 17
Cervantes. See Don Quixote
Chatman, Seymour, 1
The Chronicles of Kazam series, 42; The Eye of Zoltar, 58; Jennifer Strange, 42, 56–58, 141; The Last Dragonslayer, 11, 56–58, 141; The Song of the Quarkbeast, 58; Tiger Prawns, 42, 56–58
The Chronicles of Prydain, 56, 61, 63, 141; The Castle of Llyr, 63
Cleary, Beverly, 91, 141
Collins, Suzanne. See The Hunger Games series
comic books, 2, 7–9, 16, 22–23, 32, 36, 43–51, 62, 112, 117–118, 120–121, 123, 128, 139, 141
The Contender, 16
Coogan, Peter, 4, 9, 22, 45
Cormier, Robert, 16
Crisis on Infinite Earths, 45, 64

149

Culler, Jonathan, 1

Dan the Detective, 44
The Dark Knight, 118
The Dark Knight Returns, 8, 42, 47–49, 122, 126
The Dark Knight Rises, 118
Dark Tower series, 92
Day, Sara K., 103
DC Cinematic Universe, 8
Deadpool, 117, 118
Deadpool 2, 118
detective characters and sidekicks, 44
Dirda, Michael, 17
Donelson, Kenneth L., 10, 19
Don Quixote, 21; Don Quixote, 21–22, 25, 27; Sancho Panza, 21–22, 25, 27
Doty, William, 76
Doyle, Christine, 101, 102, 107, 108, 109, 112
Doyle, Sir Arthur Conan, 11, 16, 17, 118, 135. See also See also *Sherlock Holmes* series
Dr. Who, 16–17
Duncan, Lois, 16
Dune, 42, 51–53; Jessica Atreides, 42, 52–53; Paul Atreides, 42, 51–53

Earthsea series, 10, 12, 34, 64, 70, 81, 84, 88; *The Farthest Shore*, 82, 85; Ged, 34–36, 42, 53–54, 81–84, 87; *The Other Wind*, 85; *Tales from Earthsea*, 81, 85; Tehanu, 82, 84–86; Tenar, 12, 81–87; Therru, 84, 85, 86, 87; *The Tombs of Atuan*, 81–82, 84, 85, 86; Vetch, 34–36, 42, 53–54; *A Wizard of Earthsea*, 16, 34–36, 53–54
Edlund, Ben, 22
Edwards, Owen, 18–19
Elementary, 2, 17
Ender's Game series, 12; Bean, 12, 100–112; Ender, 100–112; *Ender's Game*, 12, 92, 100–101, 104, 106, 107, 110; *Ender's Shadow*, 12, 92, 100–106, 103–105, 106, 107, 108, 110, 111–112; mythification of Ender, 106, 108, 109, 111; Nikolai, 105–106
Entwicklungsroman, 21, 70
eucatastrophe, 28, 31

face, 122–123
familial relationships: brother-brother, 42, 53; father-daughter, 47–49; father-son, 42, 44–47; hero/sidekick triad, 43, 61–63, 70, 71; mother-daughter, 49–51; mother-son, 42, 51–53; romantic, 42, 58–61; sister-brother non-romantic, 42, 56–58; sister-sister, 42, 54–56
Faulkner, William, 92
Ferraiolo, Jack. See *Sidekicks*
Fforde, Jasper. See *The Chronicles of Kazam* series
fictive revisions, 95–97
The Force Awakens, 2
foundling, 56–57
frenemies, 94, 140
Frye, Northrop, 5

Garbowski, Christopher, 28
Gardner, John, 92
Geaman, Kristen L., 45
Gilgamesh, 2, 9
graphic novel, 4, 8, 46, 49, 92, 95, 99, 112
Grayson, Devin, 46
The Green Hornet, 118
Grendel, 92
Grey, 92

"Harrison Bergeron," 93
Harry Potter series, 12, 24, 31, 64, 69, 70, 71, 76, 79, 81, 88, 140; "could have been" Harry, 71, 76, 77, 88; destroying horcruxes, 78, 79; Harry Potter, 43, 61, 63, 70–80, 72, 140; *Harry Potter and the Chamber of Secrets*, 79; *Harry Potter and the Deathly Hallows*, 74, 79, 140; *Harry Potter and the Goblet of Fire*, 71–73; *Harry Potter and the Half-Blood Prince*, 77; *Harry Potter and the Order of the Phoenix*, 71, 73, 74, 76; Hermione Granger, 43, 61, 70, 71, 72, 73, 73–75, 77, 78, 79; Neville Longbottom, 12, 31, 70–81; Ron Weasley, 43, 61, 70, 71, 72, 73, 73–75, 77, 78, 79, 140
Harvey, W. J., 7
Henry and Ribsy, 141
Henry Huggins, 91
Herbert, Frank. See *Dune*

Hinton, S. E., 16
His Dark Materials, 141
The Hobbit, 26, 27–31, 32, 53, 96; Beorn, 29–30; Bilbo Baggins, 28–29; the dwarves, 26, 27–31; Thorin, 26, 28–31
Hogan, Walter, 41
Holland, Isabelle, 10
Hollindale, Peter, 34, 35, 84, 86
Holmes & Watson, 17
Holquist, Michael, 25
The Hunger Games series, 11, 57, 60–61; *Catching Fire*, 61; Gale Hawthorne, 60; Katniss Everdeen, 60–61; Peeta Mellark, 61

identity crisis, 120
The Iliad, 2
The Incredibles, 42, 49–51; Helen Parr, 42, 49–51; Violet Parr, 42, 49–51
Incredibles 2, 49, 64
in loco parentis, 42, 52, 53, 64
in logo parentis, 42
in parentis, 42

James, E. L., 92
Jewett, Robert, 7, 75
Jordan, Robert, 80
Jung, Carl, 6

Kerr, M. E., 16
Kick-Ass, 118
Kick-Ass 2, 118
To Kill a Mockingbird, 11, 17, 19–21, 26; Scout Finch, 19–21; Jem Finch, 19–21
King, Stephen, 92

Lawrence, John, 7, 75
Lee, Harper, 10, 11. *See also To Kill a Mockingbird*
The LEGO Batman Movie, 117
Le Guin, Ursula K., 10, 12, 16, 34, 35, 53, 64, 70, 81, 83, 84, 85. *See also Earthsea* series
Levinson, Stephen C., 122–123
Levi-Strauss, Claude, 6
The Lion King, 92
The Lion King 1 ½, 92
Lipsyte, Robert, 16
Littlefield, Holly, 83, 85

The Lord of the Rings trilogy, 32, 53–54, 140; Frodo Baggins, 32–34, 53–54; Samwise Gamgee, 2, 32–34, 53–54
love triangle, 43, 59, 60, 61, 97, 131
Lynch, Paul, 25
Lyon Clark, Beverly, 24

Martin, George R. R., 81
Marvel Cinematic Universe, 8
masks/personas, 86, 122
McCaffrey, Anne, 16
McLean, Susan, 85
Meyer, Stephenie, 92
Midnight Sun, 92
Miller, Frank, 8
Minion, 118
The Mists of Avalon, 92
morality, 126, 127, 132–134
Morrison, Grant, 44, 118
Mortimer, John, 26–27
The Multiversity: Ultra Comics, 118

Nadeau, Frances A., 51
names/naming in fantasy literature, 78, 83, 85–87
Nancy Drew series, 54–56; Bess Marvin, 42, 43, 54–56; Georgia "George" Fayne, 42, 43, 54–56; Nancy Drew, 42, 43, 54–56
Nikolajeva, Maria, 7, 42, 43
Nilsen, Alleen Pace, 10, 19
Nolan, Christopher, 8, 118

O'Higgins, Harvey J., 44
Otherwise Known as Sheila the Great, 92
The Outsiders, 16

Pagnucci, Gian, 9
parallel novel, 92, 96, 100, 101, 103, 110, 112, 139
Peck, Richard, 16
Percy Jackson and the Olympians series, 43, 142; Annabeth Chase, 43, 61, 63; Grover Underwood, 43, 61–62, 142; *The Lightning Thief*, 62; Percy Jackson, 43, 61–63; *The Sea of Monsters*, 62; *The Titan's Curse*, 62, 63
Peterfreund, Diana, 97–99
Phaedrus, 2

Picower, Bree, 130
Pierce, Tamora, 11, 42, 58. *See also Song of the Lioness* series
Plato, 2
Poe, Edgar Allan, 16, 44
positive youth development, 124
Prieto-Pablos, Juan, 51
Pullman, Philip, 141
The Punisher, 118

Ramona the Pest, 91
Return of the Jedi, 141
Reynolds, Richard, 8, 47
Rhys, Jean, 92
Riordan, Rick. *See Percy Jackson and the Olympians* series
Robertson, Robin, 32, 33
Robin, 9, 120; Carrie Kelly, 8, 42, 47–49, 51, 64, 127; Damian Wayne, 44; Dick Grayson, 9, 42, 44–47, 48, 49, 64, 70, 88, 120, 121, 122; Jason Todd, 121; Tim Drake, 44
Robinson, Kimberly Downing, 94
Romagnoli, Alex, 9
Ross, Alex. *See Kingdom Come*
Rowling, J. K., 12, 31, 61, 63, 64, 70, 73, 76, 77, 80, 81. *See also Harry Potter* series
Rozencrantz and Guildenstern Are Dead, 92

Sachdeva, Sonya, 127
Schatz, Thomas, 22
Schmidtz, David, 133
Schoon, Ingrid, 124
Shackleford, Dean, 19, 20
Sherlock Holmes series, 17–19; Dr. John Watson, 17–19, 55, 118, 135; Sherlock Holmes, 17–19, 55, 118, 135; *A Study in Scarlet*, 11, 17, 18, 21
sidekick: animal sidekick, 141–142; as antagonist, 140; comic relief, 11, 26–31; devil's advocate, 11, 21–25; elevation, 12, 69, 70, 88, 92, 95, 99, 110, 117, 139; foil, 11, 31–36; narrative gateway, 11, 16–21; secondary hero, 12, 70–88, 139; self-aware sidekick, 12, 117–135, 140; sidekick sequel, 12, 91–112, 139; whole universe, 140

Sidekicked, 12, 118; Andrew Bean, 12, 119, 128–135; The Fox, 130, 132, 133, 134; Gavin, 131–132; H.E.R.O., 128–129, 131, 132, 134; Jenna, 128, 130–134; Superhero Sidekick Code of Conduct, 129, 133, 134; The Titan, 129–130, 134
Sidekicks, 12, 118; Allison Mendes/Monkeywrench, 122, 123–128; Edward Simmons/Dr. Chaotic, 121, 122, 123, 124, 125, 127; Scott Hutchinson/Bright Boy, 12, 119–128, 135; Trent Clancy/Phantom Justice, 119–128
Smith, Sidonie, 20
Song of the Lioness series, 42, 58–60; Alanna, 42, 58–60; Jonathan, 42, 59–60
Standard Hero Behavior, 118
Star Trek, 17, 21; *Deep Space Nine*, 17; *Enterprise*, 17; *The Next Generation*, 17; *Star Trek Beyond*, 2; *Voyager*, 17
Star Wars, 2, 96, 99, 140
Star Wars: The Clone Wars, 140
Stein, Joel, 93
Stewart, Susan Louise, 102, 107, 108, 109, 112
Stoppard, Tom, 92
Superman, 5, 7, 44, 117; *Death of Superman*, 5; *Kingdom Come*, 5

Tales of a Fourth Grade Nothing, 91
Tallerico, Brian, 117
Teen Titans, 8
Teen Titans Go!, 8
Teen Titans Go! To the Movies, 8, 117, 118
The Tick, 25–24, 71; Arthur, 22–24, 25, 71; Paul the Samurai, 23
The Tick, 22–24, 25
Thomas, Trudelle, 78
Tipton, Nathan, 47, 48, 49
Titans, 8
Tolkien, J. R. R., 26, 53, 96. *See also The Hobbit*; *The Lord of the Rings* trilogy
Tom Sawyer, Detective, 44
Toner, Christopher, 28
tools of inaction, 130
Trites, Roberta Seelinger, 20, 42, 70
Twain, Mark, 24, 44. *See also The Adventures of Huckleberry Finn*; *The Adventures of Tom Sawyer*

Twilight, 92

Uglies Series, 92, 94, 112; *Cutters*, 92, 95, 97, 99; *Extras*, 92; *Pretties*, 92, 95, 98; Shay, 12, 93–99, 112; *Shay's Story*, 92, 95, 97, 99, 101; *Specials*, 92, 95, 101; Tally Youngblood, 93–99, 112; *Uglies*, 92, 93, 94–97, 99, 101

Vonnegut, Kurt, 93

Waid, Mark, 5, 45, 46
Walker, Jeanne Murray, 35
Ware, Michele S., 57
Wasserman, Robin, 97–98, 99

Watson, Julia, 20
Werlin, Nancy, 57
Westerfeld, Scott, 12, 93, 112
Wide Sargasso Sea, 92
Wodehouse, P. G., 26, 27; Jeeves, 26–27, 30–31; Wooster, 26–27
Woloch, Alex, 1
Wood, Daniel Davis, 25
Wright, Bradford W., 9

Young Adult Literature (YA): definition, 9; historical use of term, 16

Zemeckis, Robert, 92
Zindel, Paul, 16

About the Author

Stephen M. Zimmerly, PhD, is an assistant professor of English at the University of Indianapolis, where he teaches a variety of courses, including Young Adult literature. Growing up, he always pretended he was Robin, not Batman. He lives in Indianapolis, IN, with his wife Rachel and their four children.

www.ingramcontent.com/pod-product-compliance
Lightning Source LLC
Chambersburg PA
CBHW020125010526
44115CB00008B/974